THE OFFICIAL
F.A. Premier

League
Football Guide

THIS IS A CARLTON BOOK

First published by Carlton Books Limited in 1997

ISBN   1 85868 417 X (Hardback)
            1 85868 327 0 (Paperback)

A CIP catalogue record for this book is available from the British Library

10 9 8 7 6 5 4 3 2 1

Project Editor: Martin Corteel
Editorial Assistant: Roland Hall
Picture Research: Lorna Ainger
Project Art Direction: Paul Messam
Production: Garry Lewis

Author's Acknowledgements
I would like to thank the following for their help with this book: Debbie Millett; Roland Hall and Martin Corteel at Carlton; David Prole; Peter Neish; Steve Pearce; John Kelly.

(opposite) **The Young Ones: Fans this age have known only success at Manchester United**

The publishers would like to thank the following sources for their kind permission to reproduce the pictures in this book:

Allsport UK Ltd 9l, 13l, 35b, 81, 96t/Shaun Botterill 9r, 15l, 33b, 64r, 65, 84l, 96b, 101; Clive Brunskill 11l, 23, 90, 94, 102; Phil Cole 108l; Graham Chadwick 35t; Mike Cooper 41, 62; Stu Forster 82, 113, 117; Ross Kinnaird 21l, 29l, 85, 86, 125l; Gary M.Prior 66, 68l, 120bl,tr; Ben Radford 25, 29cl, 30, 32, 33t, 46, 49, 54, 88b, 93, 97, 98, 100t,b; Mark Thompson 14, 26, 48, 56, 76tl, 125r. Colorsport 19r, 22, 42, 44r, 45, 48cb, 50, 52r, 68r, 80l, 88t, 104r, 114, 123, 124. Empics Sports Photo Agency 3, 25, 28, 29r, 56l, 57, 76tr, 89, 92b, 118/Matthew Ashton 24, 34, 72b, 84r, 116l; Barrington Coombes 11r, 16, 72t, 74, 116r; Mike Egerton 108tr, 109; Laurence Griffiths 12, 13r, 19l, 20, 92t, 104bl; David Hewitson 17l, 18, 70; Tony Marshall 31, 53, 104tl, 112bc; Mike Poole 17r, 76cb; Neal Simpson 8, 21r, 73, 78, 106, 112tl; Michael Steele 58; Aubrey Washington 61, 80cb, 110. John Parkinson Jones FBIPP 39. Popperfoto 10, 27t, 44l, 69, 121/Dave Joyner 64l; SAG 60t. Sky Sports 38br/Kerry Ghais 6, 38bl; Sam Teare 40. Sporting Pictures (UK) Ltd. 52l, 60b.

Every effort has been made to acknowledge correctly and contact the source and/copyright holder of each picture, and Carlton Books Limited apologises for any unintentional errors or omissions which will be corrected in future editions of this book.

THE OFFICIAL F.A. Premier League Football Guide

GAVIN HAMILTON

CARLTON

Contents

Foreword by Andy Gray **6**

Review of the Season 1996–97

    August 8

    September 10

    October 12

    November 14

    December 16

    January 18

    February 20

    March 22

    April 24

Coca-Cola Cup Final 1997 . . . . **26**

    May 28

FA Cup Final 1997 . . . . **30**

European Cup-winners' Cup Final 1997 **32**

Champions Cup Final 1997 . . . . **33**

Division One Play-offs 1997 . . . . **34**

Anatomy of a Football Boot **36**

Anatomy of a Stadium **38**

The Teams of the Premier League **40**

Arsenal **42**

At Highbury they are getting used to the French revolution, the Arsène Wenger revolution to be precise.

Aston Villa **46**

Under manager Brian Little, Aston Villa are firmly re-established among the elite of English football.

Barnsley **50**

Danny Wilson's side are in the top division for the first time in their 110-year history.

Blackburn Rovers **54**

Blackburn Rovers are pinning their hopes on new boss Roy Hodgson, one of Europe's most experienced and respected coaches.

Bolton Wanderers . . . **58**

Back in the big time after a trailblazing season in division one, with new players and a brand new stadium.

Chelsea **62**

Under player-manager Ruud Gullit, the Continental changes are sweeping through Stamford Bridge.

Coventry City **66**
Against all the odds, they did it again. They escaped relegation from the Premier League by the skin of their teeth.

Crystal Palace **70**
Back in the Premier League, where they believe they belong, and only one thing on their minds – survival.

Derby County **74**
Steady, unexceptional progress in last season's Premier League – and they would not have had it any other way.

Everton **78**
Lost their final home game of last season 2–1 to Chelsea, but a more significant event took place off the pitch that day.

Leeds United **82**
Under George Graham, goals became a scarce commodity – Graham's tactics were not pretty, but they were effective.

Leicester City **86**
As they lifted the Coca-Cola League Cup, the progress made under manager Martin O'Neill was there for all to see.

Liverpool **90**
The most successful club in the history of English football – but without a championship since 1990.

Manchester United . . **94**
Undisputed heavyweight champions of the Premier League, last season's title triumph was United's fourth in five seasons.

Newcastle United **98**
At St James' Park, Kenny Dalglish is out to prove that there can be life AK – After Keegan.

Sheffield Wednesday . **102**
All the qualities needed to be one of England's leading clubs; strong support, a famous stadium and top quality players.

Southampton **106**
In the top division since 1978, they are living proof that small clubs can survive in the Premier League.

Tottenham Hotspur . **110**
One of English football's most high-profile clubs but have won only one trophy in the past 13 years.

West Ham United . . . **114**
Small when compared with the likes of Manchester United and Liverpool, but continuing to play skilful, attractive soccer.

Wimbledon **118**
One of the most dramatic success stories to have gripped English football in the past 20 years.

F.A. Premier League Records **122**

F.A. Premier League Tables **124**

F.A. Premier League Fixtures 1997–98 . . . . **126**

Index **128**

Foreword

The FA Carling Premier League is the most exciting League in the world, where the biggest stars of the world's greatest game can be seen – week in, week out.

In my 20 years as a player, with Dundee United, Glasgow Rangers, Aston Villa, Wolverhampton Wanderers, Everton and West Bromwich Albion, I thought I'd experienced enough excitement to last a lifetime. But the game has never been more exciting than it is today. The entertainment, the intrigue, the stars! They're out there every week for you – the fan – to enjoy.

My playing days are well and truly over, but I'm doing the next best thing. On the opening weekend of the season yours truly will be in the Sky gantry for Tottenham Hotspur's clash with Manchester United – there's no better place to be to catch all the action than with Sky Sports. Our exclusive live broadcasts and unrivalled reporting team give you the best possible coverage of the FA Carling Premier League. It means you can keep bang up to date with all the latest action, news and views.

The *Official Premier League Football Guide* is the perfect companion to Sky Sports' coverage. This superb book, crammed with colour photographs, is a real treasure-trove of information. It gives you the lowdown on all the teams and their stars, and there are hundreds of player statistics and facts. You'll find it both informative and entertaining.

In the end Alex Ferguson's Manchester United were comfortable winners of the FA Premier League last season. But can they do it again? I'm not so sure. Without the man from Marseille, Eric Cantona, United could struggle. Other teams certainly won't make things easy for them. Liverpool will be there, as will Arsène Wenger's revamped Arsenal. Kenny Dalglish has been busy at Newcastle, and I like the look of Ruud Gullit's Chelsea. And don't rule out my old club Aston Villa now that they've signed Stan "The Man" Collymore. We're guaranteed loads of great goals, some super saves and top quality action from all the teams.

The 1997–98 Premier League season promises to be a cracker from start to finish. It's going to be a fascinating contest, a real rollercoaster ride of emotions – and we'll be with you all the way on Sky Sports.

Enjoy the book, and enjoy the season,

Andy Gray
Sky Sports Commentator, London, July 1997

Review of the Season

of the

1996-97

1996-97

 ## August

England's gallant exploits at Euro 96 were already a fading memory as the new season kicked off in August. Much was expected from the teams who had spent heavily in the summer transfer market, particularly Newcastle United, but Manchester United were still the team to beat.

On Target: Cantona scores in the Charity Shield

The big kick-off

Newcastle's world-record signing of Alan Shearer – a cool £15 million – had raised expectations on Tyneside to fever pitch. Down the road in Middlesbrough, Bryan Robson was spending money like it was going out of fashion. Italian international striker Fabrizio Ravanelli, who had just won the European Cup with Juventus, was Boro's biggest signing yet.

Liverpool, who had been noticeable for their lack of activity on the transfer front, landed the catch they had been waiting for all summer; Patrik Berger, the Czech Republic international who had scored but still been on the losing side in the Final of Euro 96.

There were movers and shakers elsewhere, too. Aston Villa paid Bolton £4 million for Serbian midfielder Sasa Curcic, American goalkeeper Kasey Keller moved to Leicester from Millwall and Arsenal signed French midfielder Patrick Vieira from AC Milan. Vieira was the choice of the Arsenal manager-in-waiting, Arsène Wenger. The French coach was being lined up for a move to Highbury but could not join from Japan until the autumn. In a bizarre move to clear the way for Wenger, Arsenal sacked manager Bruce Rioch before the season had even started. Manchester United boss Alex Ferguson had also been busy buying and selling players. Karel Poborsky, who had scored the goal of the tournament at Euro 96, for the Czech Republic against Portugal, arrived from Slavia Prague for £3.5 million. Jordi Cruyff, son of Johan and a member of the Dutch squad at Euro 96, checked in from Barcelona. United, the double double-winners, paid for their new purchases by selling Lee Sharpe to Leeds.

MANAGER OF THE MONTH

David Pleat

The Sheffield Wednesday manager had been quietly building a useful side at Hillsborough. At the end of August, after three straight wins, Wednesday were top of the Premier League.

PLAYER OF THE MONTH

David Beckham

A Charity Shield success, goal of the season and an England call-up. It was quite a month for Manchester United's exciting young midfielder.

Beckham's wondergoal

Despite their new foreign contingent, which also included Norwegians Ole Gunnar Solskjaer and Ronny Johnsen, it was a United youngster who grabbed the headlines in August. David Beckham, 21, had been widely tipped as the brightest of the exciting crop of young players to emerge under Ferguson at Old Trafford. He was soon to show everybody why he was so highly rated.

In the Charity Shield at Wembley, all eyes were on Newcastle and record signing Alan Shearer. But United spoiled the party, winning 4–0, with Beckham among the scorers. A week later he scored a wondergoal, a 50-yard strike from his own half. The youngster had scored the goal of the season...on the first day of the season. If this was the shape of things to come, it promised to be one hell of a season.

PREMIER LEAGUE STANDINGS

August 30

		P	W	D	L	F	A	Pts
1	Sheffield Wednesday	3	3	0	0	6	2	9
2	Chelsea	3	2	1	0	3	0	7
3	Arsenal	3	2	0	1	4	2	6
4	Aston Villa	3	2	0	1	4	2	6
5	Manchester United	3	1	2	0	7	4	5
6	Sunderland	3	1	2	0	4	1	5
7	Liverpool	3	1	2	0	5	3	5
8	Everton	3	1	2	0	4	2	5
9	Tottenham Hotspur	3	1	2	0	3	1	5
10	Nottingham Forest	3	1	1	1	5	5	4
11	Leeds United	3	1	1	1	4	5	4
12	West Ham United	3	1	1	1	3	4	4
13	Leicester City	3	1	1	1	2	3	4
14	Newcastle United	3	1	0	2	3	4	3
15	Middlesbrough	3	0	2	1	4	5	2
16	Derby County	3	0	2	1	4	6	2
17	Southampton	3	0	1	2	2	4	1
18	Blackburn Rovers	3	0	1	2	2	5	1
19	Coventry City	3	0	1	2	1	6	1
20	Wimbledon	3	0	0	3	0	6	0

MILESTONES OF THE SEASON

AUGUST 2
Czech Republic midfielder Patrik Berger, a star of his country's Euro 96 side, joins Liverpool for a fee of £3.25 million.

AUGUST 6
Sheffield Wednesday pull out of a deal to sign Italian midfielder Attilio Lombardo from Juventus after learning of his "crazy" pay demands.

AUGUST 11
Manchester United sell Lee Sharpe to Leeds for £4.5 million. Alan Shearer, Newcastle's new £15 million striker, has a terrible day in the Charity Shield as his team are thrashed 4–0 by champions Manchester United.

AUGUST 13
Arsenal sack manager Bruce Rioch with no explanation while completing the signings of Frenchmen Patrick Vieira and Remi Garde. Speculation mounts that Frenchman Arsène Wenger is lined up to be the new boss at Highbury.

AUGUST 17
The new Premier League season kicks off with hat-tricks for Fabrizio Ravanelli (Middlesbrough) and Kevin Campbell (Nottingham Forest). David Beckham starts the season as he means to go on by scoring with an audacious 50-yard strike from his own half against Wimbledon at Selhurst Park.

AUGUST 20
Kenny Dalglish resigns as Director of Football at Blackburn Rovers. Aston Villa sign Sasa Curcic from Bolton for £4 million.

AUGUST 22
Manchester United wonderboy David Beckham is called up to the full England squad by Glenn Hoddle. Everton's Andy Hinchcliffe also gets the call for the first time.

AUGUST 24
Newcastle's shaky start to the season continues when they lose at home to Sheffield Wednesday, who go top after three straight wins. Gianluca Vialli scores his first goal for Chelsea against Coventry.

AUGUST 29
Newcastle striker Alan Shearer is appointed England captain by Glenn Hoddle for the World Cup qualifier against Moldova in Chisinau.

Ups and downs at Arsenal

Off-the-pitch affairs at Arsenal grabbed the headlines this month. Frenchman Arsène Wenger was finally named as the new boss at Highbury, making him the club's fourth manager of the season.

Wenger took charge from Pat Rice, who had held the fort after Stewart Houston had decamped to Queens Park Rangers. Ironically Houston was joined at QPR by Bruce Rioch, sacked by Arsenal to make way for Wenger in August. No sooner had Wenger been appointed than he was having to deal with allegations that the club was out of control after captain Tony Adams confessed to battling against alcoholism. Adams had reportedly hit the bottle after England's semi-final defeat on penalties to Germany at Euro 96.

While Adams battled to save his career, another self-fessed alcoholic at Arsenal, Paul Merson, enjoyed a glorious return to form which resulted in a recall to the England squad. And despite their behind-the-scenes problems, Arsenal were doing remarkably well in the Premier League.

A 4–1 home victory over early leaders Sheffield Wednesday confirmed the belief that things were looking up at Highbury. Ian Wright scored a hat-trick in that game, which included his 100th League goal for the Gunners. There was more good news at with the impressive debut of French midfielder Patrick Vieira against Sheffield Wednesday. By the end of the month, Arsenal were in second place having lost just once, to leaders Liverpool.

Liverpool look good

Roy Evans' side were unbeaten in the first two months of the League campaign and were looking good early bets for the title. One of Liverpool's biggest problems in recent seasons had been their inability to score goals from midfield. In Patrik Berger, many believed they had found the answer.

The Czech Republic international exploded on to the Premier League scene this month, scoring twice away at Leicester. If he could keep this form up, Liverpool would surely be challenging for the title come May. Berger was also doing his bit for Liverpool in Europe, scoring against MyPa of Finland as Liverpool progressed in the European Cup-winners' Cup.

In the UEFA Cup, Newcastle came through unscathed against Halmstads of Sweden. However, other English teams were not so successful. Arsenal lost out to Germany's Borussia Mönchengladbach, failing to overturn a 3–2 defeat at Highbury in the second leg in Germany. Aston Villa were the biggest disappointment, losing on away goals to Swedish part-timers Helsingborgs.

In the UEFA Champions League, Manchester United travelled to Turin to face Juventus in their opening group match. The 1–0 scoreline, courtesy of Alen Boksic's goal, did not reflect Juventus's dominance.

There were more comings and goings on the domestic front. Southampton signed Norwegian striker Egil

Ton Up: Ian Wright scored his 100th League goal for Arsenal, against early leaders Sheffield Wednesday

MANAGER OF THE MONTH

Roy Evans

Evans' Liverpool side finished the month still unbeaten and top of the Premier League. Had Evans finally got the Anfield ship back on course for the title?

PLAYER OF THE MONTH

Patrik Berger

Seven goals in four games in a remarkable 12-day period confirmed the view of many that Berger is one of the best attacking midfielders in Europe. His early form for his new club also suggested that Liverpool had signed a potential title-winner.

Ostenstad. Howard Wilkinson was sacked by Leeds, just days after a humiliating 4–0 home defeat by Manchester United. Leeds turned to former Arsenal boss George Graham, who had by now completed a year-long worldwide ban for allegedly receiving transfer "bungs".

The champions were motoring along quite nicely in the League. Czech Karel Poborsky scored the goal of the month, against Leeds, which suggested that he may be settling down at Old Trafford after an uncertain start.

Another of United's foreign legion, Norwegian striker Ole Gunnar Solskjaer, was also on target, scoring in a 4–1 defeat of Nottingham Forest and staking a claim as a player well worth keeping an eye on.

Wimbledon worth watching

The Dons, after losing the first three games of the season, then notched up five straight wins to end the month in fourth place. Fabrizio Ravanelli was the Premier League top scorer as Middlesbrough cruised along in mid-table, with no hint of the problems to come. England began a new era under coach Glenn Hoddle with a 3–0 win in a World Cup qualifier in Moldova, with goals from Nicky Barmby, Paul Gascoigne (a rare header) and new captain Alan Shearer, and debuts by Manchester United youngster David Beckham and Everton's Andy Hinchcliffe.

MILESTONES OF THE SEASON

SEPTEMBER 1
Glenn Hoddle's England kick off their World Cup qualifying campaign in style, beating Moldova 3–0 with goals from Nick Barmby, Paul Gascoigne and Alan Shearer.

SEPTEMBER 9
Nottingham Forest and England midfielder Steve Stone injures his knee and will be out for the rest of the season.

SEPTEMBER 10
Leeds sack Howard Wilkinson and replace him with former Arsenal manager George Graham.

SEPTEMBER 11
Manchester United kick off their Champions League campaign in Turin, where they go down 1–0 to holders Juventus.

SEPTEMBER 13
Stewart Houston quits as caretaker boss of Arsenal to take charge of QPR, leaving Pat Rice as caretaker boss at Highbury.

SEPTEMBER 14
Arsenal captain Tony Adams admits to being an alcoholic.

SEPTEMBER 16
Arsène Wenger is named as the new manager of Arsenal.

SEPTEMBER 21
New boy Patrik Berger scores twice on his full debut for Liverpool as Roy Evans' men win 5–1 at Anfield to end Chelsea's unbeaten run and go top of the table.

SEPTEMBER 24
Aston Villa go out of the UEFA Cup to Helsingborgs of Sweden. York City knock Everton out of the Coca-Cola Cup.

SEPTEMBER 25
Arsenal fail to overturn a 3–2 first-leg defeat by Borussia Mönchengladbach in the UEFA Cup, while Manchester United beat Rapid Vienna in the Champions League.

PREMIER LEAGUE STANDINGS

September 30

		P	W	D	L	F	A	Pts
1	Liverpool	8	6	2	0	18	2	20
2	Newcastle United	8	6	0	2	14	10	18
3	Manchester United	8	4	4	0	18	6	16
4	Arsenal	8	5	2	1	17	8	17
5	Wimbledon	8	5	0	3	12	7	15
6	Chelsea	8	3	4	1	11	10	13
7	Sheffield Wednesday	8	4	1	3	9	11	13
8	Aston Villa	8	3	3	2	11	9	12
9	Middlesbrough	8	3	2	3	14	13	11
10	Leicester City	8	3	2	3	6	9	11
11	Derby County	8	2	4	2	8	10	10
12	Sunderland	8	2	3	3	6	6	9
13	Everton	8	2	3	3	8	10	9
14	Tottenham Hotspur	8	2	2	4	6	8	8
15	West Ham United	8	2	2	4	7	12	8
16	Nottingham Forest	8	1	4	3	9	14	7
17	Leeds United	8	2	1	5	6	13	7
18	Southampton	8	1	2	5	10	12	5
19	Coventry City	8	1	2	5	3	13	5
20	Blackburn Rovers	8	0	3	5	5	11	3

This was the month that Manchester United wobbled, Newcastle went clear at the top and Wimbledon continued their unbeaten run.

Manchester United get the wobbles

United started the month in style, beating Liverpool 1–0 at Old Trafford thanks to a crucial David Beckham goal. But then Alex Ferguson's side went to pieces. They lost at home to Fenerbahce in the Champions League, their first home defeat in 40 years of European competition. Four days later on Tyneside, Newcastle gained revenge for their Charity Shield mauling in August with a 5–0 thrashing of the champions. Newcastle's final goal, when Belgian defender Philippe Albert had chipped Peter Schmeichel, was the final insult on a humiliating afternoon for United.

Six days later, there was more embarrassment. Ferguson's men visited Southampton, where a year earlier they had famously excused a defeat by complaining they could not pick each other out in their new grey strip. Southampton, already resigned to another battle against relegation, were 3–1 up by half-time. Again Peter Schmeichel had been lobbed, this time by Matthew Le Tissier. The match ended in a staggering scoreline, 6–3, and left many predicting that, with the champions floundering, it was going to be one of the most open title races for years.

For Newcastle manager Kevin Keegan, his team's trouncing of the champions must have been particularly satisfying after his outburst ("I'd love it if they lost!") during the title run-in the previous season. The Magpies were starting to put a decent run together and Alan Shearer was doing exactly what he had been bought to do – score goals. The England captain scored against Aston Villa in a thrilling match at St James' Park which ended 4–3 in Newcastle's favour; scored the only goal in his side's win at Derby; and then played a major part in Newcastle's demolition of Manchester United, scoring one and setting up two for his team-mates.

Arsenal back on track

Down in London, Arsène Wenger was keeping the Arsenal ship on course after a shaky start to the season. Wins over Blackburn and Leeds, on George Graham's return to Highbury, helped the Gunners stay in second place. Liverpool weren't far behind, but the defeat at Manchester United suggested the Anfield side, midfield, still lacked a killer instinct.

Wimbledon's progress continued unabated. Wins over Sheffield Wednesday (4–2 at home) and Chelsea (4–2 away) and a draw at Middlesbrough maintained the Dons' unbeaten run of form. Joe Kinnear's side had been written off by many at the start of the season (this was the year they would be found out, it was claimed) but they were showing they were a match for the best in the land.

However, Wimbledon nearly came unstuck in the Coca-Cola Cup third round, when they could only draw with lowly Luton. Another second division side went one better. Stockport County

On Top: Philippe Albert outjumps Eric Cantona during Newcastle's 5–0 mauling of the champions

MANAGER OF THE MONTH

Joe Kinnear

After three defeats at the start of the season, Kinnear took Wimbledon on an unbeaten run and the talk was now of Europe, not relegation.

PLAYER OF THE MONTH

Alan Shearer

His goals took Newcastle to the top of the Premier League and England to the top of their World Cup qualifying group.

secured a stunning result, winning 1–0 at Blackburn – a result which led to the resignation of Rovers boss Ray Harford.

Elsewhere, Ruud Gullit's cosmopolitan Chelsea side were knocked out by first-division Bolton, a match that was overshadowed by the death of Matthew Harding. The Chelsea director, who had invested millions in the club, was killed when his helicopter crashed on its way back to London.

European successes

In Europe, Liverpool and Newcastle continued to progress. Roy Evans' Liverpool took on Sion of Switzerland in the Cupwinners Cup and came through comfortably. Newcastle travelled to Budapest, Hungary, for the first leg of their UEFA Cup second round tie against Ferencvaros. Kevin Keegan's side were 2–0 down within 17 minutes, but bounced back with goals from

Shearer and Ferdinand. The 3–2 defeat left Newcastle needing at least a 1–0 win back at St James' Park. They duly obliged, thanks to a spectacular volleyed goal from Frenchman David Ginola, the highlight of a 4–0 second-leg victory.

On the international front, Glenn Hoddle made his home debut as England coach in the World Cup qualifier against Poland at Wembley. Few expected the Poles to offer much of a threat, but they surprised everyone by taking an early lead through Marek Citko, who was to become a transfer target for Blackburn Rovers. England bounced back with two goals from, predictably, Alan Shearer. The 2–1 win put England on top of the qualifying group, ahead of Italy on goal difference.

PREMIER LEAGUE STANDINGS

October 30

		P	W	D	L	F	A	Pts
1	Liverpool	10	7	2	1	20	7	25
2	Arsenal	11	7	3	1	22	8	24
3	Newcastle	11	8	0	3	20	12	24
4	Wimbledon	11	7	1	3	20	11	22
5	Manchester United	11	5	4	2	22	17	19
6	Chelsea	12	5	4	2	19	16	19
7	Tottenham Hotspur	11	4	2	5	11	11	16
8	Aston Villa	11	4	3	4	13	11	15
9	Everton	10	4	3	3	11	11	15
10	Sheffield Wednesday	11	4	3	4	12	16	15
11	West Ham United	11	4	2	5	11	15	14
12	Leicester City	11	4	2	5	9	13	14
13	Middlesbrough	11	3	4	4	16	17	13
14	Sunderland	11	3	4	4	9	11	13
15	Southampton	11	3	3	5	20	16	12
16	Derby County	11	2	5	4	10	14	11
17	Leeds United	11	3	1	7	8	18	10
18	Nottingham Forest	11	1	5	5	10	18	8
19	Coventry City	11	1	5	5	4	14	8
20	Blackburn Rovers	11	0	4	7	7	16	4

MILESTONES OF THE SEASON

OCTOBER 5
Manchester United deny speculation that they are to bid £10 million for Fabrizio Ravanelli after Andy Cole breaks both legs in a reserve match.

OCTOBER 9
England beat Poland 2–1 at Wembley in a France 98 World Cup qualifier.

OCTOBER 10
Sheffield Wednesday sign Benito Carbone from Internazionale. Tomas Brolin threatens to quit the game rather than play for Leeds again.

OCTOBER 12
Mark Bosnich faces disciplinary action from the FA after a Nazi salute to Spurs fans at White Hart Lane.

OCTOBER 16
In Turkey, Manchester United win 2–0 against Fenerbahce in the Champions League.

OCTOBER 18
Paul Gascoigne's future with England is placed in doubt after allegations of wife-beating.

OCTOBER 20
Newcastle gain revenge for the Charity Shield defeat by Manchester United when they hammer the champions 5–0 at St James' Park.

OCTOBER 22
Chelsea director Matthew Harding is killed in a helicopter crash.

OCTOBER 26
Ray Harford resigns as manager of Blackburn Rovers.

November

The title race remained wide open during November, with Arsenal taking over at the top after a crucial win at St James' Park on the final weekend of the month.

All to play for in the title race

Small But Effective: Gianfranco Zola proved to be one of the best buys of the season for Ruud Gullit's Chelsea.

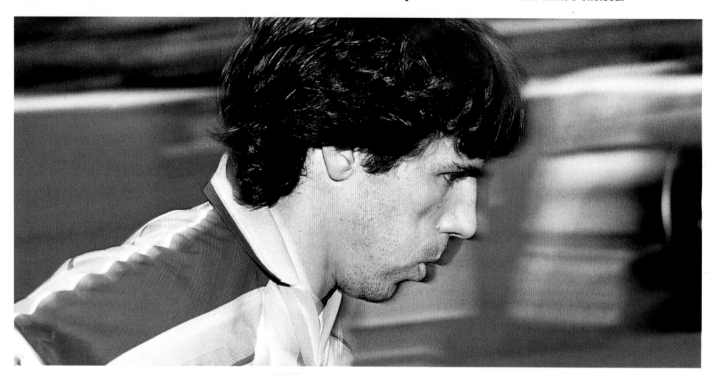

Under new coach Arsène Wenger, Arsenal had discovered a team spirit and sense of adventure that few thought existed at Highbury. Wenger had been expected to make sweeping changes at the club, with older players such as Steve Bould and Lee Dixon making way for a new Continental class. Instead, the French coach stuck with the existing players, often offering them new, extended contracts.

The result was a resurgent Arsenal. Captain and centre-back Tony Adams was encouraged to get further forward and discovered hitherto-unknown attacking talents. Patrick Vieira proved a rock in midfield, providing the thoughtful passing that had been lacking for some years. In attack, Ian Wright was a changed man. The 33-year-old striker, who had been on the verge of quitting Highbury after disagreements with previous manager Bruce Rioch, weighed in with some crucial goals against Wimbledon, Tottenham and Newcastle. Wright's striking partner Dennis Bergkamp also discovered a rich vein of form, scoring a memorable goal against Spurs in the North London derby at Highbury on a rain-soaked Sunday afternoon. The Gunners won 3–1.

Arsenal, 16–1 outsiders for the title at the start of what threatened to be a difficult season, were suddenly looking championship material. Not even a 1–0 defeat at Old Trafford could dampen the optimistic mood at Highbury.

United stumble

Champions Manchester United stayed in touch with the League leaders at home, but manager Alex Ferguson insisted that his team's priority was to qualify for the quarter-finals of the Champions League. They were not doing a very good job of it. The home defeat by Fenerbahce, United's first in 40 years of European competition, was followed by a second defeat at Old Trafford, this time at the hands of the holders Juventus. The 1–0 defeat meant the champions had to beat Rapid Vienna away to be sure of qualifying for the quarter-finals.

Newcastle continued to improve on previous seasons' showings in Europe, drawing 1–1 against Metz in the first leg of the UEFA Cup third round, with Peter Beardsley scoring the crucial away goal from the penalty spot.

Liverpool, having already qualified for the quarter-finals of the Cup-winners' Cup, were able to concentrate on the domestic title race, albeit with mixed results. They crashed 3–0 at Blackburn, who were still without a manager, drew 1–1 at home to Wimbledon and won 2–0 at Leeds.

Wimbledon kept up their challenge, completing another unbeaten month, while other sides showing improvement were Aston Villa, Derby County and Sunderland. The relegation zone already had a familiar look to it, with Nottingham Forest, Coventry

MANAGER OF THE MONTH

Arsène Wenger

In a matter of weeks at Highbury, Arsenal's French coach guided his side to the top of the Premier League table, a feat few thought possible at the start of the season.

PLAYER OF THE MONTH

Patrick Vieira

The young French midfielder provided a taste of what was to come at Highbury under Arsène Wenger with a series of polished displays.

City, Southampton and Middlesbrough all in the bottom five.

The pressure was beginning to tell at the bottom. Ron Atkinson was effectively sacked by Coventry, being moved "upstairs" to the position of Director of Football while Gordon Strachan, still playing at a sprightly 40, took control of team affairs. In the Nationwide first division, former Manchester United favourite Steve Coppell quit as Manchester City manager after just 33 days in charge at Maine Road, citing the pressure of the job.

Zola zooms in

On the transfer scene, the Premier League's growing foreign legion was joined by another world-class player. Gianfranco Zola, the Italian international striker, signed for Ruud Gullit's Chelsea from Parma. Spurs, already suffering from a glut of injuries, signed the young Norwegian forward Steffen Iversen. Also on the move were John Spencer, from Chelsea to QPR, and Darren Huckerby, a £1 million buy for Coventry from Newcastle.

Glenn Hoddle continued to impress as England coach, albeit against mediocre opposition, making it three out of three with a win in Tbilisi, Georgia. Hoddle chose to back Paul Gascoigne, subject to intense media criticism after allegations of wife-beating, and the gamble paid off. In the absence of the injured Alan Shearer, goals from Sheringham and Ferdinand secured a comfortable 2–0 win.

On the domestic Cup front, Tottenham were pulverized 6–1 by first-division Bolton in the Coca-Cola Cup fourth round. Eventual winners Leicester pulled off a memorable 2–0 win at Filbert Street over champions Manchester United. In the two biggest games of the round, Middlesbrough put paid to Newcastle's hopes 3–1 at the Riverside stadium, while Liverpool again got the better of Arsenal at Anfield, winning 4–2.

PREMIER LEAGUE STANDINGS

November 30

		P	W	D	L	F	A	Pts
1	Arsenal	15	9	4	2	29	13	31
2	Newcastle United	15	9	2	4	26	17	29
3	Liverpool	14	8	4	2	24	13	28
4	Wimbledon	15	8	4	3	26	16	28
5	Manchester United	15	7	5	3	29	22	26
6	Aston Villa	15	7	3	5	19	15	24
7	Chelsea	14	6	6	2	23	19	24
8	Everton	15	6	5	4	23	18	23
9	Derby County	15	5	6	4	17	17	21
10	Sheffield Wednesday	15	5	6	4	16	18	21
11	Tottenham Hotspur	14	6	2	6	15	14	20
12	Sunderland	15	4	5	6	13	18	17
13	West Ham United	15	4	5	6	13	18	17
14	Leicester City	15	5	2	8	14	21	17
15	Leeds United	14	5	1	8	13	20	16
16	Middlesbrough	15	3	5	7	20	26	14
17	Southampton	15	3	4	8	23	28	13
18	Blackburn Rovers	15	2	6	7	15	20	12
19	Coventry City	15	1	7	7	9	21	10
20	Nottingham Forest	15	1	6	8	12	25	9

MILESTONES OF THE SEASON

NOVEMBER 2
Blackburn, still without a manager, upset Liverpool 3–0. Southampton's Matthew Le Tissier sets a personal record by scoring in his sixth successive game.

NOVEMBER 6
Gordon Strachan is appointed manager of Coventry as Ron Atkinson steps upstairs to become Director of Football.

NOVEMBER 9
England win a World Cup qualifier in Georgia with goals from Sheringham and Ferdinand.

NOVEMBER 10
Steve Coppell quits as manager of Manchester City after just 33 days in charge at Maine Road.

NOVEMBER 11
Italy striker Gianfranco Zola joins Chelsea from Parma.

NOVEMBER 14
Everton defeat Southampton 7–1, the biggest win so far in this season's Premier League.

NOVEMBER 20
Manchester United lose 1–0 to Juventus at Old Trafford in the Champions League.

NOVEMBER 24
First division leaders Spurs are dumped out of the Coca-Cola Cup, thrashed 6–1 at Bolton.

NOVEMBER 30
Arsenal's 2–1 win at Newcastle takes the Gunners to top spot.

All change at the top

December was another topsy-turvy month in the League, with Liverpool back on top while Manchester United got their domestic title challenge on track again after qualifying for the quarter-finals of the Champions League.

Four for Fowler: the Liverpool striker humiliated Boro

Wins over Middlesbrough, Tottenham and Forest confirmed Liverpool as the team that everybody else had to beat, but Roy Evans' side were showing an alarming inability to kill games off. Sheffield Wednesday travelled to Anfield early in the month and came away with a 1–0 victory. Liverpool had created a host of chances, but failed to take any of them.

A week later Liverpool bounced back, hitting five past Middlesbrough, with Robbie Fowler scoring four times. However, the feeling persisted that Liverpool's midfield lacked steel. If another team could put a run of wins together, the title was there for the taking.

Manchester United manager Alex Ferguson had been arguing all season that his team's priority had been to get through the Champions League group stages and qualify for the quarter-finals. The Premier League campaign had taken a back seat during October and November, but United were now ready for a concerted challenge.

United bounce back

During December United's League form returned with a vengeance, and there were wins over Leeds, Nottingham Forest and Sunderland. The 4–0 victory over lowly Forest, who were now managed by Stuart Pearce following Frank Clark's resignation, was particularly pleasing for Ferguson. His side won at the City Ground on Boxing Day with goals from Beckham, Butt, Solskjaer and Cole.

The form of striker Solskjaer was a big bonus for United. The young Norwegian international quickly earned the nickname 'Baby-faced Assassin' after a series of crucial goals for his new club. He had been expected to ease into the first team slowly, but took to Old Trafford like a duck to water, scoring goals in both Europe and the Premier League for the champions. Solskjaer's form meant Ferguson had a surplus of strikers when Andy Cole returned from injury.

Arsenal kept in touch with the title race with wins over Southampton and draws with Sheffield Wednesday and Aston Villa, but had striker Ian Wright sent off in a 2–1 loss at Nottingham Forest.

Wimbledon, meanwhile, were confounding all the critics. They suffered their worst defeat of the season, 5–0 at Aston Villa, which ended their unbeaten run. However, away wins at Sunderland and Everton confirmed that the Crazy Gang's fighting spirit was alive and well. A place in Europe at the season's end seemed well within their grasp.

Newcastle in the goals

Newcastle had a good month, turning on the style for what were to be manager Kevin Keegan's final games in charge. They overcame French side Metz in the third round of the UEFA Cup. A 2–0 win in the second leg at St James', thanks to goals from the Colombian Faustino Asprilla, set up a quarter-final clash with French League leaders Monaco.

In the League, there were draws with Liverpool and Forest

MANAGER OF THE MONTH

Kevin Keegan

It was one last hurrah for the Geordie Messiah, with Newcastle earning rave reviews for their wins over Metz in the UEFA Cup and Tottenham in the League.

PLAYER OF THE MONTH

Ole Gunnar Solskjaer

Manchester United's young Norwegian striker weighed in with some crucial goals as the champions put their title challenge back on track after concentrating on the Champions League.

and a disappointing 2–1 defeat at Coventry, where Darren Huckerby scored against his old side, before a staggering 7–1 mauling of Tottenham.

Injury deprived Spurs of new signing John Scales, who had turned down a move from Liverpool to Leeds at the last minute in favour of a move south to Tottenham. Centre-back Scales was to have been George Graham's first signing at Leeds: instead, Graham turned his attention to Oldham's Gunnar Halle, making it clear that his priority at Elland Road was to sort out Leeds' leaky defence.

Middlesbrough's battle at the bottom of the Premier League was not helped by injuries or by their refusal to turn up for the fixture at Blackburn. Bryan Robson said he did not have enough fit players to put a team out. It was to prove costly – the FA would dock Boro three crucial points.

PREMIER LEAGUE STANDINGS

December 31

		P	W	D	L	F	A	Pts
1	Liverpool	21	2	6	3	38	19	42
2	Manchester United	20	10	7	3	42	25	38
3	Arsenal	20	10	7	3	37	20	37
4	Wimbledon	19	11	4	4	33	23	37
5	Newcastle United	20	10	4	6	35	22	34
6	Aston Villa	20	10	4	6	29	19	34
7	Chelsea	20	8	8	4	32	29	32
8	Everton	20	7	7	6	29	27	28
9	Sheffield Wednesday	20	6	10	4	21	22	28
10	Tottenham Hotspur	20	8	4	8	22	26	28
11	Derby County	20	5	8	7	20	25	23
12	Leicester City	20	6	5	9	20	27	23
13	Sunderland	20	6	5	9	19	28	23
14	Leeds United	20	6	4	10	16	24	22
15	West Ham United	19	5	6	8	18	25	21
16	Coventry City	20	4	7	9	18	27	19
17	Middlesbrough	20	4	6	10	25	38	18
18	Blackburn Rovers	19	3	8	9	17	22	16
19	Southampton	20	4	4	12	28	37	16
20	Nottingham Forest	20	2	8	10	18	36	14

MILESTONES OF THE SEASON

DECEMBER 1
Middlesbrough's Brazilian midfielder Emerson returns to Teesside after going absent without leave, amid rumours that he is to be sold to Bobby Robson's Barcelona.

DECEMBER 3
Newcastle reach the quarter-finals of the UEFA Cup after beating Metz at St James' Park. Faustino Asprilla scores twice but is booked for an over-elaborate goal celebration and will miss the quarter-final first leg.

DECEMBER 4
Manchester United reach the quarter-finals of the Champions Cup after beating Rapid Vienna 2–0 in Austria. They will play Portuguese champions FC Porto.

DECEMBER 7
John Scales turns down Leeds at the 11th hour in favour of a move from Liverpool to Tottenham.

DECEMBER 8
Joao Havelange announces he is to step down as president of FIFA, football's world governing body.

DECEMBER 9
Leeds sign Gunnar Halle from Oldham.

DECEMBER 16
Blackburn say Swede Sven-Goran Eriksson will be their manager for next season.

DECEMBER 17
Wembley is confirmed as the site of the new national stadium.

DECEMBER 21
Manchester United return to form in the League, beating Sunderland 5–0 at Old Trafford. Middlesbrough fail to turn up for a League match at Blackburn, citing a lack of fit players as their reason.

DECEMBER 22
Wimbledon's three-month unbeaten run ends with a 5–0 thrashing at Aston Villa.

DECEMBER 26
Boxing Day action sees Manchester United win 4–0 at struggling Nottingham Forest, while Chelsea win 2–0 at Aston Villa and Middlesbrough are 4–2 winners over Everton.

DECEMBER 28
Newcastle thrash Tottenham 7–1 at St James' Park.

DECEMBER 29
Former Nottingham Forest boss Frank Clark takes over at Manchester City.

Keegan's resignation stuns Newcastle

The resignation of Newcastle boss Kevin Keegan dominated the headlines as the Premier League season entered the new year.

Message to Kevin: Newcastle fans make their point outside St James' Park

Keegan had been showing signs of stress over the Christmas period and as speculation mounted that he was about to quit, he clashed with reporters after his side's 1–1 draw with Charlton in the FA Cup third round. Nevertheless his departure took everybody by surprise, not least Newcastle, who had the tough task of finding a successor.

"I've taken the club as far as I can", was Keegan's official reason for quitting. He said the look on the face of Tottenham boss Gerry Francis after Newcastle had beaten Spurs 7–1 at Christmas had brought home to him just how stressful football management could be. It has since emerged that the club was pressuring Keegan to commit to a long-term contract so they could go ahead with a Stock Exchange flotation. Kevin couldn't give Newcastle a guarantee that he would be around in the long term, so he quit.

Assistant manager Terry McDermott took charge of Newcastle on a temporary basis while the club searched for a replacement. Former England manager Bobby Robson was the first choice, but he declined to break his contract with Barcelona, so Newcastle turned to Kenny Dalglish, ironically the man who replaced Keegan as a player at Liverpool in 1977.

Dalglish's first game in charge was the FA Cup third-round replay against Charlton at St James' Park. The Magpies won, but not with any great style. After nearly five glorious years, during which Newcastle had been saved from the old third division and been taken to the top of the Premier League, the Keegan era was well and truly over.

Upsets in the Cup

Bad weather and a crowded fixture list combined to disrupt the FA Cup third round. When all the ties were finally played, there were some big surprises. Southampton crashed out to First Division Reading, a game which left Saints boss Graeme Souness fuming about having to play on a frozen pitch. West Ham were held to a draw in the snow by Second Division Wrexham, then beaten at Upton Park in the replay. Non-League Woking came so very close to the biggest upset, drawing with Premier League Coventry City at Highfield Road before losing by a solitary goal in the home replay.

The FA Cup fourth round kicked off with some third-round ties unresolved, but in the game of the round Chelsea mounted a remarkable comeback against Liverpool at Stamford Bridge, winning 4–2 after being 2–0 down at half-time. Italian striker Gianfranco Zola was the man of the match, scoring a goal. Mark Hughes got one and Gianluca Vialli scored two for the Blues. Elsewhere, the fourth round produced upsets for Everton (losers at home to Bradford courtesy of a stunning goal from Chris Waddle), Newcastle (beaten at home by Nottingham Forest) and Manchester United (defeated 1–0 by Wimbledon).

Wimbledon were on course for Wembley in both cup competitions. They reached the Coca-Cola Cup semi-finals after a 2–0 win at runaway first division leaders Bolton. Joe Kinnear's side were joined by Leicester City, Middlesbrough (2–1 winners over Liverpool) and Second Division Stockport County (who had continued a remarkable run by beating Southampton in a fiercely-contested replay).

MANAGER OF THE MONTH

Alex Ferguson

The double double-winning manager masterminded a fightback for Manchester United which, after a shaky November, saw the champions back in contention in the Premier League.

PLAYER OF THE MONTH

Gianfranco Zola

The little Italian delighted everyone at Stamford Bridge with a fantastic performance against Liverpool in the FA Cup fourth round, showing just why he is rated as one of the best players in the world.

United catching up

In the Premier League Liverpool led the way, but Manchester United were catching up fast thanks to wins over Spurs, Coventry and Wimbledon. Alex Ferguson's team were up to second place by the end of the month.

Chelsea were continuing to make progress in the League and FA Cup under Ruud Gullit, while Leeds and Blackburn were also moving up the table. It was beginning to look bleak for Middlesbrough, though: they remained rooted to the bottom and, worse still, the FA docked Boro three points for failing to turn up for the game at Blackburn in December.

January also saw former Leeds manager Howard Wilkinson appointed as FA Technical Director and there were some important transfers too. Liverpool signed Norwegian centre-back Bjorn Kvarme from Rosenborg, Dutch defender Robert Molenaar joined Leeds and Matt Elliott moved from Oxford to Leicester.

Arsenal signed French teenager Nicolas Anelka from under the noses of Paris St Germain, while Everton moved for Danish midfielder Claus Thomsen.

Two other foreigners, however, left England. West Ham were glad to part company with troublesome Romanian Florin Raducioiu, and Tomas Brolin returned to Italy after his difficult time at Leeds.

PREMIER LEAGUE STANDINGS

January 31

		P	W	D	L	F	A	Pts
1	Manchester United	23	13	7	3	48	27	46
2	Arsenal	24	13	7	4	44	23	46
3	Liverpool	24	13	7	4	41	20	46
4	Newcastle United	24	12	6	6	46	27	42
5	Wimbledon	22	11	5	6	35	28	38
6	Chelsea	23	10	8	5	36	32	38
7	Aston Villa	23	10	5	8	31	25	35
8	Sheffield Wednesday	23	8	10	5	26	27	34
9	Tottenham Hotspur	23	9	4	10	26	31	31
10	Leeds United	24	8	5	11	21	27	29
11	Sunderland	24	7	8	9	23	31	29
12	Everton	24	7	7	10	32	38	28
13	Leicester City	23	7	6	11	22	31	27
14	Coventry City	24	6	8	10	23	33	26
15	Derby County	23	5	10	8	22	29	25
16	Blackburn Rovers	23	5	9	9	24	24	24
17	Nottingham Forest	24	5	8	11	23	38	23
18	West Ham United	23	5	7	11	19	30	22
19	Southampton	22	5	5	12	31	39	20
20	Middlesbrough	23	5	6	12	29	43	18

MILESTONES OF THE SEASON

JANUARY 4
The FA Cup third round is hit by bad weather. Of the ties that do go ahead, West Ham are held by Wrexham and Southampton are beaten 3–1 by Reading.

JANUARY 5
Manchester United beat injury-hit Tottenham 2–0 and Newcastle draw with Charlton in the third round of the FA Cup.

JANUARY 7
Howard Wilkinson is appointed Technical Director of the FA.

JANUARY 8
Kevin Keegan quits as manager of Newcastle United.

JANUARY 9
Leeds boss George Graham signs another defender, Dutchman Robert Molenaar.

JANUARY 10
Liverpool sign Norwegian defender Bjorn Tore Kvarme from Rosenborg.

JANUARY 14
Newcastle appoint Kenny Dalglish as a replacement for Kevin Keegan. Middlesbrough have three points deducted for failing to turn up for the League match at Blackburn in December.

JANUARY 15
Newcastle beat Charlton, just, in Dalglish's first game in charge. Arsenal sign French wonderkid Nicolas Anelka from Paris St Germain. Everton sign Danish international Claus Thomsen from Ipswich.

JANUARY 23
Leeds loan Swede Tomas Brolin back to Parma.

JANUARY 25
West Ham go out of the FA Cup to Wrexham in a third-round replay. Everton are beaten by Bradford in round four.

JANUARY 26
Chelsea beat Liverpool 4–2 in a thrilling FA Cup fourth-round tie at Stamford Bridge.

February

England botch the Italian job

Wembley Woe: Gianfranco Zola scores against England

Glenn Hoddle's England faced their biggest test of his brief but so far successful management when Italy arrived in town for a crucial World Cup qualifier. Italy, of course, were no strangers to England, boasting Premier League players Fabrizio Ravanelli, Roberto Di Matteo and Gianfranco Zola among their ranks. They also had a new manager, Cesare Maldini, father of Paolo, who all the players were keen to impress.

The Italians went to Wembley with a game plan which they aimed to stick to: defending in numbers and taking the offensive only occasionally with swift, incisive counter-attacks. Glenn Hoddle knew Italy would be hard to break down and controversially selected Southampton's Matthew Le Tissier, a player he believed could be the key to unlocking a tight Italian defence.

Hoddle's plan backfired. Le Tissier had little or no influence on the game, even though England were forced to attack for much of the match after the Italians took an early lead. With less than 20 minutes gone, Italian defender Alessandro Costacurta launched a hopeful clearance forward. Gianfranco Zola, watched closely (but not closely enough) by Stuart Pearce and Sol Campbell, controlled the ball with an exquisite first touch and unleashed a fierce shot past stand-in goalkeeper Ian Walker.

Italy defended resolutely and England, with Alan Shearer not fully fit, rarely came close to scoring. The Italians' 1–0 victory left them firmly in control of the World Cup qualifying group and England contemplating second place and a play-off to qualify for the finals of France 98.

United on top

Manchester United went top of the Premier League after a crucial win over Arsène Wenger's Arsenal at Highbury. The champions arrived at the top after a 16-game unbeaten run. The win over Arsenal was not without its problems, however. The game saw a clash between United's Peter Schmeichel and Gunners striker Ian Wright which went unseen by the referee but was the result of a long-running feud between the two players. At the heart of the dispute were allegations from Wright of racism against Schmeichel.

While United drew strength from their troubles, Liverpool were finding goals hard to come by. Robbie Fowler was failing to convert chances that had been so easy earlier in the season, while Patrik Berger was unable to live up to the high standards which he had set for himself with some spectacular goals in the autumn.

While Liverpool were struggling to find the net, Newcastle's fortunes took a nosedive with the news that Alan Shearer, a hat-trick hero against Leicester on the second day of the month, was injured and out of action for up to six weeks.

There were further upsets in the Cups, the most notable being Second Division Chesterfield's fifth-round FA Cup victory over Premier League Nottingham Forest. The Spireites' win set up an intriguing quarter-final clash with fellow giant-slayers Wrexham, who had won away at Birmingham. Another big-name casualty was Leeds, knocked out of the fifth round by First Division Portsmouth.

There was controversy as well. Leicester and Chelsea had fought out an exciting 2–2 draw at Filbert Street and met back

MANAGER OF THE MONTH

Alex Ferguson

Manchester United's progress continued unabated, with Ferguson's decision to concentrate on the Champions League in October and November paying dividends. It was business as usual with United top of the Premier League.

PLAYER OF THE MONTH

Roy Keane

Nobody represented Man United's determination to retain their title better than Roy Keane. The Irishman's aggression and will to win was evident throughout February.

at Stamford Bridge in the replay. It was a close match, with Leicester working hard to contain Chelsea's Continental challenge, which went to extra time. Things looked set for penalties until, with three minutes remaining, Chelsea defender Erland Johnsen clumsily fell over in the Leicester penalty area. Referee Mike Reed awarded a penalty which was converted by Frenchman Frank Leboeuf. Television replays confirmed that it was a cruel and unjust way for Leicester's FA Cup challenge to end. But it also confirmed many people's belief that this was going to be Chelsea's year.

Tough at the bottom

The relegation dogfight was shaping up as a struggle between bottom-placed Middlesbrough, Southampton, West Ham, Forest and Coventry. Ironically, the three teams promoted from the first division – Derby, Sunderland and Leicester – who many had predicted would be heading straight back down at the end of the season – were pulling away from the relegation zone.

Of the teams in trouble, West Ham seemed most likely to pull clear, especially after they splashed out nearly £7 million on strikers Paul Kitson (Newcastle) and John Hartson (Arsenal). It seemed a lot of money to pay for two reserve team players, but they soon started to repay their hefty fees with goals.

Elsewhere Blackburn confirmed that Roy Hodgson would be their manager next season, after Swede Sven-Goran Eriksson had turned them down, and England launched a bid to host the 2006 World Cup, with Germany their main rivals.

PREMIER LEAGUE STANDINGS

February 28

		P	W	D	L	F	A	Pts
1	Manchester United	27	15	9	3	53	30	54
2	Liverpool	27	15	8	4	46	20	53
3	Newcastle United	26	14	6	6	51	30	48
4	Arsenal	28	13	9	6	45	26	48
5	Wimbledon	25	12	7	6	37	28	43
6	Aston Villa	27	12	7	8	34	26	43
7	Chelsea	25	11	9	5	39	34	42
8	Sheffield Wednesday	26	9	12	5	31	31	39
9	Leeds United	27	10	5	12	23	31	35
10	Tottenham Hotspur	26	9	5	12	30	37	32
11	Everton	26	8	8	10	30	38	32
12	Leicester City	25	8	6	11	29	37	30
13	Sunderland	26	7	8	11	23	33	29
14	Blackburn Rovers	25	6	10	9	28	25	28
15	Derby County	27	6	10	11	27	37	28
16	Coventry City	27	6	10	11	24	35	28
17	West Ham United	26	6	7	13	24	36	25
18	Nottingham Forest	26	5	9	12	23	40	24
19	Southampton	25	5	6	14	34	40	21
20	Middlesbrough	26	5	7	14	30	48	19

MILESTONES OF THE SEASON

FEBRUARY 2
Alan Shearer scores a hat-trick as Newcastle come from 3–1 down to beat Leicester 4–3 at St James' Park.

FEBRUARY 8
England launch a bid to stage the 2006 World Cup finals.

FEBRUARY 12
England lose 1–0 to Italy at Wembley, coach Hoddle's first defeat.

FEBRUARY 15
Second-division Chesterfield knock out Nottingham Forest to reach the quarter-finals of the FA Cup.

FEBRUARY 16
Chelsea and Leicester City draw 2–2 at Filbert Street in the FA Cup fifth round.

FEBRUARY 19
Manchester United beat Arsenal 2–1 at Highbury to stay top of the Premier League.

FEBRUARY 24
A new consortium, led by former Tottenham chairman Irving Scholar, takes control of Nottingham Forest.

FEBRUARY 25
Blackburn announce that Roy Hodgson will take charge next season.

FEBRUARY 26
Chelsea beat Leicester at Stamford Bridge in the FA Cup fifth-round replay with a controversial extra-time penalty.

FEBRUARY 27
Dave Bassett quits Crystal Palace to join Nottingham Forest as general manager.

United on song in Europe

Europe was back on everyone's minds in March, with Manchester United, Liverpool and Newcastle all in action on the Continent.

Ryan's Express: United's Giggs was on outstanding form

It was a great month for Manchester United, who stayed on course for a League and Champions Cup double. The champions maintained top spot in the Premier League while overpowering Portuguese champions FC Porto in the quarter-finals of the Champions Cup.

Porto arrived at Old Trafford with a fearsome reputation. Many doubted if United could reach the semi-finals, especially as their form in the Champions League group stages had been far from impressive.

In the end, though, we were left wondering why Porto had been so highly rated. United's stunning 4–0 win in the home leg, in which Ryan Giggs and Eric Cantona were outstanding, was followed by a 0–0 draw in Portugal. The second leg was memorable more for the violent treatment of United fans by Portuguese police than for the quality of the football, but the English champions were in the semi-finals of the European Cup for the first time since 1969.

League wins over Coventry, Sheffield Wednesday and Everton kept United on course for a fourth Premier League title in five seasons.

It was a great month, too, for Liverpool striker Robbie Fowler, who slotted home a sensational last-minute winner in his side's thrilling 4–3 victory over Newcastle at Anfield and then scored twice as Liverpool eliminated Brann Bergen of Norway from the European Cup-winners' Cup, although he was fined by UEFA for displaying a T-shirt in support of striking Liverpool dockers. The month ended on a high for Fowler with praise from FIFA for his sportsmanship, after he refused to accept the award of a penalty in Liverpool's favour in the crucial match against Arsenal at Highbury, insisting that goalkeeper David Seaman had not tripped him. Then, a few days later, Fowler scored his first senior goal for England, in a friendly against Mexico at Wembley.

Highbury hopes ended

The match at Highbury, which finished 2–1 to Liverpool, effectively ended Arsenal's title hopes, according to Gunners boss Arsène Wenger. Although his side finished the month in third place and within striking distance of leaders Manchester United, Wenger conceded that the home defeats by Liverpool and Wimbledon had effectively ended his team's chances of winning the Premiership.

While Manchester United and Liverpool progressed in European competition, there was disappointment for Newcastle in the UEFA Cup. Kenny Dalglish's side proved to be a clear second best when they came up against French League leaders Monaco. They lost 1–0 at St James' Park in the first leg and 3–0 in the return leg in Monte Carlo, and were clearly missing the striking power of the injured Alan Shearer.

While the Premier League's big guns concentrated on Europe and the League title race, some lesser-known teams were sparkling in the Cups, none more so than Chesterfield.

In an all-second-division FA Cup quarter-final, they got the better of Wrexham 1–0 to set up a semi-final against Premier League Middlesbrough, who ran out 2–0 winners over Derby, largely thanks to the form of Juninho.

Chelsea on course

In the other FA Cup quarter-finals, Chelsea swept past Portsmouth while Wimbledon reached the semi-finals at the expense of Sheffield Wednesday. For Wimbledon, the FA Cup offered a second chance

MANAGER OF THE MONTH

Alex Ferguson

United's manager kept his team on course for yet another Premier League title and steered his side into the semi-finals of the European Cup for the first time since 1969.

PLAYER OF THE MONTH

Robbie Fowler

Goals in Europe and the Premier League, praise from FIFA, a first goal for England and a fine for a political protest. All in a month's work for Liverpool's prolific young striker.

to reach Wembley following their defeat by Leicester in the semi-finals of the Coca-Cola Cup.

Leicester were joined in the League Cup Final by Middlesbrough, who had ended the brave challenge of second-division Stockport. For Bryan Robson's Middlesbrough, the Cup campaigns provided some relief from their dreadful League form. Despite the money spent on stars such as Ravanelli and Emerson, relegation was still a distinct possibility.

Other struggling sides reinforced their survival bids before the transfer market closed. Nottingham Forest, now with general manager Dave Bassett, signed Dutch striker Pierre Van Hooijdonk from Celtic, while Chris Waddle joined Sunderland.

Everton were not in serious danger of relegation, but their mid-table position was deemed not to be good enough and Joe Royle became the latest Premier League manager to bite the dust.

PREMIER LEAGUE STANDINGS

March 31

		P	W	D	L	F	A	Pts
1	Manchester United	31	18	9	4	61	33	63
2	Liverpool	31	17	9	5	53	26	60
3	Arsenal	32	16	9	7	52	28	57
4	Newcastle United	30	15	7	8	59	36	52
5	Aston Villa	31	14	8	9	37	27	50
6	Chelsea	31	13	10	8	51	44	49
7	Sheffield Wednesday	31	12	13	6	41	37	49
8	Wimbledon	30	12	10	8	42	37	46
9	Leeds United	32	11	8	13	26	34	41
10	Tottenham Hotspur	31	11	6	14	38	43	39
11	Leicester City	31	10	9	12	37	44	39
12	Blackburn Rovers	31	8	12	11	33	32	36
13	Everton	31	9	9	13	37	45	36
14	Derby County	31	8	11	12	35	47	35
15	West Ham United	31	8	9	14	31	41	33
16	Sunderland	32	8	9	15	29	48	33
17	Middlesbrough	31	9	8	14	44	52	32
18	Nottingham Forest	33	6	13	14	28	49	31
19	Coventry City	32	6	12	14	27	46	30
20	Southampton	31	6	9	16	39	51	27

MILESTONES OF THE SEASON

MARCH 2
Aston Villa beat Liverpool 1–0 at Villa Park.

MARCH 4
Newcastle lose 1–0 at home to Monaco in the UEFA Cup.

MARCH 5
Manchester United thrash FC Porto 4–0 at Old Trafford in the quarter-finals of the Champions League. Fabrizio Ravanelli scores a hat-trick as bottom club Middlesbrough thrash Derby 6–1.

MARCH 6
Liverpool draw 1–1 against Brann Bergen in Norway in the Cup-winners' Cup.

MARCH 8
Middlesbrough reach the FA Cup semi-finals after a win over Derby.

MARCH 9
Second-division Chesterfield reach the FA Cup semi-finals after a 1–0 win over Wrexham. Chelsea beat Portsmouth, and Wimbledon go through after beating Sheffield Wednesday 2–0.

MARCH 10
Liverpool beat Newcastle 4–3 at Anfield with a late winner from Robbie Fowler

MARCH 15
Leeds' Ghanaian striker Tony Yeboah throws his shirt at manager George Graham after being substituted in the League match at Spurs.

MARCH 16
Chelsea thrash Sunderland 6–2 at Stamford Bridge.

MARCH 19
Manchester United hold out for a 0–0 draw with FC Porto in Portugal to reach the semi-finals of the Champions League.

MARCH 20
Liverpool beat Brann Bergen 3–0 at Anfield to reach the semi-finals of the Cup-winners' Cup.

MARCH 21
Robbie Fowler is fined £900 by UEFA for his T-shirt protest during the game against Brann Bergen.

MARCH 24
Liverpool beat Arsenal 2–1 at Highbury.

MARCH 26
Manager Joe Royle parts company with Everton after a string of poor results.

MARCH 29
England beat Mexico 2–0 in a friendly at Wembley.

April

Ups and down for United

It was a month of mixed fortunes for champions Manchester United, who lost their Champions League semi-final to Borussia Dortmund but beat Liverpool at Anfield, virtually guaranteeing them a fourth Premier League title in five years.

Champagne Celebration: FA Cup heroes Chesterfield

Alex Ferguson had made it clear that winning the Champions League was to be United's priority for the season. Reaching the semi-finals was a success in itself – Arsenal, Leeds, Blackburn and United themselves had all failed in recent seasons – but winning Europe's top prize had become a personal crusade for the United manager.

In the end, United came very close, but ultimately Fergie's young side were not good enough. They were beaten 1–0 in both legs of the semi-final by Borussia Dortmund, with United's lack of finishing the key factor in their defeat.

However, major consolation came with a 3–1 victory over Liverpool at Anfield which all but secured another Premier League title – United's fourth in five years. Liverpool knew this was a match they could not afford to lose if they were to have any chance at all of breaking United's monopoly on the Premier League title.

The scoreline reflected not so much that United were a good side, but that their opponents were not good enough to take the title from them. Liverpool could not compete with United in midfield and handed the champions their goals with a mixture of bad defending (Gary Pallister's two headers, both from corners) and bad goalkeeping (David James's terrible handling of the cross that handed Andy Cole a goal on a plate).

The defeat by United was followed a few days later by elimination from the Cup-winners' Cup at the hands of Paris St Germain. The losses meant another disappointing season for Liverpool by their own very high standards.

To make matters worse, Robbie Fowler had been sent off in the Merseyside derby against Everton, earning him a three-match ban for the last three League games of the season. It meant Liverpool faced one hell of a battle with Newcastle and Arsenal for second place and the resulting qualification for the Champions League.

Chesterfield on Cup trail

In the FA Cup, Chesterfield was the name on everybody's lips. The Second Division side had, quite remarkably, reached the semi-finals of the Cup for the first time in their history and were bidding to become the first club from the second division to make the Final. Middlesbrough – Ravanelli, Juninho and company – stood between Chesterfield and a place in the history books.

The two teams played out one of the most memorable semi-finals in FA Cup history. The record books will say that the match ended 3–3 after extra time, with Boro comfortably winning the replay 3–0. What will never be recorded, tragically, is that Chesterfield had a perfectly good goal disallowed by

MANAGER OF THE MONTH

Martin O'Neill

Guided Leicester to a League Cup success and maintained the club's Premier League status. Nobody could have asked for more.

PLAYER OF THE MONTH

Juninho

The little Brazilian was at his brilliant best as he steered 'Boro to the FA Cup Final for the first time in their history.

referee David Elleray. The goal, if given, would have put the match beyond Middlesbrough.

Chelsea were comprehensive victors in the other semi-final, the all-London affair against Wimbledon. The result ended the Dons' assault on Wembley's twin towers, Leicester having knocked them out of the Coca-Cola Cup semi-finals on away goals.

Foxes on form

Leicester, in turn, were involved in an epic battle with Middlesbrough in the Coca-Cola Cup Final. After the game at Wembley had ended 1–1 after extra time, it was Leicester who emerged triumphant from the replay at Hillsborough, with striker Steve Claridge the Foxes' extra-time hero.

Middlesbrough's Cup exploits only served to increase their relegation worries. By the end of the month, Bryan Robson's

side, despite the brilliant individual form of Juninho, were staring relegation in the face.

Nottingham Forest were in even worse trouble, despite the presence of new striker Pierre van Hooijdonk and new general manager Dave Bassett. Also up against it were Coventry and Sunderland, now facing a fight for their Premier League lives.

MILESTONES OF THE SEASON

APRIL 7
Speculation mounts that Chelsea's unhappy Italian striker Gianluca Vialli will return to Italy at the end of the season.

APRIL 9
Manchester United lose 1–0 to German champions Borussia Dortmund in the Champions Cup semi-final first leg.

APRIL 10
Liverpool lose 3–0 to Paris St Germain in the Cup-winners' Cup semi-final first leg in France.

APRIL 13
Chelsea beat Wimbledon 3–0 to reach the FA Cup Final, while Middlesbrough and Chesterfield draw 3–3 in a thrilling match at Old Trafford. Alan Shearer is voted Player of the Year in the annual PFA poll. David Beckham wins the Young Player award.

APRIL 16
A Steve Claridge goal in extra time gives Leicester victory over Middlesbrough in the Coca-Cola Cup Final replay at Hillsborough. Robbie Fowler is sent off for fighting in the Merseyside derby.

APRIL 17
Chelsea agree to sign Nigerian full-back Celestine Babayaro from Anderlecht of Belgium for next season.

APRIL 19
Manchester United win 3–1 at Anfield in the crucial Premier League match against Liverpool.

APRIL 23
Manchester United lose 1–0 (2–0 on aggregate) to Borussia Dortmund in the Champions League semi-final at Old Trafford.

APRIL 24
Liverpool beat Paris St Germain 2–0 at Anfield in the Cup-winners' Cup semi-final second leg but go out 3–2 on aggregate.

APRIL 25
Newcastle agree to release French winger David Ginola at the end of the season.

PREMIER LEAGUE STANDINGS

April 30

		P	W	D	L	F	A	Pts
1	Manchester United	34	20	9	5	69	39	69
2	Arsenal	36	18	11	7	59	30	65
3	Liverpool	35	18	10	7	58	33	64
4	Newcastle United	34	17	9	8	67	40	60
5	Aston Villa	36	16	10	10	44	31	58
6	Sheffield Wednesday	35	14	14	7	48	44	56
7	Chelsea	36	15	10	11	56	54	55
8	Wimbledon	35	13	10	12	45	44	49
9	Tottenham Hotspur	36	13	7	16	42	47	46
10	Leeds United	36	11	11	14	27	37	44
11	Derby County	36	10	13	13	42	54	43
12	Everton	36	10	12	14	43	52	42
13	Blackburn Rovers	35	9	14	12	40	37	41
14	Leicester City	35	10	10	15	39	50	40
15	Southampton	36	9	11	16	48	55	38
16	Coventry City	36	8	14	14	35	51	38
17	West Ham United	35	9	11	15	34	45	38
18	Sunderland	36	9	10	17	32	52	37
19	Middlesbrough	34	9	9	16	44	54	33
20	Nottingham Forest	36	6	15	15	30	53	33

Coca-Cola Cup Final

Resilient Foxes take the prize

The 1997 Coca-Cola League Cup Final won't be remembered as a classic, but that won't bother Leicester City. Steve Claridge was the extra-time hero for the Foxes, scoring the only goal of the replay against Middlesbrough at Hillsborough. The victory was Leicester's first major trophy since 1964 when they won ... the League Cup. Europe and the UEFA Cup now beckon.

Flat Out:
Middlesbrough's
Emerson tangles
with Leicester's
Heskey at Wembley.

The teams' big day out at Wembley 10 days earlier had ended in a 1–1 stalemate after a late, late strike by Leicester's Emile Heskey had cancelled out Fabrizio Ravanelli's goal for Boro. The two teams could not have been more different. Middlesbrough, the cosmopolitan stars, against Leicester, the poor relations who had grafted their way to the final. Middlesbrough had Ravanelli, Juninho and Emerson. Leicester had Walsh, Parker and Claridge.

Few could doubt either team's right to be there, though. Middlesbrough had put out Newcastle and Liverpool, two of the competition's favourites, en route to Wembley. In the semi-final they faced Stockport County, not everybody's idea of a tough match, but the conquerors of West Ham and Blackburn no less. Leicester had seen off Manchester United in a memorable win at Filbert Street in the fourth round, and Wimbledon in the two-legged semi-final.

Graft defies flair

Middlesbrough were everybody's favourites to beat Leicester. Bryan Robson's side had struggled to find their form in the League, but could do no wrong in the Cups, reaching the finals of both domestic competitions. Given the money Boro had invested in their foreign stars, success was expected on Teesside. Relegation was still a possibility, but they were going to enjoy themselves in the Cups.

Leicester, in contrast, were seen as the battlers. They were

LEICESTER 1 (0) (Heskey 118)
MIDDLESBROUGH 1 (0) (Ravanelli 95)
After extra time
HT: 0–0. 90 min.: 1–1.
Attendance: 76,757. Referee: M Bodenham

Leicester: Keller, Grayson, Whitlow (Robins 105), Walsh, Izzet (Taylor 108), Lennon, Claridge, Parker, Heskey, Kaamark, Prior.

Middlesbrough: Schwarzer, Cox, Pearson, Emerson, Mustoe, Beck, Juninho, Ravanelli, Fleming, Festa, Hignett.

LEICESTER 1 (0) (Claridge 100)
MIDDLESBROUGH 0 (0)
After extra time
HT: 0–0. 90 min.: 0–0.
Attendance: 39,428. Referee: M Bodenham

Leicester: Keller, Grayson, Whitlow (Lawrence 109), Walsh, Izzet, Lennon, Claridge (Robins 117), Parker, Heskey, Kaamark, Prior.

Middlesbrough: Roberts, Cox (Moore 105), Pearson, Emerson, Kinder, Mustoe, Juninho, Ravanelli, Blackmore, Festa (Vickers 76), Hignett (Beck 105).

expected to put up a fight, but ultimately Boro's international class would prove too much for them. That was the plan.

However, Leicester boss Martin O'Neill has built a team in his own image: gritty, determined and never afraid to get stuck in. With that in mind, it perhaps wasn't a surprise that the Wembley final was such a disappointment. Leicester had a game-plan and they stuck to it. Uppermost in O'Neill's mind was the need to stop Juninho, so Pontus Kaamark was delegated to man-mark the little Brazilian. Leicester's Swedish defender did a terrific job, sticking so close to Boro's midfield danger man that Juninho must have been surprised when Kaamark did not follow him on to Boro's coach for the journey back north.

With Leicester snapping at the heels of Boro at every opportunity, the match dragged on into extra time. So when Juninho escaped his marker to set up Ravanelli to score, people thought it was all over. They hadn't reckoned with Leicester, and Emile Heskey in particular.

With two minutes remaining, another cross was pumped into the Middlesbrough area. Heskey headed against the crossbar, the ball bounced down and an almighty scramble ensued. Eventually the ball fell kindly at the feet of Heskey, who tapped home from a matter of inches.

It was scrappy goal which summed up a scrappy game. It meant the teams had to do it all over again 10 days later in Sheffield.

Here we go again

The replay was a better game, but only just. Again Boro's foreign stars tried to the grab the glory, again Leicester tried to stop them. Again there was stalemate after 90 minutes, albeit after a marginally more entertaining game. The game was crying out for a hero, someone who could settle the matter once and for all.

Step forward Steve Claridge, the striker who plays with his socks rolled down but his head held high. The centre-forward who never gives up. What he lacks in skill he makes up for in effort. It was Claridge who had secured Leicester's place in the Premier League with a last-minute extra-time winner in the play-off final against Crystal Palace. And it was Claridge who won the cup for Leicester. After 220 minutes of the final, Garry Parker floated another long ball into the Boro penalty area, Steve Walsh flicked the ball on, and Steve Claridge somehow summoned up the energy to volley home.

After the goal, there was little that Middlesbrough could do. For a tiring 20 minutes Leicester defended frantically, but successfully.

On The Up… : Gianluca Festa beats Steve Claridge to a high ball in the Wembley final.

… And Up: Captain Steve Walsh proudly displays his newly-acquired silverware.

May

United win title but lose Eric

Manchester United won the 1996–97 Premier League title without even playing. With two games still to play, Liverpool and Newcastle both travelled to London knowing only victories would keep the title race open.

Liverpool's defeat by Wimbledon, coupled with Newcastle's failure to win against West Ham, meant Alex Ferguson's team could crack open the champagne at home to West Ham on the last day of the season. Old Trafford duly celebrated United's fourth title in five years – but days later the newly-crowned champions were rocked by a sensational announcement.

Eric Cantona, United's lucky charm for the past five seasons, announced that he had played his last game for the club. The enigmatic Frenchman, who was about to turn 31, said he wanted to quit while he was at the top. His shock decision left United reeling and English football mourning the loss of one of its most talented players.

If truth be told, United had not played brilliantly in defence of their title. They had been thrashed 5–0 and 6–3 by Newcastle and Southampton respectively, but had always had the edge on their closest rivals, Liverpool and Arsenal, who were not good enough to knock United off their perch.

Boro go down

While United were busy clinching the title, a former Old Trafford great was experiencing the agonies of football management. Bryan Robson had spent more than £20 million on players but could not prevent Middlesbrough from being relegated. Their failure to turn up for a match at Blackburn, and the subsequent docking of three points, was to prove fatal.

Boro's failure to beat Leeds on the last day of the season sent them down after just two seasons back in the Premier League. They were joined by Nottingham Forest and fellow north-east strugglers Sunderland, who were condemned to the drop by Coventry's miraculous escape at Spurs, where they won 2–1.

Kenny grabs second spot

Newcastle's promising run under Kenny Dalglish was rewarded with a second-place finish in the League, thus pipping Arsenal and Liverpool to the lucrative Champions League spot. Under Dalglish, Newcastle lost some of the showmanship that had so dazzled the fans on Tyneside, but the defensive solidity brought results. The Magpies even finished the season off with a flourish, thrashing Forest, who had gone down 5–0 with two weeks of the season to go.

Chelsea clinch the Cup

Wembley played host to some big games in May. The biggest of them all, the FA Cup Final, was won by Ruud Gullit's Chelsea, 2–0 winners over Middlesbrough, who became the first team ever to lose two Wembley finals and be relegated all in the same season. Crystal Palace returned to the Premier League after winning the first division Play-off final against Sheffield United with a dramatic last-minute winner.

In Europe, Brazilian striker Ronaldo was the goal hero as Barcelona, managed by former England boss Bobby Robson, beat Paris St Germain 1–0 in Rotterdam to win the European Cup-winners' Cup. A fortnight later German side Borussia Dortmund pulled off the shock of the European season by beating the defending European champions Juventus in the Champions League Final in Munich. Glenn Hoddle's England side warmed up for a crucial France 98 with a 2–1 friendly victory over South Africa at Old Trafford. A week later in Katowice the striking partnership of Alan Shearer and Teddy Sheringham produced the goals as England secured a vital 2–0 win over Poland and set up an intriguing final group match against Italy in Rome in October.

Champions: United celebrate a fourth title in five years

MANAGER OF THE MONTH

Alex Ferguson

Manchester United's Scottish manager guided his side to their fourth League title in five seasons, an astonishing record which earned Ferguson the Manager of the Year award.

PLAYER OF THE MONTH

Eric Cantona

English football was rocked by the announcement that United's French forward was retiring. Despite his volatile temperament, Cantona had inspired much of United's recent success and he will be sorely missed at Old Trafford.

SAS Strikeforce: Shearer and Sheringham got the goals in Poland

PREMIER LEAGUE STANDINGS

May 31

		P	W	D	L	F	A	Pts
1	Manchester United	38	21	12	5	76	44	75
2	Newcastle United	38	19	11	8	73	40	68
3	Arsenal	38	19	11	8	62	32	68
4	Liverpool	38	19	11	8	62	37	68
5	Aston Villa	38	17	10	11	47	34	61
6	Chelsea	38	16	11	11	58	55	59
7	Sheffield Wednesday	38	14	15	9	50	51	57
8	Wimbledon	38	15	11	12	49	46	56
9	Leicester City	38	12	11	15	46	54	47
10	Tottenham Hotspur	38	13	7	18	44	51	46
11	Leeds United	38	11	13	14	28	38	46
12	Derby County	38	11	13	14	45	58	46
13	Blackburn Rovers	38	9	15	14	42	43	42
14	West Ham United	38	10	12	16	39	48	42
15	Everton	38	10	12	16	44	57	42
16	Southampton	38	10	11	17	50	56	41
17	Coventry City	38	9	14	15	38	54	41
18	Sunderland	38	10	10	18	35	53	40
19	Middlesbrough	38	10	12	16	51	60	39
20	Nottingham Forest	38	6	16	16	31	59	34

MILESTONES OF THE SEASON

MAY 3
Nottingham Forest are relegated after only managing a draw at home to Wimbledon.

MAY 5
Manchester United come from two goals down to draw 3–3 with relegation-threatened Middlesbrough at Old Trafford.

MAY 6
Manchester United win the Premier League title without even playing when Liverpool lose to Wimbledon and Newcastle fail to beat West Ham.

MAY 10
In the first division Play-off semi-final first legs, Crystal Palace beat Wolves 3–1 at Selhurst Park while Sheffield United and Ipswich draw 1–1 at Bramall Lane.

MAY 11
On the last day of the season, Middlesbrough (who draw 1–1 at Leeds) and Sunderland (beaten 1–0 at Wimbledon) are relegated. Newcastle thrash Nottingham Forest 5–0 to take second place ahead of Arsenal and Liverpool.

MAY 14
Crystal Palace lose 2–1 to Wolves but win on aggregate and Sheffield United beat Ipswich on away goals in the first division Play-off semi-finals. Barcelona win the European Cup-winners' Cup after beating Paris St Germain.

MAY 16
Gianfranco Zola, Chelsea's Italian forward, is voted Footballer of the Year by the Football Writers' Association.

MAY 17
Chelsea beat Middlesbrough 2–0 in the FA Cup Final.

MAY 18
Manchester United's Eric Cantona shocks the world of football by announcing his retirement.

MAY 25
England beat South Africa 2–1 in a friendly at Old Trafford.

MAY 26
A stunning last-minute goal gives Crystal Palace victory in the first division Play-off final at Wembley.

MAY 28
In the European Champions League Final, German champions Borussia Dortmund beat favourites Juventus 3–1.

MAY 31
England beat Poland 2–0 in Katowice in a crucial World Cup qualifying match.

FA Cup Final

Chelsea paint Wembley blue

Blue was the colour to be wearing at Wembley when Chelsea won their first major trophy for 26 years, beating Middlesbrough 2–0 in the 1997 FA Cup Final. It was an afternoon of records. Chelsea boss Ruud Gullit became the first foreign manager to lead out an FA Cup Final team. Italian midfielder Roberto Di Matteo scored with the fastest goal in Wembley Cup Final history – just 42 seconds. Blues striker Mark Hughes became the first player this century to win four FA Cup winners' medals. There were two more foreigners than Englishmen in the starting line-ups – and Middlesbrough became the first team to reach two Wembley Cup Finals and be relegated in the same season.

It was a day for Chelsea fans to savour, but for Middlesbrough's followers it was the final insult in a humiliating season. A week earlier Boro had lost their Premier League status. A month earlier Bryan Robson's side had been beaten in extra time in the Coca-Cola Cup Final replay by Leicester. Boro's red army of fans drifted out of Wembley knowing they had probably seen the last of their foreign stars – Juninho, Ravanelli and Emerson – in a Middlesbrough shirt.

Blue is the Colour: Chelsea celebrate with the Cup

The foreigners' final

The match had been billed as the foreigners' final. Only nine of the starting 22 players were English. Alongside them were Italians, Brazilians, a Frenchman, a Romanian, a Norwegian, an Irishman, a Scot and a couple of Welshmen. Chelsea had another Italian, Gianluca Vialli, on the substitutes bench, while Boro had a Dane and Slovakian among their reserves. It seemed only right that the first goal should be scored by a foreigner.

Roberto Di Matteo had been overlooked in the pre-match hype about the battle of the little big men, Juninho and Gianfranco Zola, but he took just 42 seconds to send shockwaves around Wembley Stadium. People were still settling into their seats when Dennis Wise robbed Boro's Robbie Mustoe inside the Middlesbrough half. Wise, the Chelsea captain, sent a short pass to Di Matteo,

FINAL (May 17, Wembley Stadium)

CHELSEA 2 (1) (Di Matteo 1, Newton 82)
MIDDLESBROUGH 0
Attendance: 79,160

TEAMS

Chelsea: Grodas, Clarke, Leboeuf, Sinclair, Minto, Petrescu, Newton, Di Matteo, Wise, Zola (Vialli 89), Hughes.

Middlesbrough: Roberts, Fleming, Pearson, Festa, Blackmore, Stamp, Mustoe (Vickers 29), Emerson, Hignett (Kinder 74), Juninho, Ravanelli (Beck 24).

who set about running at the heart of the Middlesbrough defence. The Italian carried on running and, when it became clear that no Boro player was going to challenge him, unleashed a fierce, dipping shot from 25 yards out. The pace and swerve of the ball deceived Boro keeper Ben Roberts, who was helpless to prevent the ball crashing in off the underside of the crossbar. With 42 seconds on the clock, Roberto Di Matteo and Chelsea were in the Wembley record books.

Ravanelli crashes out

If Middlesbrough were to have any hope of coming back from such a deadly setback, they needed their foreign stars to be at their best. But with barely a quarter of the match gone, Fabrizio Ravanelli pulled up in the Chelsea penalty area, unable to continue with a damaged hamstring. Without their Italian striker, Boro lacked a cutting edge. Juninho battled bravely, as he had done all season, but the talented Brazilian lacked support. A first-half injury to Mustoe left Boro exposed in midfield and Juninho was forced to come deeper to get possession, further limiting his effectiveness as an attacking force.

Boro did get the ball in the Chelsea net, but Gianluca Festa's header from Phil Stamp's cross in first-half injury time was ruled offside. In the second half, Bryan Robson's side showed more fight, but Chelsea's defence, superbly marshalled by Frenchman Frank Leboeuf, held firm.

Gianfranco Zola, the Footballer of the Year, had a relatively quiet match but saved his best for the end. He had already exposed the Boro defence, dribbling past Vickers and Blackmore before shooting straight at Roberts. Then, with eight minutes remaining, Zola's delightful back heel of Petrescu's cross set up Eddie Newton to score the goal which clinched the Cup for Chelsea.

Wembley was a sea of blue on the final whistle as Chelsea, led by captain Dennis Wise, lifted the Cup. Ruud Gullit watched from the pitch and was quick to pay tribute to Matthew Harding, the Chelsea director whose millions had made the signing of Zola and Di Matteo possible but who had tragically died in a helicopter crash earlier in the season. "Matthew has been with us all year," Gullit said. "All the time since he died we've known he was with us. He was there for us and we will never forget the contribution he made."

No Go Zola: Chelsea's Italian forward is crowded out by Emerson, Pearson and Vickers

Cup-Winners' Cup Final

Bobby's Barça strike gold

Spot On: Barcelona striker Ronaldo scores the decisive penalty

Liverpool may have been knocked out of last season's Cup-winners' Cup in the semi-final by Paris St Germain, but an Englishman still won the trophy. Bobby Robson, former manager of England, masterminded Barcelona's triumph over Paris St Germain in the Final in Rotterdam.

Victory for Barcelona was a personal triumph for Robson. After a long and successful career at home and abroad, Robson had taken the Barcelona job in the summer of 1996 at the age of 63 knowing that he had to deliver success. Barcelona, the biggest football club in the world, demand and expect only the best.

Robson's job was made slightly easier by the presence in the ranks of Brazilian Ronaldo, named earlier in the season by FIFA

as the World Footballer of the Year. The young striker, still only 20, was sensational for Barcelona last season and he made his mark on the Cup-winners' Cup Final in Rotterdam, scoring the goal, from the penalty spot just before half-time, which won the Cup for Barcelona.

Barcelona, a team studded with stars and internationals, had numerous chances to increase their lead (Fernando Couto had a headed goal from a corner mysteriously disallowed) but a refreshingly open Final finished 1-0 to the Catalans.

Paris Saint Germain, the Cup-holders who had reached the Final after surviving a fierce fightback by Liverpool in the semi-final second leg at Anfield, were bidding to become the first team in the history of the Cup-winners' Cup to retain the trophy. Their best chance of the match came 15 minutes into the second half when French international Patrice Loko hit a post; the rebound fell to the Brazilian Leonardo, an international team-mate of Ronaldo's, but he blasted his shot over the crossbar.

In the end, though, the evening belonged to the two Rs – Ronaldo and Robson – as Barcelona won the European Cup-winners' Cup for a record fourth time.

FINAL (May 14, Feyenoord, Rotterdam)

Barcelona 1 (0) (Ronaldo pen 38)
Paris St Germain 0 (0)
Attendance: 45,000. Referee: Merk (Ger).

TEAMS

Barcelona: Vitor Baia, Ferrer, Fernando Couto, Abelardo, Sergi, Guardiola, Luis Enrique (Pizzi 89), De la Pena (Stoichkov 83), Popescu (Amor 46), Figo, Ronaldo.
Paris SG: Lama, Fournier (Algerino 58), N'Gotty, Le Guen (Dely Valdes 68), Domi, Leroy, Rai, Guerin, Cauet, Leonardo, Loko (Pouget 77).

Champions

Cup Final

Dortmund – kings of Europe

Borussia Dortmund became champions of Europe for the first time in their history following their surprise defeat of the favourites, and defending champions, Juventus. The German side ran out 3–1 winners over the Italians in Munich's famous Olympic stadium.

Juventus had been backed by almost everybody to overcome Dortmund, but it was the German side, conquerors of Manchester United in the semi-finals of the Champions Cup, who proved to be the better side on the night.

Juventus, nicknamed the "Old Lady" of Italian football, had had a barnstorming season, winning the Italian League, the World Club Championship and the European Supercup. They needed to win the European Cup, the prize at stake in the Champions

Dortmund celebrate their triumph

Cup Final, to collect a clean sweep of all the major footballing prizes, a feat which had never been achieved before in the same season.

Juventus had such strength in depth that their golden boy, Alessandro Del Piero, had to be content with a place on the substitutes bench in Munich. The Italians started well enough, but found themselves 2–0 down by half-time, the victims of two knockout blows from corner-kicks, both converted by Dortmund striker Karlheinz Riedle, who said afterwards that he had had a dream that he would score twice!

Del Piero was brought on at half-time by Juventus and quickly pulled a goal back for the Italians with a delightful back heel. But just as it seemed Juventus would draw level, Dortmund scored again with one of the most remarkable goals ever seen in a European Cup Final. Substitute Lars Ricken had been on the pitch a matter of seconds when he was played through by Andy Möller and lobbed Juventus keeper Angelo Peruzzi with his first touch of the game.

Dortmund had ground Juventus down with a masterly display of technique and gritty determination. Matthias Sammer was outstanding in defence for Dortmund as they became the first German team to lift the European Cup since Hamburg in 1983. That they did it on home soil in Munich was fitting in one of the most exciting European Cup Finals of recent years.

FINAL (May 28, Olympia, Munich)

Borussia Dortmund 3 (2) (Riedle 29, 34, Ricken 71)
Juventus 1 (0) (Del Piero 64)
Attendance: 59,000. Referee: Puhl (Hung).

TEAMS

Dortmund: Klos, Sammer, Kree, Köhler, Sousa, Lambert, Heinrich, Möller (Zorc 89), (Ricken 70), Riedle (Herrlich 67). Reuter, Paulo Chapuisat

Juventus: Peruzzi, Ferrera, Montero, Porrini (Del Piero 46), Juliano, Di Livio, Deschamps, Zidane, Jugovic, Boksic (Tacchinardi 87), Vieri (Amoruso 72).

**Cup Final Hero: Dortmund's Karlheinz Riedle
celebrates the first of his two goals**

Division One

Play-offs

Eagles flying high

Crystal Palace returned to the Premier League after two seasons in division one when a dramatic last-minute goal from midfielder David Hopkin gave Steve Coppell's side a 1–0 victory over Sheffield United in the Play-off Final at Wembley.

Palace were no strangers to a winner in the dying seconds of a Play-off Final. The year before they had been on the receiving end of the Steve Claridge strike which took Leicester City into the Premier League with virtually the last kick of extra time.

Sheffield United had been one of the bookies' favourites for automatic promotion at the start of the season. Manager Howard Kendall, the former Everton and Manchester City boss, had steered United away from the relegation zone in the 1995–96 season and their future looked promising. During the whole of last season the Blades were never out of contention for automatic promotion, but eventually finished in fifth place, behind champions Bolton Wanderers, Barnsley, Wolves and Ipswich.

Palace finished sixth after a poor run of form in the spring had seen them drop out of the play-off places. Ironically, much of their early season success had been achieved under Dave Bassett, the former Sheffield United manager who Kendall had replaced at Bramall Lane. When Bassett left for Nottingham Forest, former Palace boss Steve Coppell, the most successful manager in the club's history, agreed to return to Selhurst Park.

The Wembley Final was Palace's third appearance in the play-off decider. In 1989, Coppell's men had beaten Blackburn Rovers over two legs in a home-and-away Final to win promotion to the old first division, but the memory of 1996's devastating last-minute defeat at the hands of Leicester still weighed heavily on the minds of many at Palace this time round.

For Sheffield United, it was their first experience of a Play-off Final. Under Dave Bassett, the Blades had played at Wembley in

Last-Minute Winner: Palace's Dave Hopkin grabs the glory

FINAL (April 6, Wembley Stadium)

Crystal Palace 1 (Hopkin 90)
Sheffield United 0
Attendance: 64,383.

TEAMS

Crystal Palace: Nash, Edworthy, Gordon, Roberts, Tuttle, Linighan, Hopkin, Muscat, Shipperley, Dyer, Rodger.

Sheffield United: Tracey, Ward, Nilsen, Hutchison (Sandford), Tiler, Holdsworth, White, Spackman (Walker), Fjortoft, Katchuro (Taylor), Whitehouse.

PREVIOUS FINALS

1992
Blackburn Rovers 1 (Newell pen). Leicester City 0.
1993
Swindon Town 4 (Hoddle, Maskell, Taylor, Bodin pen).
Leicester City 3 (Joachim, Walsh, Thompson).

1994
Leicester City 2 (Walsh 2). Derby County 1 (Johnson).
1995
Bolton Wanderers 4 (Coyle, De Freitas 2, Paatelainen).
Reading 3 (Nogan, Williams, Quinn). After extra time.
1996
Leicester City 2 (Parker, Claridge). Crystal Palace 1 (Houghton). After extra time.

the all-Sheffield FA Cup semi-final against neighbours Wednesday in 1993, but a year after losing that match United had been relegated on the last day of the season. They had needed a draw with Chelsea to stay up, but lost to an agonising last-minute winner at Stamford Bridge.

United came through a tightly-fought semi-final against Ipswich, winning only on away goals. The first leg in Sheffield had ended 1–1 and although Ipswich were the better side in the return leg, United held on for a 2–2 draw.

Palace had a slightly easier ride against Wolves in their semi-final, winning the first leg at Selhurst Park 3–1. Wolves threw all they had at Palace in the second leg at Molineux and went 1–0 up just before half-time, only for David Hopkin to grab a vital away goal for Palace. Hopkin was again the goal hero for the South London side in the Wembley Final. His last-minute strike broke the deadlock of what had been a tense finale to the first division season.

The heat stifled the early exchanges at Wembley, but there were good chances in the first-half for Palace's Andy Roberts and Neil Shipperley, which were not taken. United's prospects were not helped by the departures through injury of midfielder Don Hutchison and striker Petr Katchuro, but Kendall's side came back strongly in the second half, with Jan Aage Fjortoft going closest to giving his side the lead.

Then, just as everybody was preparing for extra

Going Up: Palace, the better side on the day, earned promotion to the Premier League the hard way

time, Hopkin scored the goal that took Palace into the Premier League. A corner was headed away by the Sheffield United defence and collected 25 yards out by the ginger-haired Hopkin, who trapped the ball with his left foot and switched to his right before curling a fabulous shot past the outstretched Simon Tracey in the United goal. It was a goal worthy of winning any Wembley final and it won the match for Palace with seconds to spare.

It was a heartbreaking way for Sheffield United to lose, but Palace had been the better side on the day and had experienced similar heartache a year earlier.

Semi-Final Success: Palace's Bruce Dyer with Wolves' Keith Curle

Anatomy of a Football Boot

The best quality boots put a spring in their wearers' feet – literally – by being manufactured from kangaroo leather. The goalkeeper facing a penalty from the likes of Ryan Giggs or Robbie Fowler might feel a little more secure knowing that his boots are made of Kevlar – the same tough, energy-absorbing plastic material used to make bullet-proof vests.

Here, we take a look at the state-of-the-art design skills and craftsmanship which go into making a pair of modern football boots...

The Upper

The upper part of a football boot can be made of either leather or a synthetic material. 'Leather' can actually be kangaroo, calfskin, goatskin, cowhide or oxhide and comes in three qualities: higher, medium and lower grades. Synthetic materials used include Kevlar, which has ten times the tensile strength of leather; Diatex; Pelletech; Polyvinyl chloride (PVC); and polyurethane (PU).

The Insole

The insole consists of the lasting board and the sockliner, or footbed. The lasting board, to which the outsole is attached, can be made of Texon, which is thin, stable and light; leather, now becoming less common; or a leather/canvas composite known as 'soft board'. On top of the lasting board is the sockliner or footbed, the padding material on which the foot rests. This can be made of Ethylene Vinyl Acetate (EVA), Frelene foam or Polynylon lined foam, and is either removable or glued in place.

Football has come a long way since the days of the last century, when the players wore kits and boots that bore little resemblance to modern-day football attire.

Nothing symbolises the rapid development of football in the modern age more than the changes that have taken place to the humble football boot. Where once players nailed studs into the soles of workman's boots, they now play in football boots designed using the very latest technology and made of the most up-to-date manmade materials.

In the 1990s, the football boot industry is now such big business that the top players are paid thousands of pounds every season to wear a particular company's boot.

The first purpose-built football boots were developed in the 1930s, but they were still boots which covered the ankle. The breakthrough in football boot technology came in 1958 with the launch of what we know today as the modern-day football boot. The boot featured specially-prepared leather, screw-in nylon studs and, most importantly, was a below-the-ankle shoe rather than a boot.

The boot developed further during the 1960s, 1970s and 1980s and the modern-day boot is now unrecognisable when compared with its ancestors.

The Midsole

The midsole is the hardest-working part of the boot, absorbing the shock of the foot hitting the ground. It is usually made of either EVA or PU. EVA is a synthetic fibre which is made of a vinyl compound mixed with a derivative of vinegar. The EVA is usually compressed and heated during the moulding process which makes it lighter and longer lasting.

The alternative, PU, is injected with air to make it lighter and enhance the cushioning effect.

The Heel

The heel counter is the cup construction which protects and supports the heel. This can be pre-moulded in different sizes to suit different kinds of boot in all sizes or standard sized to fit all kinds of boot at each size.

The heel counter can be made of Thermoplastic PU, Nylon or PVC. Thermoplastic PU is considered best as it is strong and pliable. Nylon is strong but not as pliable as PU. PVC is used in standard heel cups only. It is very rigid but not very strong.

The Outsole

There are three basic types of outsole – the bottommost part of the boot.

Single-density outsoles are one single pre-molded piece; dual-density outsoles have a base plate which is made from one type of material and cleats or studs made from another, different material; and Tri-density outsoles resemble the dual-density design, but include yet a third type of material at the tip of each stud or cleat.

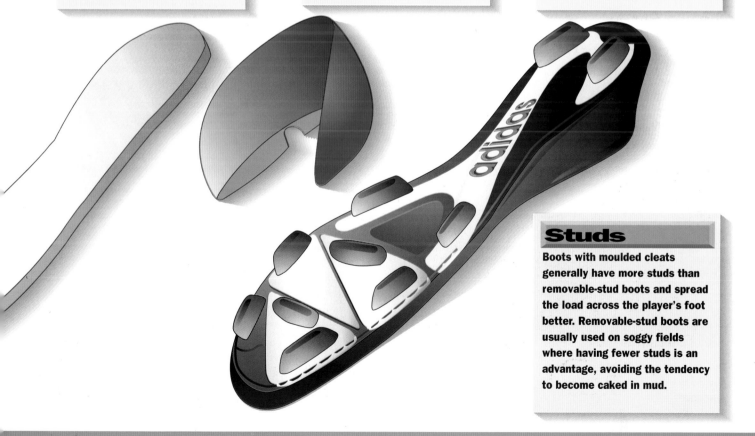

Studs

Boots with moulded cleats generally have more studs than removable-stud boots and spread the load across the player's foot better. Removable-stud boots are usually used on soggy fields where having fewer studs is an advantage, avoiding the tendency to become caked in mud.

Anatomy of a Football Stadium

The new 25,000-seater Reebok stadium built by Bolton Wanderers to coincide with their re-entry into the Premier League is the most expensive stadium ever built in Britain, over £1,000 per seat being spent on constructing it. The overall design is in accordance with the recommendations laid down by Lord Justice Taylor in his report which followed the Hillsborough disaster and the pitch has been constructed to comply with FIFA and UEFA recommendations. More than 2,000 car parking spaces are available on match days and the stadium is part of a larger development which includes shops, a bowling alley, tennis centre and cinema.

The importance of TV to the modern game means camera positions were considered at an early stage in the design process

The needs of the media are taken care of with modern facilities and a well-appointed commentary box

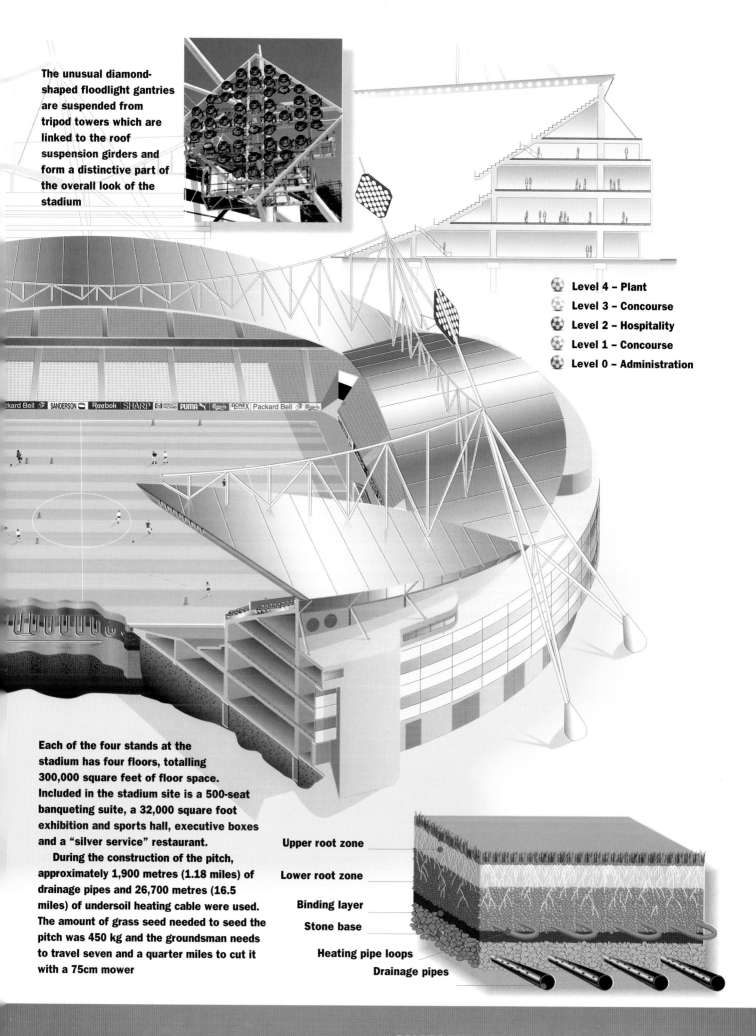

The unusual diamond-shaped floodlight gantries are suspended from tripod towers which are linked to the roof suspension girders and form a distinctive part of the overall look of the stadium

⚽ Level 4 – Plant
⚽ Level 3 – Concourse
⚽ Level 2 – Hospitality
⚽ Level 1 – Concourse
⚽ Level 0 – Administration

Packard Bell · SANDERSON · Reebok · SHARP · HEWLETT PACKARD · PUMA · Carlsberg · EIONEX · Packard Bell · Carlsberg

Each of the four stands at the stadium has four floors, totalling 300,000 square feet of floor space. Included in the stadium site is a 500-seat banqueting suite, a 32,000 square foot exhibition and sports hall, executive boxes and a "silver service" restaurant.

During the construction of the pitch, approximately 1,900 metres (1.18 miles) of drainage pipes and 26,700 metres (16.5 miles) of undersoil heating cable were used. The amount of grass seed needed to seed the pitch was 450 kg and the groundsman needs to travel seven and a quarter miles to cut it with a 75cm mower

Upper root zone
Lower root zone
Binding layer
Stone base
Heating pipe loops
Drainage pipes

Teams of the premier league

Manchester United may have won the championship four times in the last five seasons, but no other league in the world boasts as many big-name clubs as the FA Premiership. From United and Liverpool to Arsenal and Newcastle, through to Chelsea, Aston Villa, Leeds and Everton, English football has strength in depth – and plenty of world-class stars to boot.

United have dominated the Premier League since the start in 1992, largely thanks to one man, Eric Cantona. With the Frenchman's retirement and United concentrating more than ever before on winning the European Cup, the door could be open for a team to knock United off their pedestal. Liverpool will again be leading the challenge, with Arsenal, Newcastle and Aston Villa not far behind.

Chelsea, last season's FA Cup-winners, are looking to transfer their success in the knockout competitions to the League, as will be Leicester, Coca-Cola Cup holders, and Wimbledon, semi-finalists in both Cups last season.

The Premier League is full of teams with great traditions – Tottenham, Everton, Sheffield Wednesday, Blackburn Rovers, Leeds United – whose fans demand success, as well as those who are happy just to avoid last season's battle against relegation: Derby County, Coventry City, West Ham United and Southampton.

The next pages list full squad details of every Premiership team for the 1997–98 season. The "Appearances" and "Goals" statistics are for the Premiership only, so any new teams, and some new players, will have zero appearances and zero goals.

(right) All Good Friends: Robbie Fowler and co. celebrate a goal with an unsuspecting referee
(below) Lights, Camera, Action: Charity Shield losers Newcastle United parade past the Manchester fans

Arsenal
The Gunners

At Highbury they are getting used to the French revolution, the Arsène Wenger revolution to be precise. Arsenal's French manager is determined to bring success to North London, and make the Gunners one of Europe's top clubs in the process.

Wenger arrived at Highbury from Japan at one of the most difficult times in the club's history. The Frenchman was the fourth manager in a matter of weeks, following Bruce Rioch, Stewart Houston and Pat Rice. Club captain Tony Adams confessed to being an alcoholic just as former manager George Graham (banned from football for allegedly receiving a transfer "bung") took charge at Leeds.

Everybody thought the new manager would steady a very shaky ship and then hope for the best. Highbury was in for a difficult season, with little chance of any success. In fact, Arsenal finished the season in third place and in better shape than for many years, with European success in the UEFA Cup now a distinct possibility.

Wenger was quick to ring the changes at Highbury, although the bulk of the first team remained unchanged. Reserves Paul Dickov (Manchester City), Glenn Helder (Benfica), David Hillier (Portsmouth), Chris Kiwomya (Cannes), Andy Linighan (Crystal Palace), Eddie McGoldrick (Manchester City), Steve Morrow (QPR), John Jensen (Brondby) and John Hartson (West Ham Utd) all left the club during the course of last season. In their place, Wenger installed a new Continental class: Frenchmen Patrick Vieira, Remi Garde and Nicolas Anelka arrived, with the promise of more to come.

Under George Graham, Arsenal fans had got used to success (two League titles, the FA Cup, Cup-winners' Cup and two League Cups) but at the expense of attractive football. The arrival of Bruce Rioch as manager in the summer of 1995 promised changes, especially with the signing of Dutch striker Dennis Bergkamp. But Bergkamp took time to settle in and Rioch also had problems. The former Bolton Wanderers boss steered Arsenal away from Graham's more direct style and into the UEFA Cup but had run-ins with key players, notably Ian Wright, and Highbury bosses decided to move for Frenchman Wenger, who took charge at Highbury at the start of October last year.

Despite all the comings and goings at Highbury, Arsenal were doing very nicely thank you. They were second in the table behind early leaders Liverpool and performing much better than their early-season title odds of 16–1 had suggested.

Vieira makes his mark

Patrick Vieira made his Arsenal debut against Sheffield Wednesday at Highbury and quickly

French Resistance: young midfielder Patrick Vieira

ARSENAL

Formed: 1886.
Nickname: The Gunners.
Stadium: Highbury.
Capacity: 38,500.
Address: Arsenal Stadium, Highbury, London N5 1BU.
Telephone: 0171 704 4000.
Clubcall: 0891 202021.
Fax: 0171 704 4001.
Website: www.fa-carling.com/club/a.fc
Manager: Arsène Wenger.

COLOURS

RECORDS

Record Premier League victory: 5–1 (v Ipswich T, Mar 5, 1994; v Norwich, April 1, 1995).
Record Premier League defeat: 3–0 (v Leeds U, Nov 21, 1992; v Coventry, Aug 14, 1993; v Liverpool, Aug 28, 1994).
Record transfer fee received: £2.8 million from Nottingham F for Kevin Campbell, July 1995.
Record transfer fee paid: £7.5 million to Inter for Dennis Bergkamp, June 1995.
Record attendance: 73,295, v Sunderland, Division 1, March 9, 1935.

HONOURS

League (10): 1930–31, 1932–33, 1933–34, 1934–35, 1937–38, 1947–48, 1952–53, 1970–71, 1988–89, 1990–91.
FA Cup (6): 1930, 1936, 1950, 1971, 1979, 1993.
League Cup (2): 1987, 1993.
European Cup-winners' Cup (1): 1994.
European Fairs Cup (1): 1970.

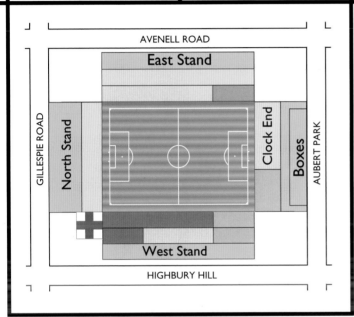

established himself as the passing influence which Arsenal had lacked since the days of Paul Davis. "We discovered we needed players to bridge the gap between defence and attack," says Dennis Bergkamp. "Now Vieira forms the link we were missing. Patrick has the ability to attack and defend, and that gives us so much more power."

The Wenger revolution at Arsenal has not just taken place on the pitch. Players now follow strict diets and plans are well advanced to build a new training complex which will incorporate a youth development centre.

On the personnel front, Wenger has money to spend but intends to use it wisely. Arsenal splashed out £7 million on Dutch winger Marc Overmars. The French connection was maintained by the signing of Emmanuel Petit and Gilles Grimandi from Wenger's old club, Monaco. Wenger is also bringing in young English players – he paid £1 million for Luton's teenage defender Matthew Upson. In an attempt to balance the books a little, Wenger and the Highbury board made the shock sale of fans' favourite Paul Merson to freshly-relegate Middlesbrough, towards the end of the summer. The sum was around £4.5 million.

The future looks good for the Gunners. Arsenal may have just missed out on this season's Champions League, but Arsène Wenger is building a team which, make no mistake about it, will be challenging for honours in the very near future.

FIXTURES 1997–98

9 AUG	LEEDS UNITED	A	____	:	____
11 AUG	COVENTRY CITY	H	____	:	____
23 AUG	SOUTHAMPTON	A	____	:	____
27 AUG	LEICESTER CITY	A	____	:	____
30 AUG	TOTTENHAM HOTSPUR	H	____	:	____
13 SEPT	BOLTON	H	____	:	____
21 SEPT	CHELSEA	A	____	:	____
23 SEPT	WEST HAM UNITED	H	____	:	____
27 SEPT	EVERTON	A	____	:	____
4 OCT	BARNSLEY	H	____	:	____
18 OCT	CRYSTAL PALACE	A	____	:	____
26 OCT	ASTON VILLA	H	____	:	____
1 NOV	DERBY COUNTY	A	____	:	____
9 NOV	MANCHESTER UNITED	H	____	:	____
22 NOV	SHEFFIELD WEDNESDAY	A	____	:	____
29 NOV	LIVERPOOL	H	____	:	____
8 DEC	NEWCASTLE UNITED	A	____	:	____
13 DEC	BLACKBURN ROVERS	H	____	:	____
22 DEC	WIMBLEDON	A	____	:	____
26 DEC	LEICESTER CITY	H	____	:	____
28 DEC	TOTTENHAM HOTSPUR	A	____	:	____
10 JAN	LEEDS UNITED	H	____	:	____
17 JAN	COVENTRY CITY	A	____	:	____
31 JAN	SOUTHAMPTON	H	____	:	____
7 FEB	CHELSEA	H	____	:	____
14 FEB	BOLTON	A	____	:	____
21 FEB	CRYSTAL PALACE	H	____	:	____
28 FEB	WEST HAM UNITED	A	____	:	____
7 MAR	DERBY COUNTY	H	____	:	____
14 MAR	MANCHESTER UNITED	A	____	:	____
28 MAR	SHEFFIELD WEDNESDAY	H	____	:	____
4 APR	LIVERPOOL	A	____	:	____
11 APR	NEWCASTLE UNITED	H	____	:	____
13 APR	BLACKBURN ROVERS	A	____	:	____
18 APR	WIMBLEDON	H	____	:	____
25 APR	BARNSLEY	A	____	:	____
2 MAY	EVERTON	H	____	:	____
10 MAY	ASTON VILLA	A	____	:	____

PREMIER LEAGUE TABLES

SEASON	POS.	P	W	D	L	F	A	PTS	TOP SCORER	AV. GATE
1992–93	10th	42	15	11	16	40	38	56	Wright 14	24,403
1993–94	4th	42	18	17	7	53	28	71	Wright 23	30,563
1994–95	12th	42	13	12	17	52	49	51	Wright 18	35,330
1995–96	5th	38	17	12	9	49	36	63	Wright 15	37,568
1996–97	3rd	38	19	11	8	62	32	68	Wright 23	37,822

Ian Wright

Love him or loathe him, you just can't ignore Ian Wright. He's aggressive, he's argumentative, he's often downright rude, but Arsenal fans adore him. It's easy to see why.

It's more than 12 years since Crystal Palace signed a 21-year-old Wright from non-League Greenwich Borough, where he was playing his football after being rejected by Millwall and Brighton. His goals helped Palace to promotion and in the 1990 FA Cup Final, when Wright came off the bench to score twice in the 3–3 draw with Manchester United.

Wright joined Arsenal in October 1991 for £2.5 million, then a record but a bargain compared with today's soaraway prices. His time at Highbury has been nothing short of phenomenal. Last season he scored his 100th League goal for the Gunners and he ended the campaign high in the overall top scorers list with 23.

With 118 League goals for Arsenal already in the bag, Wright has his sights set on overtaking the club record of 178, set by Cliff Bastin between 1930 and 1947. Wright may be approaching the age when most players consider calling it a day, but he has no plans to quit. "He seems to get

Striking Target: Ian Wright has Cliff Bastin's record in sight

better as he gets older," says England manager Glenn Hoddle, who recalled Wright to the international set-up last season.

One thing's for sure, we haven't heard the last of Ian Wright.

Dennis Bergkamp

It has taken time for Dennis Bergkamp to settle in at Highbury, but Arsenal fans are starting to see the best of the man known simply as the Iceman.

Bergkamp started his career in his native Holland with Ajax, the Amsterdam club famous around the world for its youth policy. He made his debut for Ajax as a teenager just as another Ajax legend, Marco Van Basten, was leaving. Bergkamp took over Van Basten's goalscoring role for Ajax and the Dutch national team and eventually followed his hero to Italy.

However, Dennis's time in Italy, with Milan club Internazionale, was not a happy one, but he did win the UEFA Cup. Arsenal broke the bank to bring him to England in the summer of 1995, paying Inter a club record £7.5 million. He took time to score his first goal for the Gunners – Highbury waited what seemed like ages, but it was a memorable strike when it did arrive, against Southampton on September 23, 1995.

Until the appointment of Arsène Wenger last autumn, many fans thought Arsenal were too reliant on Ian Wright for goals.

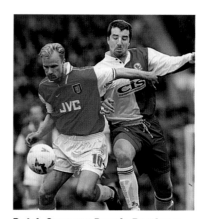

Dutch Courage: Dennis Bergkamp

Now Dennis Bergkamp (14 League and Cup goals last season) is weighing in with some crucial contributions.

Tony Adams

After his much-publicised problems, Arsenal captain Tony Adams has found a new lease of life at Highbury under manager Arsène Wenger.

The England defender – whose trademark was, and still is, the arm held aloft, appealing for offside – can often be seen in unfamiliar places these days. Adams, a one-club man with nearly 400 appearances for Arsenal since his debut 14 years ago, has been encouraged by Wenger to get forward into attacking positions more often. So Adams can now be seen strolling over the half-way line and into the opposition penalty area.

George Graham probably isn't very impressed with Adams's new-found forward thinking, but Arsenal now have the tactical flexibility they lacked under their old manager.

Patrick Vieira

Few if any people knew much about Frenchman Patrick Vieira when he arrived at Highbury from Milan last summer, but it didn't take long for Arsenal fans to realize the club had unearthed a real find.

Last season the 21-year-old midfielder provided the link between defence and attack that had been lacking at Highbury in recent years. His intelligent passing, combined with

Player Records

	BORN	NATIONALITY	HEIGHT	WEIGHT	APPS	GOALS	PREVIOUS TEAMS
GOALKEEPERS							
John Lukic	11.12.60 Chesterfield	English	6-4	13-12	593	0	Leeds U, Arsenal, Leeds U.
David Seaman	19.9.63 Rotherham	English	6-4	14-10	556	0	Leeds U, Peterborough U, Birmingham C, QPR.
DEFENDERS							
Tony Adams	10.10.66 London	English	6-3	13-11	395	27	none
Steve Bould	16.11.62 Stoke	English	6-4	14-2	435	11	Stoke C, Torquay U.
Lee Dixon	17.3.64 Manchester	English	5-8	11-8	502	31	Burnley, Chester C, Bury, Stoke C.
Remi Garde	3.4.66 L'Arbresle	French	5-8	11-4	11	0	L'Arbresle, Lyon, Strasbourg (Fra).
Gilles Grimandi	11.1.70 Gap	French	5-11	11-11	0	0	Monaco (Fra).
Martin Keown	24.7.66 Oxford	English	6-1	12-4	400	6	Arsenal, Brighton & HA, Aston Villa, Everton.
Gavin McGowan	16.1.76 Blackheath	English	5-8	11-7	5	0	none
Scott Marshall	1.5.73 Edinburgh	Scottish	6-1	12-5	48	2	Rotherham U, Oxford U, Sheffield U.
Emmanuel Petit	22.9.70 Dieppe	French	6-1	12-6	0	0	Monaco (Fra).
Matthew Upson	18.4.79 Hartismere	English	6-1	11-5	1	0	Luton T.
Nigel Winterburn	11.12.63 Coventry	English	5-8	11-4	511	15	Birmingham C, Oxford U, Wimbledon.
MIDFIELDERS							
Stephen Hughes	18.9.76 Wokingham	English	6-0	12-8	16	1	none
Alberto Mendez Rodriguez	24.10.74 Nuremburg	German	5-9	11-8	0	0	Feucht (Ger).
Ray Parlour	7.3.73 Romford	English	5-10	11-12	135	6	none
Marc Overmars	29.3.73 Emst	Dutch	5-7	10-8	0	0	Go Ahead Eagles, Willem II, Ajax (Hol).
Ian Selley	14.6.74 Chertsey	English	5-9	10-1	41	0	none
Patrick Vieira	26.6.76 Dakar	French	6-3	12-10	31	2	Cannes (Fra), Milan (Ita).
David Platt	10.6.66 Chadderton	English	5-10	11-12	412	146	Crewe, Aston Villa, Bari, Juventus, Sampdoria (all Italy)
FORWARDS							
Nicolas Anelka	14.3.79 Versailles	French	6-0	12-2	4	0	Paris St Germain (Fra).
Dennis Bergkamp	18.5.69 Amsterdam	Dutch	6-0	12-5	62	23	Ajax (Hol), Internazionale (Ita).
Luis Boa Morte	4.8.77 Lisbon	Portuguese	5-9	11-2	0	0	Sporting Lisbon (Por).
Paul Shaw	4.9.73 Burnham	English	5-11	12-2	30	9	Burnley, Cardiff C, Peterborough U.
Ian Wright	3.11.63 Woolwich	English	5-9	11-8	422	207	Crystal Palace.

tough tackling, provided the perfect base for forwards Ian Wright and Dennis Bergkamp.

Vieira's form for Arsenal earned him a full international debut for France and manager Arsène Wenger, who first spotted Vieira playing for French side Cannes in July 1994, was quick to praise him. "Patrick is remarkable for such a young player, and potentially a very big force," said the Highbury boss.

Vieira's targets for this season include winning a regular place in the French national side and acquiring some silverware with Arsenal. He has already achieved a great deal for such a young player, but the future looks bright for Patrick Vieira, and Arsenal.

Captain Marvel: Tony Adams is playing better than ever for the Gunners

Aston Villa
The Villans

At Villa Park, there is living proof that Little can go a long way. Under manager Brian Little, Aston Villa have made giant strides and are firmly re-established among the elite of English football.

Brian Little was always going to be a popular choice as Aston Villa manager. A former favourite as a player, Little had developed a reputation as a promising young manager at Leicester. He joined Villa in December 1994 from Leicester, replacing the sacked Ron Atkinson. Big Ron's time at Villa Park had seen the first silverware arrive since the early 1980s, when Ron Saunders had steered Villa to the League title, the club's first since 1910. A year later, Saunders' successor Tony Barton guided the club to their finest hour yet, the European Cup. Striker Peter Withe was the hero in Rotterdam as Villa beat German champions Bayern Munich 1–0 in the Final.

Villa have never been able to match the achievements of the early 1980s. The club suffered the ignominy of relegation to the old second division in 1987, but bounced back at the first attempt under Graham Taylor, who took Villa to a second-place finish in the League before departing to take charge of England. Villa then brought in Czech manager Dr Josef Venglos, who was not a great success, before employing the flamboyant Atkinson in 1992.

Atkinson impresses

Big Ron quickly built an impressive outfit, with striker Dean Saunders a major signing, from Liverpool. Saunders finished the 1992–93 season as the club's top scorer as Villa finished in second place. The following season saw Villa's League position slip to 10th, but consolation came in the form of a League Cup Final victory over Manchester United.

A dramatic win on penalties over Italian side Internazionale in the UEFA Cup promised great things during the 1994–95 season, but by November Big Ron was gone and the call went out to Brian Little.

Former Villa hero Little did a great job in rescuing an ageing and demoralized side from relegation (Villa finished the season in 18th place) and set about building a new era at Villa Park.

Little's Big Man: Ugo Ehiogu is a tower of strength for Villa

ASTON VILLA

Formed: 1896.
Nickname: The Villans.
Stadium: Villa Park.
Capacity: 39,339.
Address: Trinity Road, Birmingham B6 6HE.
Telephone: 0121 327 2299.
Clubcall: 0891 121148.
Fax: 0121 322 2107.
Website: www.fa-carling.com/club/av.fc
Manager: Brian Little.

COLOURS

RECORDS

Record Premier League victory:
7–1 (v Wimbledon, Feb 11, 1995).
Record Premier League defeat:
5–1 (v Newcastle U, April 27, 1994).
Record transfer fee received:
£5.5 million from Bari for David Platt, Aug 1991.
Record transfer fee paid:
£7 million to Liverpool for Stan Collymore, May 1997.
Record attendance:
76,588, v Derby Co, FA Cup 6th round, Mar 2, 1946.

HONOURS

League (7): 1893–94, 1895–96, 1896–97, 1898–99, 1899–1900, 1909–10, 1980–81.
FA Cup (7): 1887, 1895, 1897, 1905, 1913, 1920, 1957.
League Cup (5): 1961, 1975, 1977, 1994, 1996.
European Cup (1): 1982.
European Supercup (1): 1982.

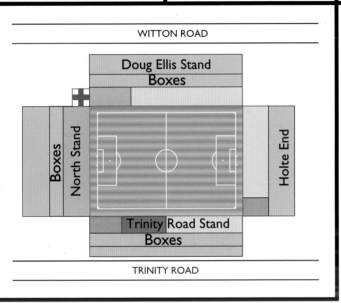

FIXTURES 1997–98

Date	Opponent	H/A		
9 AUG	LEICESTER CITY	A	___ : ___
13 AUG	BLACKBURN ROVERS	H	___ : ___
23 AUG	NEWCASTLE UNITED	A	___ : ___
27 AUG	TOTTENHAM HOTSPUR	A	___ : ___
30 AUG	LEEDS UNITED	H	___ : ___
13 SEPT	BARNSLEY	A	___ : ___
20 SEPT	DERBY	H	___ : ___
22 SEPT	LIVERPOOL	A	___ : ___
27 SEPT	SHEFFIELD WEDNESDAY	H	___ : ___
4 OCT	BOLTON	A	___ : ___
18 OCT	WIMBLEDON	H	___ : ___
26 OCT	ARSENAL	A	___ : ___
1 NOV	CHELSEA	H	___ : ___
8 NOV	CRYSTAL PALACE	A	___ : ___
22 NOV	EVERTON	H	___ : ___
29 NOV	WEST HAM UNITED	A	___ : ___
6 DEC	COVENTRY CITY	H	___ : ___
15 DEC	MANCHESTER UNITED	A	___ : ___
20 DEC	SOUTHAMPTON	H	___ : ___
26 DEC	TOTTENHAM HOTSPUR	H	___ : ___
28 DEC	LEEDS UNITED	A	___ : ___
10 JAN	LEICESTER CITY	H	___ : ___
17 JAN	BLACKBURN ROVERS	A	___ : ___
31 JAN	NEWCASTLE UNITED	H	___ : ___
7 FEB	DERBY COUNTY	A	___ : ___
14 FEB	BARNSLEY	H	___ : ___
21 FEB	WIMBLEDON	A	___ : ___
28 FEB	LIVERPOOL	H	___ : ___
7 MAR	CHELSEA	A	___ : ___
14 MAR	CRYSTAL PALACE	H	___ : ___
28 MAR	EVERTON	A	___ : ___
4 APR	WEST HAM UNITED	H	___ : ___
11 APR	COVENTRY CITY	A	___ : ___
13 APR	MANCHESTER UNITED	H	___ : ___
18 APR	SOUTHAMPTON	A	___ : ___
25 APR	BOLTON	H	___ : ___
2 MAY	SHEFFIELD WEDNESDAY	A	___ : ___
10 MAY	ARSENAL	H	___ : ___

That summer, Little brought in Gareth Southgate, Savo Milosevic and Mark Draper to join existing stars Mark Bosnich, Steve Staunton, Andy Townsend and Dwight Yorke.

The Little revolution

Patiently and without a great deal of fuss, the Little revolution has taken effect at Villa Park. Dwight Yorke has emerged as a talented goalscorer and it was his goals which took Villa to the 1996 League Cup Final, where Villa outclassed Leeds United, winning 3–0. Gareth Southgate, a midfielder at his previous club Crystal Palace, has been converted to a central defender of international standing.

Last season, Villa, like many other Premier League clubs, added a few more Continental touches with the purchases of Serbian midfielder Sasa Curcic and Portuguese defender Fernando Nelson. There was disappointment in the UEFA Cup (defeat by Swedish part-timers Helsingborgs) but compensation in the form of a top-five placing.

Brian Little has come a long way in a short space of time at Villa Park, and is not finished yet. The signing of striker Stan Collymore for a club record £7 million is an indication that Villa's ambitions extend beyond just being a top-five side. With the temperamental but undeniably gifted Collymore on board, Villa have the Premier League title firmly in their sights.

PREMIER LEAGUE TABLES

SEASON	POS.	P	W	D	L	F	A	PTS	TOP SCORER	AV. GATE
1992–93	2nd	42	24	12	6	67	31	84	Saunders 13	29,594
1993–94	10th	42	15	12	15	46	50	57	Atkinson 9	29,015
1994–95	18th	42	11	15	16	51	56	48	Saunders 15	29,758
1995–96	4th	38	18	9	11	52	35	63	Yorke 17	32,614

Squad Info
KEY PLAYERS TO WATCH

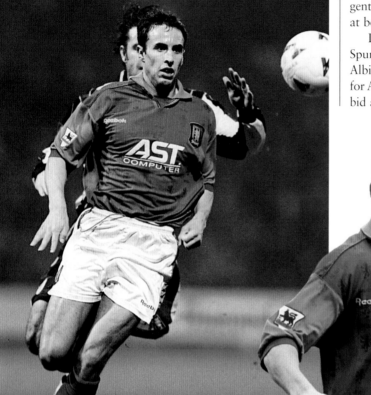

Defensive Linchpin: Gareth Southgate

Gareth Southgate

He's the man who missed that penalty and unfortunately some people will never let him forget it! But it is a great tribute to the character of Gareth Southgate that his career has survived that terrible night at Wembley, when the hopes of a whole nation fell on his shoulders.

He remains a crucial part of Brian Little's plans at Aston Villa and is a regular member of Glenn Hoddle's squad battling to qualify for the 1998 World Cup in France.

Watford-born Gareth was first called up for England duty by Terry Venables, who recognized his great versatility – he started as a full-back for Crystal Palace, making his League debut against Liverpool at Anfield in April 1991, before moving into midfield. It was as a midfielder that Southgate was first spotted by Brian Little, who was looking for players for a new-look three-man central defence at Villa Park. When Palace were relegated in 1995, Villa moved in, signing Southgate for £2 million.

Last season, 26-year-old Southgate committed himself to Aston Villa for the foreseeable future, making it likely that he will play

the best years of his career at Villa Park. Intelligent and eloquent both on and off the pitch, few would be surprised if Southgate went into football management when he retires.

Ugo Ehiogu

If there is great optimism at Villa Park about the development of the team under manager Brian Little, it is largely because of players such as Ugo Ehiogu. The young defender is a stylish, intelligent centre-back who looks set for a long and successful career at both Premier League and international level.

London-born Ehiogu started his career not with Arsenal, Spurs or West Ham, but in the Midlands with West Bromwich Albion. He made only two appearances in the 1990–91 season for Albion before Villa's Ron Atkinson stepped in with a £200,000 bid and took the tall centre-back down the road to Villa Park.

Ehiogu took his time settling in under Atkinson, making eight appearances in the 1991–92 season and four the next. His career really took off with the arrival of Brian Little. The new boss had plans for a new-look three-man defence – and Ehiogu was to play a full role alongside Paul McGrath and Gareth Southgate. Ehiogu is now firmly established at the heart of Villa's defence and has even received international recognition. He was called up by former England manager Terry Venables just prior to Euro 96 and was desperately unlucky to be left out of the tournament squad.

Mark Draper

Midfielder Mark Draper has the potential to be one of English football's leading midfielders. He has already been called up to the full England squad, and his first cap cannot be far away.

Brian Little signed Draper from his old club Leicester in the summer of 1995. The 26-year-old had spent one season at Filbert Street and despite Leicester's poor run of results (they were relegated) Draper stood out as their star performer. Villa paid £3.25 million for Draper, which gave Leicester

Midfield Dynamo: Mark Draper is tipped for England honours

Player Records

	BORN	NATIONALITY	HEIGHT	WEIGHT	APPS	GOALS	PREVIOUS TEAMS
GOALKEEPERS							
Mark Bosnich	13.1.72 Fairfield	Australian	6-1	13-7	137	1	Sydney Croatia (Aus), Manchester U.
Michael Oakes	30.10.73 Northwich	English	6-1	12-7	21	0	Scarborough, Tranmere R.
DEFENDERS							
Gary Charles	13.4.70 London	English	5-9	11-8	175	5	Nottingham F, Leicester C, Derby Co.
Ugo Ehiogu	3.11.72 London	English	6-2	13-3	144	7	West Brom.
Scott Murray	26.5.74 Aberdeen	Scottish	5-10	11-0	4	0	none
Riccardo Scimeca	13.6.75 Leamington Spa	English	6-1	12-9	34	0	none
Gareth Southgate	3.9.70 Watford	English	6-0	12-8	211	17	Crystal Palace.
Steve Staunton	19.1.69 Drogheda	Irish	6-0	12-4	256	15	Liverpool, Bradford C.
Alan Wright	28.9.71 Ashton under Lyne	English	5-4	9-5	256	4	Blackpool, Blackburn R.
MIDFIELDERS							
Sasa Curcic	14.2.72 Belgrade	Yugoslav	5-9	10-7	50	4	Partizan Belgrade (Yug), Bolton W.
Mark Draper	11.11.70 Long Eaton	English	5-10	12-4	326	47	Notts Co, Leicester C.
Simon Grayson	16.12.69	English	5-11	12-10	175	13	Leeds U, Leicester C
Fernando Nelson	5.11.71 Oporto	Portuguese	5-10	11-2	33	0	FC Porto (Por), Sporting Lisbon (Por).
Ian Taylor	4.6.68 Birmingham	English	6-1	12-0	178	35	Port Vale, Sheffield W.
Andy Townsend	27.3.63 Maidstone	Irish	5-11	12-7	397	33	Southampton, Norwich C, Chelsea.
Julian Joachim	20.9.74 Peterborough	English	5-6	12-11	125	29	Leicester C.
FORWARDS							
Stan Collymore	22.1.71 Stone	English	6-3	14-10	176	83	Crystal Palace, Southend U. Nottingham F, Liverpool.
Savo Milosevic	2.9.73 Bijelina	Yugoslav	6-1	13-5	67	22	Partizan Belgrade (Yug).
Dwight Yorke	3.11.71 Canaan, Tobago	Trinidad & Tobago	5-10	11-13	201	61	Signal Hill (Tob).

a £2 million profit on the £1.25 million they paid Draper's first club Notts County. A lot of money, but for Villa it has been money well spent.

Dwight Yorke

In Trinidad and Tobago international Dwight Yorke, Aston Villa possess a world-class striker who has a knack of scoring crucial goals at crucial times.

Last season 25-year-old Yorke again finished as Villa's top scorer and only Fabrizio Ravanelli, Alan Shearer, Robbie Fowler, Ole Gunnar Solskjaer and Ian Wright scored more goals. That's world-class company by anybody's standards.

Yorke made his debut for Villa as a fresh-faced 18-year-old way back in the 1989–90 season. Since then he has become a regular fixture at Villa Park, scoring more than 60 League goals. It was largely thanks to Yorke that Villa won the 1996 Coca-Cola League Cup – he scored five times on the way to Wembley and again in the Final against Leeds.

Unfortunately for Villa, as long as Yorke continues to score goals, other clubs will always be interested in signing him. Spanish side Atletico Madrid were reported to have bid for Yorke last season, but Villa say they are determined to hold on to him. When you see Yorke's goalscoring record, it is easy to see why.

Villa Thriller: Trinidad and Tobago star Dwight Yorke

Barnsley
The Tykes

"Que sera sera, whatever will be, will be. You're going to Barnsley!"** used to be the chant directed at teams heading for relegation from the Premier League. Not any more – Barnsley are in the top flight for the first time in their 110-year history.

Last season's promotion from the First Division was a remarkable feat for a club which has spent its entire life in the lower reaches of the Football League.

Indeed, until 1981, when the Tykes were promoted to the old second division, the club had spent only a handful of seasons outside of the third and fourth divisions. Barnsley's previous best performance had been way back in 1922, when they finished third in division two.

The club have only won one trophy, the FA Cup, in 1912. That Cup-winning side became renowned for tough tackling and gritty goalless draws. They were dubbed "battling Barnsley", an image which has stuck, sometimes unfairly. These days at Oakwell, they have a team who can battle with the best of them, but can play a bit too.

"Brazil, it's just like watching Brazil" is the song which will be heard around Premier League grounds this season when Barnsley come to town. Tykes fans might be pushing their luck a little, but you get the picture. Barnsley are a passing side and when faced with tough situations they play their way out of trouble. Unlike

their South Yorkshire rivals Sheffield United, who were consigned to the play-offs, Barnsley are an attractive side who let their football do the talking.

"At times, when it's been difficult to play football, my players have got themselves out of some tricky situations by doing just that," says player-manager Danny Wilson, who has to take the lion's share of the credit for Barnsley's success.

Danny takes charge

Wilson took over at Oakwell in 1994 from Middlesbrough-bound Viv Anderson. A former Northern Ireland international, Wilson knows all about life in the lower leagues, having spent the bulk of his playing career there with the likes of Bury, Chesterfield, Brighton and Luton. Wilson arrived at Barnsley as a player from Sheffield Wednesday in 1993 and continued to play when he took on the managerial duties. Last season he was voted manager of the year by his fellow Football League bosses.

"It's great that we're up there, and the credit's due to Danny Wilson," says last season's Player of the Year, John Hendrie. "To get a club like Barnsley competing against the big boys is quite an achievement. Danny's got a player's mentality and he knows all the tricks, which helps. He likes his little jokes and he uses his wit to diffuse awkward situations, which is more like a player than a manager.

Top Man: John Hendrie was last year's player of the season

BARNSLEY

Formed: 1887.
Nickname: The Tykes.
Stadium: Oakwell.
Capacity: 19,101.
Address: Grove St,
Barnsley,
South Yorkshire S71 1ET.
Telephone: 01226 211211.
Clubcall: 0891 121152
Fax: 01226 211444.
Website: www.fa-carling.com/club/b.fc
Manager: Danny Wilson.

COLOURS

RECORDS

Record Premier League victory:
None.
Record Premier League defeat:
None.
Record transfer fee received:
£1.5 million from Nottingham F for Carl
Tiler, May 1991.
Record transfer fee paid:
£1.5 million to Partizan Belgrade for Georgi
Hristov, June 1997.
Record attendance:
40,255 v Stoke C, FA Cup 5th round,
Feb 15, 1936.

HONOURS

League: Runners-up, Division One,
1996–97.
FA Cup (1): 1912.
League Cup: 5th round, 1982.

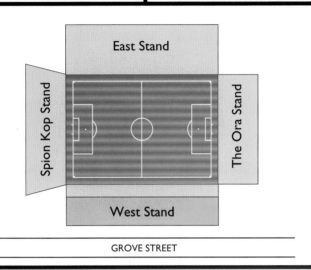

East Stand

Spion Kop Stand

The Ora Stand

West Stand

GROVE STREET

FIXTURES 1997–98

9 AUG	WEST HAM UNITED	H	____ : ____
12 AUG	CRYSTAL PALACE	A	____ : ____
24 AUG	CHELSEA	H	____ : ____
26 AUG	BOLTON	H	____ : ____
30 AUG	DERBY COUNTY	A	____ : ____
13 SEPT	ASTON VILLA	H	____ : ____
20 SEPT	EVERTON	A	____ : ____
23 SEPT	WIMBLEDON	A	____ : ____
27 SEPT	LEICESTER CITY	H	____ : ____
4 OCT	ARSENAL	A	____ : ____
20 OCT	COVENTRY CITY	H	____ : ____
25 OCT	MANCHESTER UNITED	A	____ : ____
1 NOV	BLACKBURN ROVERS	H	____ : ____
8 NOV	SOUTHAMPTON	A	____ : ____
22 NOV	LIVERPOOL	A	____ : ____
29 NOV	LEEDS UNITED	H	____ : ____
8 DEC	SHEFFIELD WEDNESDAY	A	____ : ____
13 DEC	NEWCASTLE UNITED	H	____ : ____
20 DEC	TOTTENHAM HOTSPUR	A	____ : ____
26 DEC	BOLTON	A	____ : ____
28 DEC	DERBY COUNTY	H	____ : ____
10 JAN	WEST HAM	A	____ : ____
17 JAN	CRYSTAL PALACE	H	____ : ____
31 JAN	CHELSEA	A	____ : ____
7 FEB	EVERTON	H	____ : ____
14 FEB	ASTON VILLA	A	____ : ____
21 FEB	COVENTRY CITY	A	____ : ____
28 FEB	WIMBLEDON	H	____ : ____
7 MAR	BLACKBURN ROVERS	A	____ : ____
14 MAR	SOUTHAMPTON	H	____ : ____
28 MAR	LIVERPOOL	H	____ : ____
4 APR	LEEDS UNITED	A	____ : ____
11 APR	SHEFFIELD WEDNESDAY	H	____ : ____
13 APR	NEWCASTLE UNITED	A	____ : ____
18 APR	TOTTENHAM HOTSPUR	H	____ : ____
25 APR	ARSENAL	H	____ : ____
2 MAY	LEICESTER CITY	A	____ : ____
10 MAY	MANCHESTER UNITED	H	____ : ____

"He is hard enough – you know who is the boss. But on the other hand you can have a joke with him. We are a small club so all the players have to be up for it, and Danny's door is always open."

Barnsley's success under Wilson has been all the more remarkable for the lack of money – less than £1 million – that it took to assemble the promotion-winning side. Hendrie and Paul Wilkinson, surplus to requirements at Middlesbrough following the arrival of Juninho and Ravanelli, were brought in at a knock-down price. Nor has Wilson been afraid to experiment with foreign players. Dutch defender Arjan De Zeeuw and Trinidadian forward Clint Marcelle have fully repaid Wilson's faith in them. There were more arrivals from abroad this summer: Macedonian Georgi Hristov, South African Eric Tinkler, German Lars Leese and Slovenian Ales Krizan.

Something to be proud of

Barnsley, the town, has not had a great deal to shout about in recent years, with 20,000 people losing their jobs when the coalmines were closed down. But Barnsley the football club is giving people something to shout about.

"It's much more than football," says Wilson. "They've had hard times here over the past decade and this is the sort of relief they needed. Now they can look forward to enjoying top-flight football."

After 110 years, it hasn't come a moment too soon.

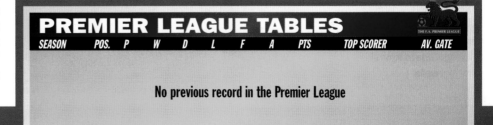

PREMIER LEAGUE TABLES										
SEASON	POS.	P	W	D	L	F	A	PTS	TOP SCORER	AV. GATE

No previous record in the Premier League

KEY PLAYERS TO WATCH

John Hendrie

The irony of Barnsley being promoted to the Premier League while Middlesbrough were relegated back to Division One has not been lost on John Hendrie. The 33-year-old striker was forced out at Boro to make way for foreign stars Juninho and Fabrizio Ravanelli. He moved to Oakwell and played a crucial role in Barnsley's promotion campaign.

Scots-born Hendrie spent six seasons with Middlesbrough before making the switch to South Yorksire last October. He finished Barnsley's League campaign with 15 goals, including a vital late winner away at promotion rivals Sheffield United. His efforts earned him the fans' Player of the Season award for last term.

Clint Marcelle

"Brazil – it's just like watching Brazil" may be a bit far-fetched, but when you see Clint Marcelle in action, it's easy to understand why Barnsley fans get so excited about the team Danny Wilson has assembled at Oakwell.

Trinidad and Tobago international Marcelle joined Barnsley in the summer of 1996 from Portuguese First Division side Felgueiras. He made an immediate impact, scoring on his debut as Barnsley won away at West Bromwich Albion and grabbed the second goal against Bradford City, which secured Barnsley's promotion to the Premiership.

His lightning pace will be a big bonus for Barnsley this season and his runs from "in the hole" could cause Premier League defenders all sorts of problems.

Caribbean Special: Trinidad & Tobago international Clint Marcelle

Captain's Example: Tykes skipper Neil Redfearn

Neil Redfearn

For club captain Neil Redfearn, playing in the Premier League will be a whole new ball game. Despite 15 seasons as a professional footballer, 32-year-old Redfearn has yet to experience life in the top flight.

The hard-working, goal-scoring midfielder has been at Oakwell since 1991, having previously played for Oldham Athletic, Watford, Crystal Palace, Doncaster Rovers, Lincoln City and Bolton Wanderers. He left both Palace and Oldham just before they won promotion to the top division, in 1989 and 1991 respectively, and moved to Watford in the summer after they were relegated from the top flight. So this time, Redfearn, Barnsley's Player of the Year in 1993–94 and top League goalscorer for the club 1996–97, is determined to be there to taste life in the Premier League success.

Paul Wilkinson

Barnsley manager Danny Wilson has had to work on a tight budget at Oakwell (the entire squad that won promotion cost less than £1 million). Striker Paul Wilkinson did not cost the Tykes a penny.

Wilkinson joined Barnsley on a free transfer in the summer of 1996. The 32-year-old forward had been at Middlebrough since 1991, but, like John Hendrie, had been struggling to hold down a first-team place since the arrival of Boro's foreign legion. He spent much of the 1995–96

Player Records

	BORN	NATIONALITY	HEIGHT	WEIGHT	APPS	GOALS	PREVIOUS TEAMS
GOALKEEPERS							
Lars Leese	18.8.69 Germany	German	6-4	14-4	0	0	Preussen Köln, Bayern Leverkusen (Ger).
David Watson	10.11.73 Barnsley	English	5-11	12-3	142	0	none
DEFENDERS							
Matt Appleby	16.4.72 Middlesbrough	English	5-10	11-10	144	8	Newcastle U, Darlington.
Steve Davis	26.7.65 Birmingham	English	5-11	12-12	397	22	Crewe Alex, Burnley.
Nicky Eaden	12.12.72 Sheffield	English	5-8	11-9	176	8	none
Ales Krizan	25.7.71 Slovenia	Slovenian	5-10	11-6	0	0	Maribor Branitz (Sloven).
Adrian Moses	4.5.75 Doncaster	English	5-5	12-8	56	3	none
Darren Sheridan	8.12.67 Manchester	Irish	5-4	10-12	120	4	none
Neil Thompson	2.10.63 Beverley	English	5-11	13-8	348	39	Hull C, Scarborough, Ipswich T.
Arjan de Zeeuw	16.4.70 Holland	Dutch	6-2	12-12	74	3	Telstar (Hol).
MIDFIELDERS							
Jovo Bosancic	7.8.70 Croatia	Croatian	25	1	25	1	Camponaoir (Por).
Martin Bullock	5.3.75 Derby	English	5-4	10-9	98	1	none
Neil Redfearn	20.6.65 Dewsbury	English	5-8	12-0	579	118	Bolton W, Lincoln C, Doncaster R, Crystal Palace, Watford, Oldham Ath.
Eric Tinkler	20.7.70 Johannesburg	South African	6-0	11-9	0	0	Cagliari (Ita).
Carel Van der Velden	3.8.72 Arnhem	Dutch	5-9	13-0	9	0	Den Bosch (Hol).
FORWARDS							
John Hendrie	24.10.63 Lennoxtown	Scottish	5-8	12-5	489	116	Coventry C, Hereford U, Bradford C, Newcastle U, Leeds U, Middlesbrough.
Laurens Ten Heuval	6.6.76 Amsterdam	Dutch	6-0	10-9	6	0	Den Bosch (Hol).
Andy Liddell	28.6.73 Leeds	English	5-6	10-9	164	23	none
Clint Marcelle	9.11.68 Trinidad	Trinidadian	40	8	40	8	Felgueiras (Por).
Paul Wilkinson	30.10.64 Louth	Scottish	6-1	12-4	447	141	Grimsby T, Everton, Nottingham F, Watford, Middlesbrough, Oldham Ath, Watford, Luton T.
Georgi Hristov	30.1.76 Macedonia	Macedonian	5-11	11-8	0	0	Partizan Belgrade (Yug)

season on loan to Oldham Athletic, Watford and Luton, and jumped at the chance of a move to Oakwell.

As a target man, Wilkinson played an important role in last season's promotion campaign, scoring 11 League goals and setting up numerous chances for teammates.

Martin Bullock

Winger Martin Bullock is one of the best young players to come out of Oakwell for a long time. Since making his debut for the Tykes three seasons ago, 22-year-old Bullock, nicknamed "Willo the Wisp", has developed into a highly promising player.

He represented the Nationwide League Under-21 side in March 1997 and his contribution to last season's promotion campaign attracted the attention of a number of other Premier League clubs.

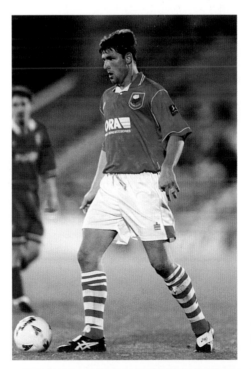

Arjan De Zeeuw

Zola, Juninho and Ravanelli may have grabbed all the headlines last season as the star foreigners in the Premier League, but Barnsley have uncovered their own foreign star in Dutch defender Arjan De Zeeuw. The centre-back was the defensive rock on which last season's promotion campaign was built. He is now in his third season with Barnsley, having joined in 1995 from Dutch side Telstar. He showed his potential early on, winning the fans' Player of the Year award in his first season.

Barnsley have other foreign players – former Yugoslav Under-21 midfielder Josa Bosancic impressed last season – but De Zeeuw was the pick of the crop.

Dutch Defender: Arjan De Zeeuw, Barnsley's fans' favourite

Blackburn Rovers

After the trials and tribulations of last season, Blackburn Rovers are pinning their hopes on new boss Roy Hodgson, one of Europe's most experienced and respected coaches.

Judging by the cheers that echoed around Ewood Park after Rovers' goalless draw with Middlesbrough in their penultimate match of last season, anybody would have thought the Premier League trophy was back in Blackburn. That Rovers had just avoided relegation says a great deal about how low

Safe Hands: In Tim Flowers, Rovers have a world-class goalkeeper

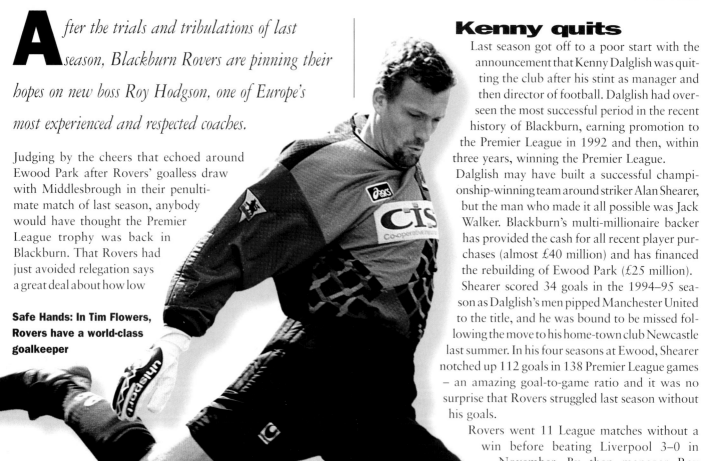

expectations have sunk since Blackburn won the League title just over two years ago.

New manager Roy Hodgson is not promising miracles, though. In the long term his plan is to get Rovers back where he believes they belong – up with the elite of English football. In the short term, though, the aim is to steady the ship and avoid the sort of hair-raising relegation scrapes and Cup humiliations that Rovers fans were forced to endure last season.

Kenny quits

Last season got off to a poor start with the announcement that Kenny Dalglish was quitting the club after his stint as manager and then director of football. Dalglish had overseen the most successful period in the recent history of Blackburn, earning promotion to the Premier League in 1992 and then, within three years, winning the Premier League.

Dalglish may have built a successful championship-winning team around striker Alan Shearer, but the man who made it all possible was Jack Walker. Blackburn's multi-millionaire backer has provided the cash for all recent player purchases (almost £40 million) and has financed the rebuilding of Ewood Park (£25 million).

Shearer scored 34 goals in the 1994–95 season as Dalglish's men pipped Manchester United to the title, and he was bound to be missed following the move to his home-town club Newcastle last summer. In his four seasons at Ewood, Shearer notched up 112 goals in 138 Premier League games – an amazing goal-to-game ratio and it was no surprise that Rovers struggled last season without his goals.

Rovers went 11 League matches without a win before beating Liverpool 3–0 in November. By then manager Ray Harford had resigned – the pressure had got too much following a home defeat by second division Stockport County in the League Cup. Harford's assistant Tony Parkes took charge of first-team affairs while the club looked for a long-term replacement.

BLACKBURN ROVERS

Formed: 1875.
Nickname: Rovers.
Stadium: Ewood Park.
Capacity: 31,367.
Address: Ewood Park, Blackburn, BB2 4JF.
Telephone: 01254 698888.
Clubcall: 0898 121179.
Fax: 01254 671042.
Website: www.fa-carling.com/club/br.fc
Manager: Roy Hodgson.

COLOURS

RECORDS

Record Premier League victory:
7–0 (v Nottingham F, Nov 18, 1995).
Record Premier League defeat:
5–0 (v Coventry C, Dec 9, 1995).
Record transfer fee received:
£15 million from Newcastle U for Alan Shearer, July 1996.
Record transfer fee paid:
£5 million to Norwich C for Chris Sutton, July 1994.
Record attendance:
61,783, v Bolton W, FA Cup 6th round, Mar 2, 1929.

HONOURS

League (3): 1911-12, 1913-14, 1994-95.
FA Cup (6): 1884, 1885, 1886, 1890, 1891, 1928.

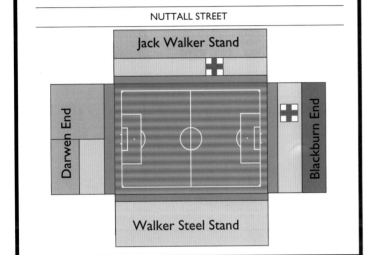

NUTTALL STREET

Jack Walker Stand

Darwen End

Blackburn End

Walker Steel Stand

Roy of the Rovers

An embarrassing episode with Swedish coach Sven-Goran Eriksson ended with the Sampdoria manager deciding to stay in Italy, but Rovers finally got their man when Roy Hodgson, one of their original choices, agreed to move to join them from Italian side Internazionale. London-born Hodgson has worked all around the Continent over the past 20 years, including a successful spell as coach of Switzerland, and is one of Europe's most respected coaches. He brings a wealth of experience to Ewood Park.

Hodgson's first task is to stabilize a shaky ship. "My job is to make sure we don't challenge for the title one year and then fight against relegation the next," he says. Jack Walker has made money available to the new manager to spend on new players. Hodgson says: "It's nice to know there's money to spend, but it's not that important."

Hodgson is well aware that there is already a wealth of talent at Ewood Park. In Tim Flowers, Blackburn have a world-class goalkeeper. There are excellent defenders in Chris Coleman, Jeff Kenna and Stephane Henchoz, recently-acquired from SV Hamburg. In midfield they can boast Garry Flitcroft, Lars Bohinen and Paul Warhurst, while up front there are Chris Sutton and Kevin Gallacher, the Scottish international who has been so unlucky with injuries in recent seasons.

There may not be immediate fire-works under new manager Roy Hodgson, but Blackburn fans can expect a season of steady progress. Bearing in mind the club's rich history, it's the least the Ewood Park faithful deserve.

FIXTURES 1997–98

9 AUG	DERBY COUNTY	H	___ : ___
13 AUG	ASTON VILLA	A	___ : ___
23 AUG	LIVERPOOL	H	___ : ___
25 AUG	SHEFFIELD WEDNESDAY	H	___ : ___
30 AUG	CRYSTAL PALACE	A	___ : ___
14 SEPT	LEEDS UNITED	H	___ : ___
20 SEPT	TOTTENHAM HOTSPUR	A	___ : ___
24 SEPT	LEICESTER CITY	A	___ : ___
28 SEPT	COVENTRY CITY	H	___ : ___
4 OCT	WIMBLEDON	A	___ : ___
18 OCT	SOUTHAMPTON	H	___ : ___
25 OCT	NEWCASTLE UNITED	A	___ : ___
1 NOV	BARNSLEY	A	___ : ___
8 NOV	EVERTON	H	___ : ___
22 NOV	CHELSEA	H	___ : ___
29 NOV	MANCHESTER UNITED	A	___ : ___
6 DEC	BOLTON	H	___ : ___
13 DEC	ARSENAL	A	___ : ___
20 DEC	WEST HAM UNITED	H	___ : ___
26 DEC	SHEFFIELD WEDNESDAY	A	___ : ___
28 DEC	CRYSTAL PALACE	H	___ : ___
10 JAN	DERBY COUNTY	A	___ : ___
17 JAN	ASTON VILLA	H	___ : ___
31 JAN	LIVERPOOL	A	___ : ___
7 FEB	TOTTENHAM HOTSPUR	H	___ : ___
14 FEB	LEEDS UNITED	A	___ : ___
21 FEB	SOUTHAMPTON	A	___ : ___
28 FEB	LEICESTER CITY	H	___ : ___
7 MAR	BARNSLEY	H	___ : ___
14 MAR	EVERTON	A	___ : ___
28 MAR	CHELSEA	A	___ : ___
4 APR	MANCHESTER UNITED	H	___ : ___
11 APR	BOLTON	A	___ : ___
13 APR	ARSENAL	H	___ : ___
18 APR	WEST HAM UNITED	A	___ : ___
25 APR	WIMBLEDON	H	___ : ___
2 MAY	COVENTRY CITY	A	___ : ___
10 MAY	NEWCASTLE UNITED	H	___ : ___

PREMIER LEAGUE TABLES

SEASON	POS.	P	W	D	L	F	A	PTS	TOP SCORER	AV. GATE
1992–93	4th	42	20	11	11	68	46	71	Shearer 16	16,246
1993–94	2nd	42	25	9	8	63	36	84	Shearer 31	17,721
1994–95	1st	42	27	8	7	80	39	89	Shearer 34	25,272
1995–96	7th	38	18	7	13	61	47	61	Shearer 31	27,716
1996–97	13th	38	9	15	14	42	43	42	Sutton 11	24,947

Tim Flowers

Since his transfer from Southampton for a British record (for a goalkeeper) of £2.4 million in November 1993, Tim Flowers has established himself as one of the most charismatic goalkeepers in the Premier League. His performances last season for Blackburn won him a player of the month award as Rovers put their early-season problems behind them.

Flowers is a regular in Glenn Hoddle's England squad after making his international debut in a 1–1 draw with Brazil in June 1993. He has since brought his total to nine caps, the last against Italy in last summer's four-nation tournament in France. However, with David Seaman established as England first-choice keeper, Flowers has been left to compete with Leeds' Nigel Martyn for second spot.

Flowers is used to being an understudy. He moved to Southampton from Wolves for £70,000 in 1986 to be Peter Shilton's number two and stayed there for eight seasons before the move to Ewood Park.

Chris Sutton

Chris Sutton became Britain's most expensive player when Blackburn signed him from Norwich for £5 million in the summer of 1994. That figure has since been eclipsed a number of times, notably by Sutton's former striking partner Alan Shearer.

It was with Shearer that Sutton formed the lethal SAS (Shearer and Sutton) partnership. Between them, the pair scored 49 League goals as Rovers won the 1994–95 title. Sutton signalled his intentions early on in that campaign with a hat–trick against Coventry. But the following season was not a happy one for Nottingham-born Sutton – he failed to score in the League and was even used in his original role at Norwich in the centre of defence.

Last season was altogether happier for Sutton. Rovers found things hard going following the £15 million sale of Alan Shearer to Newcastle, but Sutton found his form sufficiently to finish the campaign as Blackburn's top scorer.

Life after Shearer: Chris Sutton is back among the goals

Back in Business: Kevin Gallacher is scoring goals for club and country after serious injury

Kevin Gallacher

After three years plagued by injuries, Scottish striker Kevin Gallacher is finally repaying the £1.5 million Blackburn paid Coventry for his services in March 1993.

Gallacher broke a leg and played just one League game for Rovers in their 1994–95 title-winning season. He was injured almost immediately on his comeback and only re-established himself in the Rovers first team last season. He had already done enough to win a place in Scotland's Euro 96 squad, though, and he came on as a substitute against Holland at Villa Park as the Scots came mighty close to reaching the quarter-finals.

Clydebank-born Gallacher spent six-and-a-half seasons with Dundee United before moving south of the border to Coventry for a £900,000 fee.

Last season, Gallacher scored twice for Scotland against Austria in a vital World Cup qualifier. He now has his sights set firmly on reaching the World Cup finals in France – if he can stay free from injury.

Player Records

	BORN	NATIONALITY	HEIGHT	WEIGHT	APPS	GOALS	PREVIOUS TEAMS
GOALKEEPERS							
John Filan	8.2.70 Sydney	Australian	5-11	12-10	15	0	Coventry C., Cambridge Utd.
Tim Flowers	3.2.67 Kenilworth	English	6-3	14-4	403	0	Wolverhampton W, Southampton, Swindon T.
DEFENDERS							
Chris Coleman	10.6.70 Swansea	Welsh	6-2	14-3	342	15	Swansea C, Crystal Palace.
Gary Croft	17.2.74 Stafford	English	5-9	11-8	154	3	Grimsby T.
Stephane Henchoz	7.9.74 Switzerland	Swiss	6-2	12-8	0	0	Neuchatel Xamax (Swi), Hamburg (Ger).
Colin Hendry	7.1.65 Keith	Scottish	6-1	12-7	406	40	Dundee, Blackburn R, Manchester C.
Jeff Kenna	28.8.70 Dublin	Irish	5-11	12-3	192	5	Southampton.
Ian Pearce	7.5.74 Bury St Edmunds	English	6-4	14-4	55	2	Chelsea.
Adam Reed	18.2.75 Bishop Auckland	English	6-0	11-0	52	1	Darlington.
Patrick Valery	3.7.69 Brignoles	France	5-11	11-9	0	0	Monaco (Fra), Bastia (Fra).
MIDFIELDERS							
Anders Andersson	15.3.74 Tomellia	Sweden	5-9	11-9	0	0	Malmo.
Lars Bohinen	8.8.69 Vadso	Norwegian	6-1	12-1	106	13	Valerengen (Nor), Viking (Nor), Young Boys (Swi), Nottingham F.
Georgios Donis	20.10.69 Frankfurt	Greek	6-0	12-2	20	2	Panathinaikos (Gre).
Garry Flitcroft	6.11.72 Bolton	English	6-0	12-9	158	16	Manchester C, Bury.
Billy McKinlay	22.4.69 Glasgow	Scottish	5-8	11-4	266	27	Dundee U.
Stuart Ripley	20.11.67 Middlesbrough	English	6-0	13-0	412	38	Middlesbrough, Bolton W.
Tim Sherwood	2.2.69 St Albans	English	6-1	12-9	299	29	Watford, Norwich C.
Jason Wilcox	15.7.71 Bolton	English	6-0	11-0	187	24	none
FORWARDS							
Martin Dahlin	16.4.68 Sweden	Swedish	6-0	12-8	0	0	Malmo, Borussia MG (Ger), Roma (Ita)
Kevin Gallacher	23.11.66 Clydebank	Scottish	5-8	11-3	321	80	Dundee U, Coventry C.
Per Pedersen	30.3.69 Odense	Danish	6-1	13-7	11	1	Lyngby (Den), Odense (Den).
Chris Sutton	10.3.73 Nottingham	English	6-3	13-7	180	61	Norwich C.

Jason Wilcox

Despite all the millions spent on players by Blackburn in recent seasons, one of Rovers' most consistent performers has been Jason Wilcox, who did not cost the club a penny.

Bolton-born Wilcox joined the club from school and made his debut in the 1989–90 season, making him one of the few players in the current squad to have played for Rovers before they were promoted to the Premier League.

The left-midfielder's career had been blighted by injury – a serious knee injury kept him out of action for much of the 1995–96 season – but he returned to sufficient form to earn an England call-up from Terry Venables and made his international debut against Bulgaria at Wembley in May 1996.

Real Rover: Jason Wilcox

Stephane Henchoz

Swiss defender Stephane Henchoz turned down an offer from Manchester United to join Rovers in a £3 million summer transfer from German club Hamburg.

The reason? Roy Hodgson. The new Rovers boss introduced Henchoz to professional football as manager of Neuchatel Xamax, and then gave the 23-year-old defender an international debut for Switzerland in 1993 against Japan.

Henchoz, who plays in central defence but can also double up as a defensive midfielder, was Hodgson's first signing as Blackburn manager following his arrival from Italy.

The transfer was a sure sign that Hodgson intends to introduce a new Continental class to Ewood Park.

Bolton Wanderers

The Trotters

Bolton Wanderers are back in the big time after a trailblazing season in division one. With new players and a brand new stadium, Colin Todd's side are determined to be no pushovers.

Nothing demonstrates the spirit of Bolton's new era more than the club's new stadium, the space-age superdome just down the road from Burnden Park, the club's home for more than a century. The new ground, which will hold 25,000, is part of a £200 million development, making it the most expensive stadium ever built in Britain. It's a sign of Bolton's ambition and their determination to avoid a repeat of 1995–96, when they were relegated after finishing bottom.

Bolton fans have not known whether to laugh or cry in recent seasons. A series of giantkilling acts in the Cups was followed by promotion to the Premier League in 1995, only for relegation back to division one to follow. Delight at promotion as champions last season was contrasted with the sadness at leaving Burnden Park.

Wanderers are one of the oldest football clubs in the world, having been formed in 1874. Despite being founder members of the Football League, Bolton have never won the top division title. They do, however, have a fearsome reputation as a Cup side.

Bolton have won the FA Cup four times – in 1923, 1926, 1929 and 1958, when club hero Nat Lofthouse scored twice in a 2–0 win over Manchester United. The club's saddest hours also came in the Cup: in 1946, 33 people were killed when a wall collapsed during an FA Cup tie against Stoke at Burnden Park

Cup giantkillers

In the 1990s, under Phil Neal and then Bruce Rioch, Bolton achieved promotion to division one and picked up some big-name scalps in the Cups, notably Liverpool and Arsenal. In the 1994–95 season, Wanderers reached Wembley twice, losing to Liverpool in the League Cup Final, but beating Reading in a thrilling promotion Play-off Final. Mixu Paatelainen and Fabian De Freitas secured Bolton's place in the Premier League in extra time.

Under Bruce Rioch, Bolton developed a reputation for playing attractive, attacking football. Then Rioch was lured away to Arsenal in the summer of 1995, leaving his assistant Roy McFarland in charge of Wanderers' Premier League challenge. Despite the arrival of new players (Chris Fairclough, Gerry Taggart, Nathan Blake and Scott Sellars), Bolton found life tough at the top. They finished with just 29 points and without McFarland, who had resigned and been replaced by Colin Todd.

Ton Up: Scott Green scores one of Wanderers' 100 League goals last season

BOLTON WANDERERS

Formed: 1874.
Nickname: The Trotters.
Stadium: The Reebok Stadium.
Capacity: 25,000.
Address: The Reebok Stadium,
Mansell Way,
Horwich,
Bolton, BL6 7JW
Telephone: 01204 389200.
Clubcall: 01204 521101.
Fax: 01204 382334.
Website: www.fa-carling.com/club/bw.fc
Manager: Colin Todd.

COLOURS

RECORDS

Record Premier League victory:
4–1 (v Middlesbrough, Feb 17, 1996).
Record Premier League defeat:
6–0 (v Manchester U, Feb 25, 1996).
Record transfer fee received:
£4.5 million from Celtic for Alan Stubbs,
Aug 1996.
Record transfer fee paid:
£2.5 million to Newcastle U for Robbie
Elliott, July 1997.
Record attendance:
69,912, v Manchester C, FA Cup 5th round,
Feb 18, 1933 (at Burnden Park).

HONOURS

League: 3rd, Division One 1899–1900,
1920–21, 1924–25.
Champions, Division One 1996–97.
Champions, Division Two 1908–09,
1977–78.
FA Cup (4): 1923, 1926, 1929, 1958.
League Cup: Runners-up 1995.

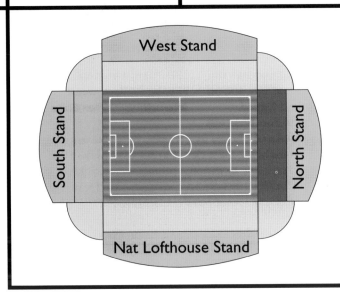

FIXTURES 1997–98

Date	Opponent	H/A	Score
9 AUG	SOUTHAMPTON	A	____ : ____
23 AUG	COVENTRY CITY	A	____ : ____
26 AUG	BARNSLEY	A	____ : ____
1 SEPT	EVERTON	H	____ : ____
13 SEPT	ARSENAL	A	____ : ____
20 SEPT	MANCHESTER UNITED	H	____ : ____
23 SEPT	TOTTENHAM HOTSPUR	H	____ : ____
27 SEPT	CRYSTAL PALACE	A	____ : ____
4 OCT	ASTON VILLA	H	____ : ____
18 OCT	WEST HAM UNITED	A	____ : ____
25 OCT	CHELSEA	H	____ : ____
1 NOV	LIVERPOOL	H	____ : ____
8 NOV	SHEFFIELD WEDNESDAY	A	____ : ____
22 NOV	LEICESTER CITY	A	____ : ____
29 NOV	WIMBLEDON	H	____ : ____
1 DEC	NEWCASTLE UNITED	H	____ : ____
6 DEC	BLACKBURN ROVERS	A	____ : ____
14 DEC	DERBY COUNTY	H	____ : ____
20 DEC	LEEDS UNITED	A	____ : ____
26 DEC	BARNSLEY	H	____ : ____
28 DEC	EVERTON	A	____ : ____
10 JAN	SOUTHAMPTON	H	____ : ____
17 JAN	NEWCASTLE UNITED	A	____ : ____
31 JAN	COVENTRY CITY	H	____ : ____
7 FEB	MANCHESTER UNITED	A	____ : ____
14 FEB	ARSENAL	H	____ : ____
21 FEB	WEST HAM UNITED	H	____ : ____
28 FEB	TOTTENHAM HOTSPUR	A	____ : ____
7 MAR	LIVERPOOL	A	____ : ____
14 MAR	SHEFFIELD WEDNESDAY	H	____ : ____
28 MAR	LEICESTER CITY	H	____ : ____
4 APR	WIMBLEDON	A	____ : ____
11 APR	BLACKBURN ROVERS	H	____ : ____
13 APR	DERBY COUNTY	A	____ : ____
18 APR	LEEDS UNITED	H	____ : ____
25 APR	ASTON VILLA	A	____ : ____
2 MAY	CRYSTAL PALACE	H	____ : ____
10 MAY	CHELSEA	A	____ : ____

Not even the most optimistic of Bolton fans could have predicted that Wanderers would have such a successful season back in division one. The loss of Premier League income forced the sale of captain and centre-back Alan Stubbs, to Celtic, and Yugoslav midfielder Sasa Curcic, to Aston Villa. Manager Todd spent the money wisely, bringing in Danes Per Frandsen and Michael Johansen and midfielders John Sheridan (from Sheffield Wednesday) and Jamie Pollock (from Spain).

Champions by a mile

The 1–1 draw at Port Vale on the opening day of the season gave little hint of what was to come. Wanderers lost just four times in the League on the way to winning the Championship in style. Goals rained down in abundance, with John McGinlay and Nathan Blake grabbing the lion's share. The season was so successful that Wanderers went into the last home game – the last-ever at Burnden Park – against Tranmere Rovers, needing a win to finish the season on 100 points. Tranmere spoiled the party, but the 2–2 draw took Bolton's goal tally into three figures, a staggering total.

This season, with new signings Robbie Elliott (from Newcastle) and Neil Cox (from Middlesbrough) and a brand new stadium, the outlook is promising. Wanderers signalled their intentions last season with Coca-Cola Cup wins over Premier League Chelsea (2–1) and Tottenham (6–1). The message is clear and simple – Bolton will be no pushovers this time around.

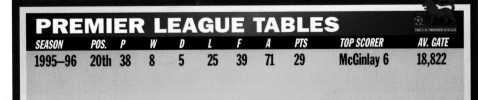

PREMIER LEAGUE TABLES

SEASON	POS.	P	W	D	L	F	A	PTS	TOP SCORER	AV. GATE
1995–96	20th	38	8	5	25	39	71	29	McGinlay 6	18,822

Alan Thompson, Robbie Elliott and Scott Sellars

The list of players who have been sold by Newcastle United in recent years, only to experience success with their new clubs, makes for interesting reading. To the names of Darren Huckerby and Paul Kitson, Bolton fans will happily add three of their own: Alan Thompson, Robbie Elliott and Scott Sellars.

Former England Under-21 midfielder Thompson failed to make the breakthrough at St James' Park and joined Bolton in 1993. At Burnden Park he has developed into an accomplished player, scoring a memorable goal in the 1995 League Cup final. Robbie Elliott, who can play in defence or midfield, nearly joined Blackburn Rover last season, but opted to join Bolton this summer in a record £2.5 million move.

Sellars arrived at Newcastle from Leeds just as Thompson was leaving. He was ever-present for Kevin Keegan's side in the 1993–94 season, but lost his place with the arrival of David Ginola.

The former Leeds and Blackburn midfielder's qualities have been put to good use at Bolton. He was unable to prevent Wanderers' last Premier League campaign from ending in disappointment, but his contribution to last season's campaign was vital.

Nathan Blake

John McGinlay may have finished as division one's top scorer last season, but Welsh striker Nathan Blake was never far behind. He finished the campaign with 24 League and Cup goals.

Despite all the goals, last year was a controversial season for 25-year-old Blake, a player who is never afraid to speak his mind. He clashed with Wales manager Bobby Gould following allegations of racism and also had run-ins with rival fans, notably at Sheffield United.

Cardiff-born Blake was on the books of Chelsea as a trainee, but made his professional debut for his home-town club, Cardiff City, in the 1989–90 season. He first came to national prominence with his goalscoring feats in Cardiff's 1993–94 FA Cup campaign. He joined Premier League Sheffield United later that season, but was powerless to prevent relegation: The Blades' fate was sealed in the last minute of the last game of the campaign, against Chelsea at Stamford Bridge.

Blake was well established in division one with United when Bolton signed him to boost their fight against relegation from the Premier League. Blake could only manage one goal as Wanderers went down, but last season he redeemed his reputation as a first-class goalscorer.

Flipping Brilliant: Welsh international Nathan Blake

John Sheridan

Since his arrival last year on loan from Sheffield Wednesday, John Sheridan has given Bolton the stability and inspiration in midfield they need to succeed at the highest level.

The former Leeds and Republic of Ireland midfielder had not been getting first-team football at Wednesday and had a spell on loan at Birmingham City towards the end of the 1995–96 season. Last season his loan deal was converted to a permanent one as the 32-year-old proved he still has a future in the top flight.

John McGinlay

It is rare for a division one footballer to play a leading part in his country's World Cup campaign, as Bolton's John McGinlay did for Scotland last season. But then McGinlay is no ordinary striker.

McGinlay finished not only as Bolton's top scorer in 1996–97, but his 30 League

Invaluable: Bolton midfielder Scott Sellars

Player Records

	BORN	NATIONALITY	HEIGHT	WEIGHT	APPS	GOALS	PREVIOUS TEAMS
GOALKEEPERS							
Keith Branagan	10.7.66 Fulham	Irish	6-0	13-2	325	1	Cambridge U, Millwall, Brentford, Gillingham, Fulham.
Gavin Ward	30.6.70 Sutton Coldfield	English	6-3	14-5	149	0	Shrewsbury T, West Brom, Cardiff C, Leicester C, Bradford C, Bolton W.
DEFENDERS							
Gudni Bergsson	21.7.65 Reykjavik	Icelandic	6-1	12-3	146	9	Valur (Ice), Tottenham H.
Simon Coleman	13.6.68 Worksop	English	6-0	10-8	271	17	Mansfield T, Middlesbrough, Derby Co, Sheffield W, Bolton W.
Neil Cox	8.10.71 Scunthorpe	English	6-0	13-2	153	9	Scunthorpe U, Aston Villa, Middlesbrough.
Chris Fairclough	12.4.64 Sheffield	English	5-11	11-2	439	34	Nottingham F, Tottenham H, Leeds U.
Steve McAnespie	1.2.72 Kilmarnock	Scottish	5-9	10-7	62	0	Raith R.
Jimmy Phillips	8.2.66 Bolton	English	6-0	12-7	512	17	Bolton W, Rangers, Oxford U, Middlesbrough.
Nicky Spooner	5.6.71 Manchester	English	5-10	119	23	2	none
Gerry Taggart	18.10.70 Belfast	Northern Irish	6-1	12-3	278	21	Manchester C, Barnsley.
MIDFIELDERS							
Robbie Elliott	25.12.73 Newcastle	English	5-10	10-13	79	7	Newcastle U.
Jamie Pollock	16.2.74 Stockton	English	5-10	14-1	155	17	Middlesbrough, Osasuna (Spa)
Scott Sellars	27.11.65 Sheffield	English	5-7	9-10	410	63	Leeds U, Blackburn R, Leeds U, Newcastle U.
John Sheridan	1.10.64 Stretford	Irish	5-10	12-1	449	74	Leeds U, Nottingham F, Sheffield W, Birmingham C.
Alan Thompson	22.12.73 Newcastle	English	6-0	12-8	140	25	Newcastle U.
Andy Todd	21.9.74 Derby	English	5-10	10-11	48	2	Middlesbrough, Swindon T.
FORWARDS							
Nathan Blake	27.1.72 Cardiff	Welsh	5-11	13-12	260	90	Cardiff C, Sheffield U.
Per Frandsen	6.2.70 Copenhagen	Danish	6-1	12-6	41	5	B1903(Den),Lille(Fra), FC Copenhagen (Den).
Michael Johansen	22.7.72 Glostrup	Danish	5-6	10-5	33	5	B1903 (Den), FC Copenhagen (Den).
John McGinlay	8.4.64 Inverness	Scottish	5-9	11-4	304	133	Shrewsbury T, Bury, Millwall.
Scott Taylor	5.5.76 Chertsey	English	5-10	11-4	40	1	Millwall.

and Cup goals also made him the leading marksman in division one. He grabbed a hat-trick when Wanderers thrashed Spurs in the Coca-Cola Cup and he was also on target for his country as the Scots beat Sweden 1–0 in Glasgow in a crucial World Cup qualifier.

It's all a far cry from the early days of McGinlay's career, which were spent in the lower reaches of the Football League with Shrewsbury, Bury and Millwall. Inverness-born McGinlay is a late developer, having made his League debut for Shrewsbury Town at the relatively mature age of 24.

McGinlay joined Bolton in the autumn of 1992 and was quick to make an impact, scoring 16 League goals in his first season. The next year was even better, with 25 goals in 39 League appearances. But last season was his best yet, and the confidence gained from such a prolific goal tally is likely to spur McGinlay to even greater heights. Premier League defences have been warned.

Goal Machine: Scottish international striker John McGinlay

Chelsea
The Blues

Under player-manager Ruud Gullit, the Continental changes are sweeping through Stamford Bridge. Last season's FA Cup victory suggests Chelsea are finally shaking off the "great underachievers" tag which has dogged them for so long.

Chelsea's first trophy for 26 years owed a great deal to two men: Ruud Gullit and the late Matthew Harding. Club director Harding, a multi-millionaire, provided the funding and Gullit, the former World and European Footballer of the Year, attracted the world-class players needed to build a winning team.

It's a far cry from the early 1980s when Chelsea struggled in the old second division having been on the brink of major success after winning the 1970 FA Cup. The club had a reputation for unruly fans and controversial chairman Ken Bates even threatened to install electric fences at Stamford Bridge to control them.

Glenn's legacy

Glenn Hoddle got the ball rolling at Stamford Bridge in 1993, before leaving to manage England three years later. It was Hoddle who signed Gullit on a free transfer from Italian Serie A side Sampdoria in the summer of 1995. Hoddle changed Chelsea's playing style to a more Continental approach, which brought immediate success – the Blues reached the 1994 FA Cup Final and the semi-final two years later, losing to Manchester United on both occasions.

Gullit was the overwhelming choice of Chelsea fans to succeed Hoddle – and he has not disappointed them. As a player, Gullit experienced phenomenal success, winning the Italian League, European Cup and World Club Cup with Milan and the 1988 European Championship with Holland. As one of the world's most famous footballers, Gullit was always going to be in a strong position to attract other world-class players to Chelsea. And he has done just that.

Viva Vialli

Italian striker Gianluca Vialli, who had just won the European Cup with Juventus and was looking for a new challenge, not to mention a final pay day, was one of Gullit's first major signings as Chelsea boss. Vialli was joined by fellow-Italian and midfielder Roberto Di Matteo, a record signing at £4.9 million, and French defender Frank Leboeuf.

Gullit changed Chelsea's training methods, employing a full-time fitness coach, former international sprinter Ade Mafe, and encouraged the players to change their diets. Chips were out, salads were in. Some players took time to adapt but Chelsea started the season well and were unbeaten in their first six League matches, before being brought down to earth when they lost 5–1 to Liverpool at Anfield. Vialli was already a hero at Stamford Bridge but another Italian was to make a bigger impact. Gianfranco Zola, who Gullit had tried to buy during the summer of 1996, fell out with his Serie A club

Making a Mark: striker Hughes continues to defy the critics

CHELSEA

Formed: 1905.
Nickname: The Blues.
Stadium: Stamford Bridge.
Capacity: 31,791.
Address: Stamford Bridge, London SW6 1HS.
Telephone: 0171 385 5545.
Clubcall: 0891 121159.
Fax: 0171 381 4831.
Website: www.fa-carling.com/club/c.fc
Manager: Ruud Gullit.

COLOURS

RECORDS

Record Premier League victory:
5–0 (v Middlesbrough, Feb 4, 1996).
Record Premier League defeat:
5–1 (v Liverpool, Sept 21, 1996).
Record transfer fee received:
£2.2 million from Tottenham H for Gordon Durie, July 1991.
Record transfer fee paid:
£4.9 million to Lazio for Roberto Di Matteo, July 1996.
Record attendance:
82,905, v Arsenal, Division 1, Oct 12, 1935.

HONOURS

League (1): 1954–55.
FA Cup (2): 1970, 1997.
League Cup (1): 1965.
European Cup-winners' Cup (1): 1971.

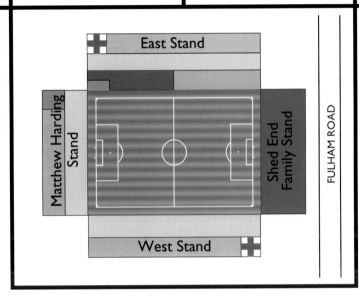

FIXTURES 1997–98

Date	Opponent	H/A	Score
19 AUG	COVENTRY CITY	A	____ : ____
24 AUG	BARNSLEY	A	____ : ____
26 AUG	WIMBLEDON	A	____ : ____
30 AUG	SOUTHAMPTON	H	____ : ____
13 SEPT	CRYSTAL PALACE	A	____ : ____
21 SEPT	ARSENAL	H	____ : ____
24 SEPT	MANCHESTER UNITED	A	____ : ____
27 SEPT	NEWCASTLE UNITED	H	____ : ____
5 OCT	LIVERPOOL	A	____ : ____
18 OCT	LEICESTER CITY	H	____ : ____
25 OCT	BOLTON WANDERERS	A	____ : ____
1 NOV	ASTON VILLA	A	____ : ____
8 NOV	WEST HAM UNITED	H	____ : ____
22 NOV	BLACKBURN ROVERS	A	____ : ____
26 NOV	EVERTON	H	____ : ____
29 NOV	DERBY COUNTY	H	____ : ____
6 DEC	TOTTENHAM HOTSPUR	A	____ : ____
13 DEC	LEEDS UNITED	H	____ : ____
20 DEC	SHEFFIELD WEDNESDAY	A	____ : ____
26 DEC	WIMBLEDON	H	____ : ____
29 DEC	SOUTHAMPTON	A	____ : ____
10 JAN	COVENTRY CITY	H	____ : ____
17 JAN	EVERTON	A	____ : ____
31 JAN	BARNSLEY	H	____ : ____
7 FEB	ARSENAL	A	____ : ____
14 FEB	CRYSTAL PALACE	H	____ : ____
21 FEB	LEICESTER CITY	A	____ : ____
28 FEB	MANCHESTER UNITED	H	____ : ____
7 MAR	ASTON VILLA	H	____ : ____
14 MAR	WEST HAM UNITED	A	____ : ____
28 MAR	BLACKBURN ROVERS	H	____ : ____
4 APR	DERBY COUNTY	A	____ : ____
11 APR	TOTTENHAM HOTSPUR	H	____ : ____
13 APR	LEEDS UNITED	A	____ : ____
18 APR	SHEFFIELD WEDNESDAY	H	____ : ____
25 APR	LIVERPOOL	H	____ : ____
2 MAY	NEWCASTLE UNITED	A	____ : ____
10 MAY	BOLTON WANDERERS	H	____ : ____

Parma and agreed to move to the Bridge last November. The little Sardinian made a huge impact, striking up a partnership with Welshman Mark Hughes which kept Vialli out of the side but took Chelsea to the FA Cup Final and 6th place in the League, their highest placing for more than a quarter of a century.

Europe awaits

This season, further progress is expected under Gullit. As FA Cup-holders, Chelsea are competing in the European Cup-winners' Cup, one of the few competitions Gullit never won as a player. Last season Gullit arranged for Chelsea to play a friendly against Milan in the famous San Siro stadium, so his players will not be strangers to the European stage.

The redevelopment of Stamford Bridge continues, with a new all-seater stand to replace the old Shed terrace opening this season. Gullit has been no slouch on the transfer market, either. Norwegian striker Tor Andre Flo and Nigerian defender Celestine Babayaro were two of his summer signings. Uruguayan midfielder Gustavo Poyet has admitted he turned down Real Madrid to move to the Bridge.

Chelsea are once again a fashionable club to support, just as they were in the late 1960s and early 1970s when the nearby King's Road was the centre of the fashion universe. However, this time round, under the clever management of Ruud Gullit, it might well be a little longer before Chelsea go out of fashion.

PREMIER LEAGUE TABLES

SEASON	POS.	P	W	D	L	F	A	PTS	TOP SCORER	AV. GATE
1992–93	11th	42	14	14	14	51	54	56	Harford/Stuart 9	18,787
1993–94	14th	42	13	12	17	49	53	51	Stein 13	19,416
1994–95	11th	42	13	15	14	50	55	54	Spencer 11	21,057
1995–96	11th	38	12	14	12	46	44	50	Spencer 13	25,466
1996–97	6th	38	16	11	11	58	55	59	Vialli 9	27,617

Frank Leboeuf

Few people knew much about Frank Leboeuf when he joined Chelsea in the summer of 1996. He had been a member of the French squad but did not play in England at Euro 96.

Any doubts about Leboeuf, though, quickly went out of the window after his opening games in a Chelsea shirt. He is that rare commodity in English football – a tough-tackling centre-back who is comfortable on the ball. He has a range of passing which few, if any, English defenders can match, although if he does have a weakness, it is in the air.

French Lesson: cultured defender Frank Leboeuf

Dennis Wise

Chelsea captain Dennis Wise revealed the secret of Chelsea's FA Cup success last season – a pair of slippers! Before the Wembley final success over Middlesbrough, he said: "We all have our little superstitious things and mine is a pair of carpet slippers which play a tune when you press a button on them. I got them at Christmas and I've pressed them before every Cup round to listen to the tune which is 'Que sera sera, whatever will be, will be'. You know the next line, 'We're going to Wembley' and it's come true. But I'll be pressing them again one more time for luck."

It worked for Wise, who won the Cup for a second time. He was a winner with Wimbledon in 1988, but was desperate for success with Chelsea, the team he supported as a boy and who he joined in 1990 from Wimbledon.

Wise took time to adapt to player-manager Ruud Gullit's new training methods last season. At one point his future at Chelsea appeared in doubt when he was left out of the side. But he is now a big fan of Gullit. "It took a while to get used to him but once you do it is easy. He is very laid back and believes that people produce their best if they are enjoying life. Nobody can say he hasn't done well. The signings he's made have been brilliant, real quality. He's got us playing really well."

Slipper Skipper: Dennis Wise

Mark Hughes

You write off Mark Hughes at your peril. Chelsea's Welsh striker spent 13 seasons with Manchester United, making more than 250 League appearances and winning numerous trophies in two spells at the club. But following the £7 million purchase of Andy Cole in January 1995, United manager Alex Ferguson sold Hughes to Chelsea for £1.5 million, only for the striker to thrive at Stamford Bridge.

Hughes took time to settle in at Chelsea, but, just as people were predicting the demise of Hughes to make way for Gianluca Vialli, the Welshman turned in a series of performances as a target man which kept Vialli on the bench.

Hughes set a record last season when he became the first player this century to collect four FA Cup winners' medals.

Celestine Babayaro and Tor Andre Flo

Ruud Gullit's Continental connections paid off for Chelsea in the summer with the signing of two of Europe's hottest properties.

Celestine Babayaro is only 19 but is already an established international for Nigeria. He was one of the stars of the Nigerian side which won the gold medal at the 1996 Atlanta Olympics in the USA. He scored for his country in the final against Argentina.

Player Records

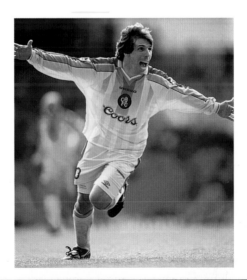

	BORN	NATIONALITY	HEIGHT	WEIGHT	APPS	GOALS	PREVIOUS TEAMS
GOALKEEPERS							
Ed de Goey	20.12.66 Gouda	Dutch	6-4	14-2	0	0	Feyenoord (Hol).
Frode Grodas	24.10.69 Norway	Norwegian	6-0	12-9	21	0	Lillestrom (Nor).
Kevin Hitchcock	5.10.62 Custom House	English	6-1	13-4	292	0	Nottingham F, Mansfield T, Northampton T, West Ham U.
Dmitri Kharine	16.8.68 Moscow	Russian	6-2	13-9	107	0	Torpedo Moscow (Rus), Dynamo Moscow (Rus), CSKA Moscow (Rus).
DEFENDERS							
Celestine Babayaro	29.8.78 Nigeria	Nigerian	5-7	10-5	0	0	Plateau U (Nig), Anderlecht (Bel).
Steve Clarke	29.8.63 Saltgate	Scottish	5-10	12-5	414	12	St Mirren.
Michael Duberry	14.10.75 Enfield	English	6-1	13-6	45	1	Bournemouth.
Bernard Lambourde	11.5.71 Guadeloupe	French	6-2	13-9	0	0	Bordeaux (Fra).
Frank Leboeuf	22.1.68 Marseille	French	6-0	11-4	32	6	Hyeres, Laval, Strasbourg (Fra)
Graeme Le Saux	17.10.68 Jersey	English	5-10	12-2	219	15	Chelsea, Blackburn R.
Dan Petrescu	22.12.67 Bucharest	Romanian	5-8	9-5	86	8	Steaua Bucharest (Rom), Foggia (Ita), Genoa (Ita), Sheffield W.
Frank Sinclair	3.12.71 Lambeth	English	5-9	12-9	153	7	West Brom.
MIDFIELDERS							
Roberto Di Matteo	29.5.70 Schaffhausen	Italian	5-10	11-9	34	7	Schaffhausen (Swi), Zurich (Swi), Lazio (Ita).
Paul Hughes	19.4.76 Hammersmith	English	6-0	11-7	12	2	none
David Lee	26.11.69 Kingswood	English	6-3	15-1	169	17	Reading, Plymouth Arg, Portsmouth.
Jody Morris	22.12.78 London	English	5-5	9-0	13	0	none
Andy Myers	3.11.73 Hounslow	English	5-10	12-11	71	2	none
Eddie Newton	13.12.71 Hammersmith	English	6-0	12-8	156	12	Cardiff C.
Mark Nicholls	30.5.77 Hillingdon	English	5-9	9-10	8	0	none
Gustavo Poyet	15.11.67 Montevideo	Uruguayan	6-1	13-0	0	0	River Plate (Uru), Grenoble (Fra), Real Zaragoza (Spa).
Dennis Wise	16.12.66 Kensington	English	5-6	10-0	353	70	Southampton, Wimbledon.
FORWARDS							
Tor Andre Flo	15.6.73 Norway	Norwegian	6-2	13-2	0	0	Tromse IL (Nor), SK Brann (Nor).
Mark Hughes	1.11.63 Wrexham	Welsh	6-0	12-4	457	145	Manchester U, Barcelona (Spa), Bayern Munich (Ger), Manchester U.
Gianluca Vialli	9.7.64 Cremona	Italian	5-11	12-1	28	11	Cremonese (Ita), Sampdoria (Ita), Juventus (Ita).
Gianfranco Zola	5.7.66 Oliena	Italian	5-5	10-3	23	8	Nuorese (Ita), Torres (Ita), Napoli (Ita), Parma (Ita).

One of three footballing brothers, Babayaro joins Chelsea from Belgian side Anderlecht, where he gained a reputation as a left wing-back who likes to get forward and score goals.

Norwegian striker Tor Andre Flo made a name for himself in Brann Bergen's Cup-winners' Cup run last season, which was ended in the quarter-finals by Liverpool. He nearly joined Everton last season, but his height will now be put to good use when he joins Chelsea in the autumn.

Small Man, Big Impact: Italian forward Gianfranco Zola

Gianfranco Zola

He may not have scored in last year's FA Cup Final, but Gianfranco Zola was the star of Chelsea's season. The little Italian only arrived in England last November, but then proceeded to show everybody why he is rated one of the world's best players. He scored outstanding goals against Manchester United, Liverpool and Wimbledon and was voted Footballer of the Year after less than a season in the Premier League.

If he does return to Italy next summer, as he has said he will, it will be a huge loss for Chelsea and the Premier League.

Coventry City
The Sky Blues

Last season, against all the odds, Coventry did it again. They escaped relegation from the Premier League by the skin of their teeth. Gordon Strachan's side looked doomed, but somehow they survived.

The Sky Blues travelled to Tottenham on the last day of the season on a wing and a prayer. They needed to beat Spurs at White Hart Lane and then hope that other results went in their favour. The 2–1 victory over Tottenham, and Middlesbrough's failure to beat Leeds and Sunderland's defeat by Wimbledon ensured Coventry's 31st consecutive season of top-flight football.

Coventry players seem to have the annual fight against relegation written into their contracts – they have been involved in the fight against the drop in nine of the past 10 seasons. Miraculously, they have survived on every occasion while other wealthier, more glamorous clubs have fallen by the wayside.

City have never been a very fashionable club, but ever since the days of Jimmy Hill, the TV pundit who as manager took them from the fourth to the first division in six years, they have been part of the elite of English football. Coventry have now been in the top division since 1967 – only Liverpool, Arsenal and Everton have been around for longer.

The Sky Blues have never experienced much success in the top division – their best placing was 6th in 1969–70 – but they have

achieved success in the FA Cup, winning it in 1987. Under joint managers John Sillett and George Curtis, City reached the FA Cup Final for the first time in their history. In an exciting match at Wembley they beat Tottenham 3–2.

Despite the Cup win, City fared no better in the League, and only survived in 1992 when Luton lost on the last day of the season. In the early 1990s, Coventry gained a reputation for starting the League campaign well, only to fade fast after Christmas. With a view to stopping that worrying trend, manager Phil Neal left the club in February 1995 and was replaced by Ron Atkinson, recently sacked by Aston Villa.

Atkinson arrives

Big Ron embarked on a major spending spree in a bid to bring success to Highfield Road. Scottish international midfielder Gary McAllister arrived from Leeds United for a club record £3 million. The defence underwent drastic changes following the sale of Phil Babb to Liverpool – in came David Burrows, Richard Shaw, Paul Williams and Liam Daish. Midfield reinforcements came in the form of John Salako, Eoin Jess and Paul Telfer, while the attack was augmented by Dion Dublin, Noel Whelan and Darren Huckerby.

True Sky Blue: club captain Dion Dublin

COVENTRY CITY

Formed: 1883.
Nickname: Sky Blues.
Stadium: Highfield Road.
Capacity: 23,500.
Address: King Richard Street,
Coventry CV2 4FW.
Telephone: 01203 234000.
Clubcall: 0891 121166.
Fax: 01203 234099.
Website: www.fa.carling.com/club/cv.fc
Manager: Gordon Strachan.

COLOURS

RECORDS

Record Premier League victory:
5–0 (v Blackburn R, Dec 9, 1995).
Record Premier League defeat:
5–0 (v Manchester U, Dec 28, 1992).
Record transfer fee received:
£3.6 million from Liverpool for Phil Babb,
Sept 1994.
Record transfer fee paid:
£3 million to Leeds U for Gary McAllister,
July 1996.
Record attendance:
51,455, v Wolves, Division 2, April 29,
1967.

HONOURS

League: Best finish 6th, Division One,
1969–70.
FA Cup (1): 1987.
League Cup: semi-finalists 1981, 1990.

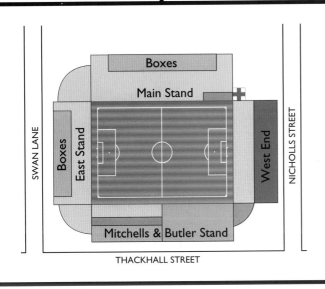

FIXTURES 1997–98

Date	Opponent	H/A	Score
9 AUG	CHELSEA	H	____ : ____
11 AUG	ARSENAL	A	____ : ____
23 AUG	BOLTON	H	____ : ____
27 AUG	WEST HAM UNITED	H	____ : ____
30 AUG	MANCHESTER UNITED	A	____ : ____
13 SEPT	SOUTHAMPTON	H	____ : ____
20 SEPT	SHEFFIELD WEDNESDAY	A	____ : ____
24 SEPT	CRYSTAL PALACE	H	____ : ____
28 SEPT	BLACKBURN ROVERS	A	____ : ____
4 OCT	LEEDS UNITED	H	____ : ____
20 OCT	BARNSLEY	A	____ : ____
25 OCT	EVERTON	H	____ : ____
1 NOV	WIMBLEDON	A	____ : ____
8 NOV	NEWCASTLE UNITED	H	____ : ____
22 NOV	DERBY COUNTY	A	____ : ____
29 NOV	LEICESTER CITY	H	____ : ____
6 DEC	ASTON VILLA	A	____ : ____
13 DEC	TOTTENHAM HOTSPUR	H	____ : ____
20 DEC	LIVERPOOL	A	____ : ____
26 DEC	WEST HAM UNITED	A	____ : ____
28 DEC	MANCHESTER UNITED	H	____ : ____
10 JAN	CHELSEA	A	____ : ____
17 JAN	ARSENAL	H	____ : ____
31 JAN	BOLTON	A	____ : ____
7 FEB	SHEFFIELD WEDNESDAY	H	____ : ____
14 FEB	SOUTHAMPTON	A	____ : ____
21 FEB	BARNSLEY	H	____ : ____
28 FEB	CRYSTAL PALACE	A	____ : ____
7 MAR	WIMBLEDON	H	____ : ____
14 MAR	NEWCASTLE UNITED	A	____ : ____
28 MAR	DERBY COUNTY	H	____ : ____
4 APRIL	LEICESTER CITY	A	____ : ____
11 APR	ASTON VILLA	H	____ : ____
13 APR	TOTTENHAM HOTSPUR	A	____ : ____
18 APR	LIVERPOOL	H	____ : ____
25 APR	LEEDS UNITED	A	____ : ____
2 MAY	BLACKBURN ROVERS	H	____ : ____
10 MAY	EVERTON	A	____ : ____

Atkinson spent almost £20 million in less than two years, but with limited success. Despite the defensive changes, City continued to leak goals. Not even the switch of striker Dion Dublin to centre-back improved matters and by November last year the Sky Blues were struggling at the wrong end of the table. Gordon Strachan had been brought in as Atkinson's assistant with a view to succeeding Big Ron in the long term. But with City's Premier League status in doubt, the changeover happened earlier than expected, with Atkinson moving upstairs to the newly-created position of "director of football".

Gordon leads fightback

Strachan, the former Aberdeen, Manchester United and Leeds midfielder, was still playing despite turning 40, thanks largely to an unlikely diet of bananas and seaweed pills. He faced a tough task in keeping Coventry in the top flight, but somehow pulled it off.

The Scot has been busy in the transfer market over the summer, paying particular attention to the Scandinavian clubs. Trond Egil Soltvedt has arrived from Norwegian club Rosenborg, Martin Johansen from FC Copenhagen and the Swedish pair Magnus Hedman and Roland Nilsson are new recruits from IFK Stockholm and Helsingborgs respectively.

Coventry, the Premier League's great survivors, have been in the top flight since 1967, they will be as determined as ever this season to preserve their elite status.

PREMIER LEAGUE TABLES

SEASON	POS.	P	W	D	L	F	A	PTS	TOP SCORER	AV. GATE
1992–93	15th	42	13	13	16	52	57	52	Quinn 17	14,951
1993–94	11th	42	14	14	14	43	45	56	Ndlovu 11	13,352
1994–95	16th	42	12	14	16	44	62	50	Dublin 13	15,980
1995–96	16th	38	8	14	16	42	60	38	Dublin 14	18,507
1996–97	17th	38	9	14	15	38	54	41	Dublin 14	19,608

Dion Dublin

Club captain Dion Dublin is the sort of player every manager likes to have in his squad. He adds pace, power and aerial punch to any attack, provides leadership on the pitch and is versatile enough to play in defence if required.

Leicester-born Dublin has come a long way since the days when he turned out for non-League Oakham United, after being released as a teenager by Norwich City. He was spotted by fourth division Cambridge City and spent the 1988–89 season in their reserves before making his League debut at Wrexham on December 13. On January 3, in only his second League appearance, he smashed a hat-trick past Peterborough. Dion Dublin had arrived.

Dublin's goals helped Cambridge into the FA Cup sixth round and promotion before Manchester United stepped in with a £1 million bid in July 1992. He scored the winner on his full debut at Southampton but broke a leg against Crystal Palace and spent the rest of the season on the sidelines. He made only a handful of appearances before moving to Coventry for £2 million in September 1994.

He has become a popular figure at Highfield Road, not just for his goals, but also for his willingness to drop back into defence when required.

Steve Ogrizovic

If Coventry have anybody to thank for their continued presence in the Premier division, it is Steve Ogrizovic. The big goalkeeper was outstanding when Coventry played Tottenham in the last game of last season, a match the Sky Blues had to win to have any chance of retaining their top-flight status. Coventry fans have got used to the sight of Ogrizovic keeping goal for City – so much so that the veteran goalkeeper has George Curtis's club record of 486 League appearances within his grasp. Ogrizovic was ever-present for Coventry last season, taking his total number of appearances for Coventry to 566 games.

Record in Sight: goalkeeper Steve Ogrizovic

Mansfield-born Ogrizovic is not quite a one-club man, having started his career with Chesterfield before moving on to Liverpool (just four League appearances in five seasons) and Shrewsbury Town, but he has been a regular fixture at Highfield Road since the summer of 1984. Ogrizovic may be about to turn 40, but, fortunately for Coventry, he is showing no signs of ending his career.

Young Gun: England Under-21 striker Darren Huckerby

Darren Huckerby

It has been a hectic 18 months for young striker Darren Huckerby. Signed by Newcastle boss Kevin Keegan from Lincoln for £500,000, 21-year-old Huckerby soon found life tough at St James' Park, especially with the arrival of £15 million man Alan Shearer. Keegan had disbanded the reserve team (they messed up the pitch at St James' Park, he claimed) and first-team football was hard to come by.

Nottingham-born Huckerby went on loan to Coventry last season, and soon found his temporary stay converted to a permanent £1 million deal after striking a rich vein of goalscoring form. His goals for the Sky Blues even earned him a call-up to the England Under-21 team. This season, he is out to prove that he is no one-season wonder.

	BORN	NATIONALITY	HEIGHT	WEIGHT	APPS	GOALS	PREVIOUS TEAMS
GOALKEEPERS							
Steve Ogrizovic	12.9.57 Mansfield	English	6-5	15-0	582	0	Chesterfield, Liverpool, Shrewsbury T.
Magnus Hedman	19.3.73 Sweden	Swedish	6-4	14-8	0	0	AIK Solna (Swe).
DEFENDERS							
Brian Borrows	20.12.60 Liverpool	English	5-10	11-12	536	11	Everton, Bolton W, Bristol C.
Gary Breen	12.12.73 London	Irish	6-1	11-12	166	2	Maidstone U, Gillingham, Peterborough U, Birmingham C.
David Burrows	25.10.68 Dudley	English	5-10	11-8	281	5	West Brom, Liverpool, West Ham U, Everton.
Liam Daish	23.9.68 Portsmouth	Irish	6-2	13-5	244	9	Portsmouth, Cambridge U, Birmingham C.
Marcus Hall	24.3.76 Coventry	English	6-1	12-2	43	0	none
Roland Nilsson	27.11.63 Sweden	Swedish	5-10	12-0	0	0	Helsingborgs (Swe), IFK Gothenburg (Swe), Sheff W., Helsingborgs (Swe).
David Rennie	29.8.64 Edinburgh	Scottish	6-0	12-0	343	21	Leicester C, Leeds U, Bristol C, Birmingham C.
Richard Shaw	11.9.68 Brentford	English	5-9	12-8	267	3	Crystal Palace, Hull C.
Paul Williams	26.3.71 Burton	English	6-0	12-10	227	30	Derby Co, Lincoln C.
MIDFIELDERS							
Willie Boland	6.8.75 Ennis	Irish	5-9	11-2	44	0	none
Marques Isias	16.11.63 Rio	Portuguese	5-10	12-10	12	2	Benfica (Por).
Gary McAllister	25.12.64 Motherwell	Scottish	6-0	12-7	529	90	Motherwell, Leicester C, Leeds U.
Michael O'Neill	5.7.69 Portadown	Northern Irish	5-11	10-10	210	45	Newcastle, Hibernian.
Kevin Richardson	4.12.62 Newcastle	English	5-7	11-7	464	36	Everton, Watford, Arsenal, Real Sociedad (Spa), Aston Villa.
John Salako	11.2.69 Nigeria	English	5-9	12-3	289	29	Crystal Palace, Swansea C.
Trond Egil Soltvedt	15.2.67 Norway	Norwegian	6-1	12-11	0	0	Rosenbor (Nor).
Gordon Strachan	9.2.57 Edinburgh	Scottish	5-6	10-6	626	138	Dundee, Aberdeen, Manchester U, Leeds U.
Paul Telfer	21.10.71 Edinburgh	Scottish	5-9	11-6	209	20	Luton T.
FORWARDS							
Dion Dublin	22.4.69 Leicester	English	6-2	12-4	267	133	Norwich C, Cambridge U, Man. U.
Andrew Ducros	16.9.77 Evesham	English	5-4	9-8	5	0	none
Simon Haworth	30.3.77 Cardiff	Welsh	6-3	13-8	0	0	Cardiff C.
Darren Huckerby	23.4.76 Nottingham	English	5-10	11-11	54	10	Lincoln C, Newcastle U.
Martin Johansen	22.7.72 Denmark	Danish	5-6	10-5	0	0	FC Copenhagen (Den).
Kyle Lightbourne	29.9.68 Bermuda	Bermudian	6-2	12-2	0	0	Scarbrough, Walsall.
Noel Whelan	30.12.74 Leeds	English	6-2	12-3	104	21	Leeds U.

Gary McAllister

Three million pounds might have been a lot to pay for a 31-year-old, but when Coventry signed Gary McAllister from Leeds United in July 1996, they were buying one of the most accomplished midfielders in the Premier League.

Despite Coventry's struggle against relegation last season, McAllister demonstrated just why he is so highly rated. He is that rare commodity – a midfielder who combines attacking flair with defensive grit. His free-kicks are some of the most feared in the Premier League, while his appetite for hard work earns him the respect of his team-mates, both at Highfield Road and with Scotland.

McAllister was Scotland's captain during Euro 96 and he suffered the humiliation of having a penalty saved against England at Wembley. However, he remains a crucial figure in his country's bid to reach the 1998 World Cup finals in France.

This season, Coventry will be hoping to see the sort of inspirational performances that McAllister contributed to Leeds' title-winning season in 1991–92. If anybody can lead Coventry away from the annual relegation dogfight, it is Gary McAllister.

Crystal Palace
The Eagles

Crystal Palace are back in the Premier League, where they believe they belong, and have only one thing on their minds – survival. Palace have experienced relegation or promotion four times in the past five years, so Steve Coppell's side are concerned simply with staying in the Premier League for more than just one campaign.

The Eagles earned promotion the hard way, coming through the Play-offs after finishing sixth in last season's first division. David Hopkin's dramatic last-minute goal, which gave Palace victory over Sheffield United, was the least Palace deserved after their heartbreaking defeat by Leicester City in the dying seconds of extra time in the previous year's Play-off Final.

Play-off precedents

Manager Steve Coppell is under no illusions as to the task ahead, especially as Palace are the bookies' favourites for relegation. In the 10-year history of the Play-offs, only Blackburn Rovers (in 1992), Leicester (1996) and Palace themselves (1989) have won a Play-off Final and gone on to maintain their top-flight status for more than one season.

Coppell has cited the example of Leicester City last season as one good reason why his young Palace side can stay up. Palace thrive on their underdog status. Coppell was the manager when they reached the 1990 FA Cup Final after beating

Young Gun: Palace striker Bruce Dyer

Liverpool 4–3 in extra time in a thrilling semi-final at Villa Park. Liverpool were the clear favourites to beat Palace that day, having thrashed them 9–0 earlier in the season. However, what Palace lacked in ability and experience, they more than made up for in team spirit.

FA Cup drama

The 1990 FA Cup Final, which Palace lost in a replay to Manchester United after drawing 3–3 in an exhilarating match, was their finest hour, but it turned out to be another false dawn for the South London club. The following season, Palace finished third in the League, their highest ever placing, but could not build on that success and in September 1991, striker Ian Wright left for Arsenal.

Palace are one of the few Premier League clubs to have played in all four divisions of the Football League. They were first promoted to the top flight in 1969 and stayed there for four seasons. Under Terry Venables, Palace won the old division two

CRYSTAL PALACE

Formed: 1905.
Nickname: The Eagles.
Stadium: Selhurst Park.
Address: Selhurst Park, London SE25 6PU.
Capacity: 26,400.
Phone: 0181 768 6000.
Clubcall: 0891 400333.
Fax: 0181 771 5311.
Website: www.fa-carling.com/club/cp.fc
Manager: Steve Coppell.

COLOURS

RECORDS

Record Premier League victory:
4–1 (v Middlesbrough, April 12, 1993; v Coventry C, Nov 2, 1994)
Record Premier League defeat:
6–1 (v Liverpool, Aug 1994).
Record transfer fee received:
£4.5 million from Tottenham H for Chris Armstrong, June 1995.
Record transfer fee paid:
£2.25 million to Millwall for Andy Roberts, July 1995.
Record attendance:
51,483, v Burnley, Division 2, May 11, 1979.

HONOURS

League: Champions, Division One 1993–94.
FA Cup: runners-up 1990.
League Cup: semi-finalists 1993, 1995.

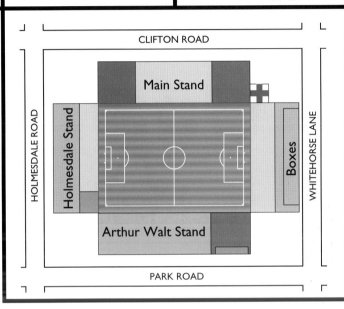

FIXTURES 1997–98

Date	Opponent	H/A	Score
9 AUG	EVERTON	A	___ : ___
12 AUG	BARNSLEY	H	___ : ___
23 AUG	LEEDS UNITED	A	___ : ___
27 AUG	SOUTHAMPTON	A	___ : ___
30 AUG	BLACKBURN ROVERS	H	___ : ___
13 SEPT	CHELSEA	H	___ : ___
20 SEPT	WIMBLEDON	A	___ : ___
24 SEPT	COVENTRY CITY	A	___ : ___
27 SEPT	BOLTON	H	___ : ___
4 OCT	MANCHESTER UNITED	A	___ : ___
18 OCT	ARSENAL	H	___ : ___
25 OCT	SHEFFIELD WEDNESDAY	A	___ : ___
3 NOV	WEST HAM UNITED	A	___ : ___
8 NOV	ASTON VILLA	H	___ : ___
24 NOV	TOTTENHAM HOTSPUR	A	___ : ___
29 NOV	NEWCASTLE UNITED	H	___ : ___
6 DEC	LEICESTER CITY	A	___ : ___
13 DEC	LIVERPOOL	H	___ : ___
20 DEC	DERBY COUNTY	A	___ : ___
26 DEC	SOUTHAMPTON	H	___ : ___
28 DEC	BLACKBURN ROVERS	A	___ : ___
10 JAN	EVERTON	H	___ : ___
17 JAN	BARNSLEY	A	___ : ___
31 JAN	LEEDS UNITED	H	___ : ___
7 FEB	WIMBLEDON	H	___ : ___
14 FEB	CHELSEA	A	___ : ___
21 FEB	ARSENAL	A	___ : ___
28 FEB	COVENTRY CITY	H	___ : ___
7 MAR	WEST HAM UNITED	H	___ : ___
14 MAR	ASTON VILLA	A	___ : ___
28 MAR	TOTTENHAM HOTSPUR	H	___ : ___
4 APR	NEWCASTLE UNITED	A	___ : ___
11 APR	LEICESTER CITY	H	___ : ___
13 APR	LIVERPOOL	A	___ : ___
18 APR	DERBY COUNTY	H	___ : ___
25 APR	MANCHESTER UNITED	H	___ : ___
2 MAY	BOLTON	A	___ : ___
10 MAY	SHEFFIELD WEDNESDAY	H	___ : ___

title in 1979 with an exciting young side, which had won the FA Youth Cup two years earlier and was dubbed the "Team of the Eighties", but the weight of expectation proved too much. Venables left to manage QPR and Palace were relegated.

The Coppell era

Palace Chairman Ron Noades took a big gamble when he appointed Steve Coppell (who had recently retired as a player through injury) as manager in 1984. The gamble paid off, though, as Coppell steered Palace through the most successful period in the club's history. Palace were relegated in 1993 on goal difference, despite having accumulated 49 points, but new manager Alan Smith took Palace back into the Premier League at the first attempt.

Under Smith, Palace reached the semi-finals of FA and League Cups, but League form suffered and the Eagles were again relegated. Coppell returned as "Technical Director" and former Sheffield United manager Dave Bassett was brought in as manager. They quickly built a young, skilful side, based around the talents of new signings Andy Roberts, Dougie Freedman and David Hopkin.

Bassett left for Nottingham Forest last season and Coppell assumed the managerial reins again with great success. Whether he can maintain that success in the Premiership remains to be seen. The signing of Juventus star Attilio Lombardo will inject some morale into the club, but morale alone will not beat the likes of Arsenal and Newcastle.

PREMIER LEAGUE TABLES

SEASON	POS.	P	W	D	L	F	A	PTS	TOP SCORER	AV. GATE
1992–93	20th	42	11	16	15	48	61	49	Armstrong 15	15,748
1994–95	19th	42	11	12	19	34	49	45	Armstrong 8	14,694

Squad Info
KEY PLAYERS TO WATCH

Old Hand: Dean Gordon is a Palace veteran at the age of 24

Bruce Dyer

Forward Bruce Dyer was one of Palace's most improved players last season. His challenge this season is to transfer the talent and ability he showed in division one on to the Premier League stage.

Dyer undoubtedly has talent, but he has often found it hard to satisfy the expectations of those who saw a bright future for him when he became Britain's most expensive teenager, joining Palace in March 1994 from Watford for £1.25 million. During Palace's last Premier League campaign, Dyer scored just once in 16 appearances – his pace caused problems for defenders, but his shooting often left a lot to be desired.

Last season, after an extended run in the first team boosted his confidence, Dyer began to show his true potential. His crossing and shooting improved and he played an important role in Palace's promotion campaign while also adding to his tally of England Under-21 caps.

Andy Roberts

Eyebrows were raised when Crystal Palace paid local rivals Millwall a club record £2.25 million for midfielder Andy Roberts in the summer of 1995. Roberts was just 21 at the time and many thought the fee too much for such a young player.

Roberts quickly silenced the doubters with a string of cultured performances for Palace in a new-look three-man central defence. The England Under-21 international had played as a central midfielder at Millwall, but Palace's coaching staff thought Roberts' thoughtful passing and clever reading of the game would be best used in defence. The switch worked and

Money Well Spent: record signing Andy Roberts

Roberts finished the 1995–96 season as Palace's Player of the Season. Roberts continued to impress last season, leaving many people at Selhurst Park with the view that he will play for England one day.

Dean Gordon

Although only 24 years old, defender Dean Gordon is one of Palace's longest-serving players. He made his debut in December 1991 against Tottenham, and despite a major knee injury has played more than 150 League games for the Eagles.

Gordon is a versatile operator who began his career as a left-winger. He was soon converted to full-back, where his furious forward runs mean he is a tricky customer. His pace and strength make him a useful defender, too, and he played a number of games for Palace last season as a centre-back.

A serious knee injury to Gordon towards the end of the 1995–96 season seriously dented Palace's promotion hopes and the player spent much of last season regaining his best form. If Palace had not won promotion, Gordon would have undoubtedly been snapped up by a Premier League club.

Player Records

	BORN	NATIONALITY	HEIGHT	WEIGHT	APPS	GOALS	PREVIOUS TEAMS
GOALKEEPERS							
Kevin Miller	15.3.69 Falmouth	English	6-1	13-0	313	0	Exeter C, Birmingham C, Watford.
Carlo Nash	13.9.73 Manchester	English	6-5	13-5	21	0	none
DEFENDERS							
Danny Boxall	24.8.77 Croydon	English	5-8	10-5	7	0	none
Gareth Davies	11.12.73 Hereford	Welsh	6-1	11-12	121	3	Hereford U.
Marc Edworthy	24.12.72 Barnstaple	English	5-8	11-10	158	1	Plymouth Argyle.
Dean Gordon	10.2.73 Thornton Heath	English	6-0	13-4	164	18	none
Andy Linighan	18.6.62 Hartlepool	English	6-4	13-10	475	27	Hartlepool U, Leeds U, Oldham Ath, Norwich C, Arsenal.
Kevin Muscat	7.8.73 Bolton	Australian	5-10	12-6	44	2	South Melbourne (Aus).
Robert Quinn	8.11.76 Sidcup	English	5-11	11-2	22	1	none
David Tuttle	6.2.72 Reading	English	6-2	12-10	132	6	Tottenham H, Peterborough U, Sheffield U.
MIDFIELDERS							
Attilio Lombardo	6.1.66 Zelo Buon Pers	Italian	5-11	11-6	0	0	Cremonese, Sampdoria, Juventus (Ita).
Darren Pitcher	12.10.69 London	English	5-9	12-2	237	8	Charlton Ath, Galway (Ire).
Alex Rae	30.9.69 Glasgow	Scottish	5-9	11-11	323	85	Falkirk, Millwall, Sunderland.
Andy Roberts	20.3.74 Dartford	English	5-10	13-0	221	7	Milwall.
Simon Rodger	3.10.71 Shoreham	English	5-9	11-9	126	5	none
Carl Veart	21.5.70 Whyalla	Australian	5-10	11-5	117	21	Sheffield U.
Paul Warhurst	26.9.69 Stockport	English	6-1	14-0	190	12	Manchester C, Oldham A, Sheffield W, Blackburn R.
FORWARDS							
Bruce Dyer	13.4.75 Ilford	English	5-11	11-3	136	37	Watford.
Dougie Freedman	21.1.74 Glasgow	Scottish	5-9	11-0	130	58	QPR, Barnet.
Leon McKenzie	17.5.78 Croydon	English	5-10	11-2	33	2	none
George Ndah	23.12.74 Camberwell	English	6-1	11-4	87	7	Bournemouth.
Neil Shipperley	30.10.74 Chatham	English	6-1	13-11	141	32	Chelsea, Watford, Southampton.

Dougie Freedman

Thoughtful passing and clever inside-forward play make Dougie Freedman the perfect foil for the pace and tenacity of striking partner Bruce Dyer. The young Scot has been a prolific goalscorer in his brief career, though his form suffered last season with injuries

Freedman's form last season was still good enough to earn him a call-up to the full Scotland squad, having previously played for the Under-21s. He missed Palace's play-off triumph at Wembley through suspension, but helped his side into the Premier League with two well-taken goals in the semi-final against Wolves.

Freedman started his career at QPR, but failed to break into the first team. Barnet signed him and he rewarded their interest with 24 goals in 42 games during the 1994–95 season. He weighed in with four more goals for Barnet at the start of the following season before Palace took him to Selhurst Park in a £800,000 transfer deal. He continued his

Great Scot: Dougie Freedman

goal-every-other-game record with 20 goals that season and scored another 14 during last season's campaign.

Leon McKenzie

Palace have gained a reputation in recent years for producing or acquiring talened young players. Leon McKenzie is the latest off the Palace production line.

Ian Wright, Gareth Southgate and Chris Armstrong are just a few of the players who have gone on to bigger and better things after getting their big break at Palace. Teenager McKenzie has gained as many headlines for his family's boxing connections (dad Clinton and uncle Duke are both former professionals) as for his exploits on the pitch. But the youngster has already made a mark on his chosen sport.

He made his Palace debut in the 1995–96 season and, although he has found first team chances limited, Leon is definitely one to watch.

DERBY COUNTY

Derby County
The Rams

Derby County made steady, unexceptional progress in last season's Premier League – and they would not have had it any other way. Twelfth place in the League would have been a disappointment for many clubs, but for Derby it made for an outstanding season. Survival had been the only target for newly-promoted County at the start of the campaign. In the end, that was achieved with ease.

The biggest disappointment of last season was the club's departure from the Baseball Ground, County's home for 102 years, for a new purpose-built all-seater stadium. But the club can embark on a new era this season at Pride Park with renewed confidence after last season's Premier League campaign.

That Derby are competing in the top flight owes a great deal to the commitment, and cash, of club chairman Lionel Pickering. His backing helped Derby to clinch promotion to the Premier League two seasons ago after two previous play-off failures.

The other person County have to thank for their recent success is manager Jim Smith. He has put together an impressive side, spending less money than most of his rivals, while having more success than most with foreign imports.

However, Smith will have to go a long way before he matches the achievements of the most successful manager in Derby's history, Brian Clough. Under Clough, County won the League in 1972 and became established in the top division, winning the title again in 1975 under Dave Mackay.

The club entered one of the darkest periods in their history during the 1980s. They were relegated to the old second division in 1980 and slumped even further in 1984, when they slipped into the third division. Under manager Arthur Cox, County clawed their way up and by 1990 were back in the big time, albeit

for just one season. After relegation back to the old second division, they faced a long haul back. Derby experienced disappointment in the 1992 play-offs semi-finals and defeat at the hands of Leicester at Wembley in 1994. Cox stayed on at the Baseball Ground until 1993 while chairman Pickering dug deep to buy success, but it eluded County.

Derby finally made the step up to the Premier League under Jim Smith, the 'Bald Eagle', who arrived in June 1995 and steered County to promotion in his first season. After being one of the biggest fish in the first division, County were now one of the smallest clubs in the Premiership. However, in manager Smith Derby had one of the shrewdest operators in the transfer market.

County High: Paolo Wanchope scored a memorable goal against Manchester United last season

DERBY COUNTY	COLOURS	RECORDS	HONOURS

DERBY COUNTY

Formed: 1884.
Nickname: The Rams.
Stadium: Pride Park Stadium.
Capacity: 30,000.
Address: Pride Park Stadium,
Pride Park, Derby DE24 8XL.
Telephone: 01332 340105.
Clubcall: 0891 121187.
Fax: 01332 360988.
Website: www.fa-carling.com/club/dc.fc
Manager: Jim Smith.

COLOURS

RECORDS

Record Premier League victory:
4–2 (v Tottenham H, Mar 22, 1997).
Record Premier League defeat:
4–2 (v Leicester C, Feb 22, 1997).
Record transfer fee received:
£2.9 million from Liverpool for Dean
Saunders, July 1991.
Record transfer fee paid:
£2.5 million to Notts Co. for Craig Short,
Sept 1992.
Record attendance:
41,826, v Tottenham H, Division 1,
20 Sept 1969.

HONOURS

League (2): 1971–72, 1974–75.
FA Cup (1): 1946.
League Cup: Semi-finalists 1968.

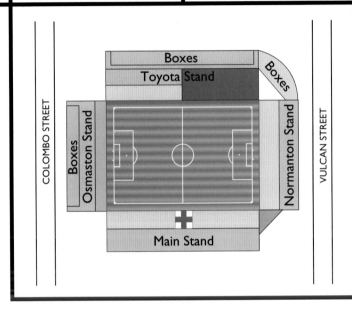

FIXTURES 1997–98

Date	Opponent	H/A	Score
9 AUG	BLACKBURN ROVERS	A	____ : ____
13 AUG	WIMBLEDON	H	____ : ____
23 AUG	TOTTENHAM HOTSPUR	A	____ : ____
30 AUG	BARNSLEY	H	____ : ____
13 SEPT	EVERTON	H	____ : ____
20 SEPT	ASTON VILLA	A	____ : ____
24 SEPT	SHEFFIELD WEDNESDAY	A	____ : ____
27 SEPT	SOUTHAMPTON	H	____ : ____
4 OCT	LEICESTER CITY	A	____ : ____
18 OCT	MANCHESTER UNITED	H	____ : ____
25 OCT	LIVERPOOL	A	____ : ____
1 NOV	ARSENAL	H	____ : ____
8 NOV	LEEDS UNITED	A	____ : ____
22 NOV	COVENTRY CITY	H	____ : ____
29 NOV	CHELSEA	A	____ : ____
6 DEC	WEST HAM UNITED	H	____ : ____
14 DEC	BOLTON	A	____ : ____
17 DEC	NEWCASTLE	A	____ : ____
20 DEC	CRYSTAL PALACE	H	____ : ____
26 DEC	NEWCASTLE UNITED	H	____ : ____
28 DEC	BARNSLEY	A	____ : ____
10 JAN	BLACKBURN ROVERS	H	____ : ____
17 JAN	WIMBLEDON	A	____ : ____
31 JAN	TOTTENHAM HOTSPUR	H	____ : ____
7 FEB	ASTON VILLA	H	____ : ____
14 FEB	EVERTON	A	____ : ____
21 FEB	MANCHESTER UNITED	A	____ : ____
28 FEB	SHEFFIELD WEDNESDAY	H	____ : ____
7 MAR	ARSENAL	A	____ : ____
14 MAR	LEEDS UNITED	H	____ : ____
28 MAR	COVENTRY CITY	A	____ : ____
4 APR	CHELSEA	H	____ : ____
11 APR	WEST HAM UNITED	A	____ : ____
13 APR	BOLTON	H	____ : ____
18 APR	CRYSTAL PALACE	A	____ : ____
25 APR	LEICESTER CITY	H	____ : ____
2 MAY	SOUTHAMPTON	A	____ : ____
10 MAY	LIVERPOOL	H	____ : ____

Transfer bargains

To Derby's existing foreign legion of Croatian sweeper Igor Stimac and Dutchman Robbie Van der Laan, Smith added Croatian midfielder Aljosa Asanovic, a star of Euro 96, Danish defender Jacob Laursen and Scottish midfielder Christian Dailly – all at knockdown prices.

Any doubts about Derby's ability to compete in the top flight were dismissed on the first day of the season when County twice came from behind to draw 3–3 with Leeds. Draws with Spurs and Manchester United followed before Smith's men travelled to Blackburn and won 2–1 in front of Sky's Monday night cameras.

During October and November, County pulled off important victories against other teams who were expected to struggle. Leicester, Middlesbrough, Sunderland and Coventry were all dispatched as Derby pulled clear of the relegation zone. In fact, County did not dip into the bottom three all season.

The highlight of the campaign came at Old Trafford in April when Paulo Wanchope, a new signing from Costa Rica, scored one of the goals of the season as County ran out 3–2 winners.

Smith spent the summer trying to hold on to his star players while signing new ones, notably Italian international midfielder Stefano Eranio from AC Milan. If this campaign is anything like last season's gallant efforts, Derby can expect a bright future in their new stadium.

PREMIER LEAGUE TABLES

SEASON	POS.	P	W	D	L	F	A	PTS	TOP SCORER	AV. GATE
1996–97	12th	38	11	13	14	45	58	46	Sturridge 11	17,889

Squad Info

KEY PLAYERS TO WATCH

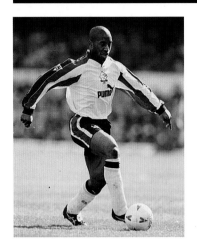

Top Gun: striker Dean Sturridge

Dean Sturridge

Dean Sturridge emerged last season as a young striker of exceptional talent and Derby quickly realised they would have to do everything in their power to hold on to him in the face of enquiries from wealthier Premier League clubs.

Birmingham-born Sturridge took time to establish himself at the Baseball Ground after making his debut in the 1991–92 season. He spent an extended period on loan to Torquay towards the end of the 1994–95 season, scoring five goals, and returned to Derby revitalized. Sturridge formed an impressive partnership with Paul Simpson and Marco Gabbiadini, striking 20 goals as Derby won promotion to the Premier League.

Last season, he finished as Derby's top scorer and hit some memorable goals, notably against Arsenal at Highbury. Sturridge is not tall (he's only 5ft 7in) but like Ian Wright, a player he resembles in so many ways, Sturridge's pace and strength make him difficult for even the most accomplished defenders to deal with.

Aljosa Asanovic

Croatian midfielder Aljosa Asanovic proved to be the bargain buy of last season's Premier League campaign. Just weeks before Newcastle paid Blackburn a world record £15 million for Alan Shearer, Derby manager Jim Smith had paid less than £1 million for Asanovic, who arrived from Hajduk Split.

Asanovic repaid his modest transfer fee a number of times over with a series of eye-catching performances for the Rams. The left-footed playmaker quickly demonstrated why Arsenal manager Arsène Wenger rates him as one of the best midfielders in Europe.

Asanovic was a regular member of the Croatia side who reached the quarter-finals of Euro 96 and had been tipped by many to go further. The midfielder had extensive experience of European football, having played in France and Spain as well as Croatia, before his performances at Euro 96 alerted many in England to his   talents – but by then Jim Smith had already snapped him up for Derby.

Clean Sweep: Croatian Igor Stimac takes control

Igor Stimac

Croatian defender Igor Stimac has, in the two seasons he has been in England, played a leading role in the Derby County success story. It would be unfair to call Stimac a central defender – he is far more than that. Stimac is a world-class sweeper who, as captain of his country, has played at the very highest level.

Derby paid £1.5 million to sign Stimac from Hajduk Split in October 1995 and he quickly adapted to English football, leading Derby's promotion challenge while also playing a crucial role in Croatia's bid to qualify for Euro 96.

His thoughtful approach on the pitch has been appreciated by Rams fans, but he has been just as important to the club off the pitch.

He was instrumental in setting up the transfer of fellow Croatian Aljosa Asanovic before he came to everybody's attention at Euro 96.

Class Act: Croatian Aljosa Asanovic

Player Records

	BORN	NATIONALITY	HEIGHT	WEIGHT	APPS	GOALS	PREVIOUS TEAMS
GOALKEEPERS							
Russell Hoult	22.11.72 Leicester	English	6-4	14-5	119	0	Leicester C, Lincoln C, Blackpool, Bolton W, Lincoln C.
Mart Poom	3.2.72 Tallinn	Estonian	6-4	13-7	8	0	FC Wil (Est), Flora Tallinn (Est), Portsmouth, Flora Tallinn (Est).
DEFENDERS							
Matt Carbon	8.6.75 Nottingham	English	6-3	13-12	85	10	Lincoln C.
Lee Carsley	28.2.74 Birmingham	English	5-9	12-7	78	3	none
Jacob Laursen	6.10.71 Veijle	Danish	5-10	12-6	36	1	Veijle (Den), Silkeborg (Den).
Chris Powell	8.9.69 Lambeth	English	5-10	11-7	317	3	Crystal Palace, Aldershot, Southend U.
Gary Rowett	6.3.74 Bromsgrove	English	6-1	12-6	156	11	Cambridge U, Everton, Blackpool.
Igor Stimac	6.9.67 Metkovic	Croatian	6-2	13-2	48	2	Hajduk Split (Cro), Cibalia Vinkovci (Cro), Cadiz (Spa), Hajduk Split (Cro).
Dean Yates	26.10.67 Leicester	English	6-2	12-6	373	36	Notts Co.
MIDFIELDERS							
Aljosa Asanovic	14.12.65 Split	Croatian	5-11	12-6	34	6	Hajduk Split (Cro), Metz (Fra), Cannes (Fra), Montpellier (Fra), Hajduk Split (Cro), Valladolid (Spa), Hajduk Split (Cro).
Stefano Eranio	29.12.66 Genoa	Italian	5-11	11-9	0	0	Genoa (Ita), Milan (Ita).
Sean Flynn	13.3.68 Birmingham	English	5-7	11-10	156	12	Coventry C.
Jonathan Hunt	2.11.71 London	English	5-10	11-0	137	22	Barnet, Southend u, Birmingham C.
Darryl Powell	15.1.71 Lambeth	English	6-1	11-2	202	22	Portsmouth.
Robin Van Der Laan	5.9.68 Schiedam	Dutch	5-11	13-8	231	32	Port Vale.
Paulo Wanchope	31.1.76 Costa Rica	Costa Rican	6-4	12-5	5	1	Herediano
FORWARDS							
Marino Rahmberg	7.8.74 Sweden	Swedish	5-11	11-9	1	0	Degerfors (Swe).
Paul Simpson	26.7.66 Carlisle	English	5-6	11-9	450	109	Manchester C, Oxford U.
Dean Sturridge	27.7.73 Birmingham	English	5-7	11-13	102	36	Torquay U.
Ashley Ward	24.11.70 Manchester	English	6-2	11-4	168	55	Manchester C, Wrexham, Leicester C, Blackpool, Crewe Alex, Norwich C.
Ron Willems	20.9.66 Epe	Dutch	6-0	12-11	49	13	PEC Zwolle (Hol), Twente (Hol), Grasshopper (Swi).
Francesco Baiano	1.9.68 Italy	Italian	5-10	11-11	0	0	Fiorentina.
Deon Burton	25.10.76 Ashford	English	5-8	10-9	67	12	Portsmouth, Cardiff City.

Stefano Eranio

County manager Jim Smith is good at spotting a bargain. And he picked the bargain of the summer when he signed Italian international midfielder Stefano Eranio on a free transfer from Milan.

Milan had been hoping to persuade Eranio to sign a new contract and stay in Italy. But the player had other ideas, and after seeing Derby's new stadium Eranio signed a three-year deal. Under the Bosman ruling, Derby paid Milan no transfer fee.

Eranio, who can play as a right-wing-back or right-sided midfielder, spent eight seasons with his home-town club Genoa before making the move to Milan in the summer of 1992. In five seasons, Eranio collected three Italian League winners' medals, a European Cup and a Supercup, as well as being a regular in the Italian national side.

Jacob Laursen

Derby manager Jim Smith has had notable successes in the foreign transfer market. While other clubs have lavished millions on stars who failed to live up to their billing, Derby picked up some bargains at the cheaper end of the market and soon discovered that cheaper was not inferior.

Danish defender Jacob Laursen, like Aljosa Asanovic, joined County after playing for his country at Euro 96. The right-back soon settled in at Derby and scored a superb goal against Manchester United last September. The Dane missed just two League games in Derby's first season back in the top flight.

Everton

The Toffees

Everton lost their final home game of last season 2–1 to Chelsea, but a more significant event took place off the pitch that day. Fans leaving the game were asked if the club should consider leaving Goodison Park for a brand-new, 60,000-capacity stadium in Kirkby. Amazingly, almost 90 per cent were in favour of Everton waving goodbye to Goodison. So before the turn of the century, the blue half of Merseyside could have a new home.

Goodison Park is still an impressive stadium and one of a handful of Premier League grounds which can hold more than 40,000 supporters. But Liverpool's Anfield, less than a mile away across Stanley Park, was chosen ahead of Goodison Park as a venue for Euro 96. And there's the rub. Everton have been playing second fiddle to Liverpool for too long, and chairman Peter Johnson feels a new stadium is the best way to put the club back on the map.

The rivalry goes back more than a century, to when the two clubs were one and the same. Everton, founder members of the Football League in 1888, played at Anfield Road. A row broke out in 1892 over the team using a pub as the club HQ. This led to Everton moving down the road to Goodison. The pub's landlord stayed at Anfield and formed a new team: Liverpool.

Everton may have lived in Liverpool's shadow in recent years but they have a pretty impressive history, enjoying three golden eras: the 1930s, the 1960s and the 1980s. They won their first title in 1891 and were runners-up six times before doing it again in 1915, by which time they had also bagged their first FA Cup, in 1906. In the 1928–29 season, striker William "Dixie" Dean set an as yet unbroken record of 60 League goals as Everton were crowned champions again.

The 1930s saw two more Championships (1932 and 1939) and an FA Cup win in 1933. However, Everton could not sustain their success after the Second World War and were relegated in 1951. They spent four seasons out of the top division before, under manager Harry Catterick, they were at last able to renew the successes of the 1930s, winning the League twice (1962–63 and 1969–70) and the FA Cup once (1966).

They were not to taste such success again until the arrival of former Everton player Howard

Northern Lad: Hull-born Nick Barmby has always preferred to play up North

EVERTON

Formed: 1878.
Nickname: The Toffees.
Stadium: Goodison Park.
Capacity: 40,200.
Address: Goodison Park,
Liverpool L4 4EL.
Telephone: 0151 330 2200.
Clubcall: 0891 121199.
Fax: 0151 286 9112.
Website: www.fa-carling/club.e.fc
Manager: Howard Kendall.

COLOURS

RECORDS

Record Premier League victory:
7–1 (v Southampton, Nov 16, 1996).
Record Premier League defeat:
5–1 (v Norwich C, Sept 25, 1993;
v Sheffield W, April 2, 1994).
Record transfer fee received:
£7 million from Fiorentina for Andrei
Kanchelskis, Mar 1997.
Record transfer fee paid:
£5.75 million to Middlesbrough for Nick
Barmby, Oct 1996.
Record attendance:
78,299, v Liverpool, Division 1,
18 Sept 1948.

HONOURS

League (9): 1890–91, 1914–15,
1927–28, 1931–32, 1938–39, 1962–63,
1969–70, 1984–85, 1986–87.
FA Cup (5): 1906, 1933, 1966, 1984,
1995.
League Cup: runners-up 1977, 1988.
European Cup-winners' Cup (1):
1985.

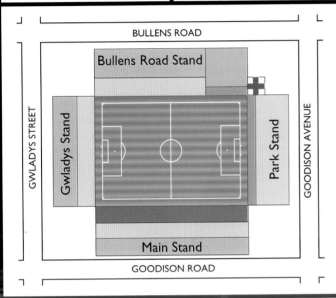

FIXTURES 1997–98

Date	Opponent	H/A	Score
9 AUG	CRYSTAL PALACE	H	____ : ____
23 AUG	WEST HAM UNITED	H	____ : ____
27 AUG	MANCHESTER UNITED	H	____ : ____
1 SEPT	BOLTON	A	____ : ____
13 SEPT	DERBY COUNTY	A	____ : ____
20 SEPT	BARNSLEY	H	____ : ____
24 SEPT	NEWCASTLE UNITED	A	____ : ____
27 SEPT	ARSENAL	H	____ : ____
4 OCT	SHEFFIELD WEDNESDAY	A	____ : ____
18 OCT	LIVERPOOL	H	____ : ____
25 OCT	COVENTRY CITY	A	____ : ____
2 NOV	SOUTHAMPTON	H	____ : ____
8 NOV	BLACKBURN ROVERS	A	____ : ____
22 NOV	ASTON VILLA	A	____ : ____
26 NOV	CHELSEA	A	____ : ____
29 NOV	TOTTENHAM HOTSPUR	H	____ : ____
6 DEC	LEEDS UNITED	A	____ : ____
13 DEC	WIMBLEDON	H	____ : ____
20 DEC	LEICESTER CITY	A	____ : ____
26 DEC	MANCHESTER UNITED	A	____ : ____
28 DEC	BOLTON	H	____ : ____
10 JAN	CRYSTAL PALACE	A	____ : ____
17 JAN	CHELSEA	H	____ : ____
31 JAN	WEST HAM UNITED	A	____ : ____
7 FEB	BARNSLEY	A	____ : ____
14 FEB	DERBY COUNTY	H	____ : ____
21 FEB	LIVERPOOL	A	____ : ____
28 FEB	NEWCASTLE UNITED	H	____ : ____
7 MAR	SOUTHAMPTON	A	____ : ____
14 MAR	BLACKBURN ROVERS	H	____ : ____
28 MAR	ASTON VILLA	H	____ : ____
4 APR	TOTTENHAM HOTSPUR	A	____ : ____
11 APR	LEEDS UNITED	H	____ : ____
13 APR	WIMBLEDON	A	____ : ____
18 APR	LEICESTER CITY	H	____ : ____
25 APR	SHEFFIELD WEDNESDAY	H	____ : ____
2 MAY	ARSENAL	A	____ : ____
10 MAY	COVENTRY CITY	H	____ : ____

Kendall as manager in 1981. Thereafter the club challenged for honours on a regular basis, winning the League (1984–85 and 1986–87), FA Cup (1984) and European Cup-winners' Cup (1985). They were losing FA Cup finalists a further three times (twice to Liverpool) and, despite 30 goals from Gary Lineker, finished second in the League behind Liverpool in 1986. The post-Heysel ruling barring English clubs from European competition denied Everton a chance at the European Cup the year after their League triumphs of 1985 and 1987, but it was still an impressive record.

Kendall left to coach Spanish side Athletic Bilbao and was replaced by his assistant Colin Harvey, who could not keep up the winning ways. Kendall returned in 1990, but to no avail. After a brief period under the stewardship of Mike Walker, during which Everton flirted with relegation, the club turned to an old hero, Joe Royle.

Royle had had great success keeping Oldham Athletic in the top division, and quickly took Everton away from the relegation zone and into the 1995 FA Cup Final. A Paul Rideout goal was enough to beat Manchester United at Wembley. The League proved a tougher nut to crack, and Royle parted company with the club last season.

The plans for a new stadium, the return of Howard Kendall for a third stint as manager and the money made available for big-name signings are further signs that Everton mean business.

PREMIER LEAGUE TABLES

SEASON	POS.	P	W	D	L	F	A	PTS	TOP SCORER	AV. GATE
1992–93	13th	42	15	8	19	53	55	53	Cottee 12	20,445
1993–94	17th	42	12	8	22	42	63	44	Cottee 16	22,876
1994–95	15th	42	11	17	14	44	51	50	Rideout 14	31,291
1995–96	6th	38	17	10	11	64	44	61	Kanchelskis 16	35,435
1996–97	15th	38	10	12	16	44	57	42	Ferguson 10	36,204

Nick Barmby

Everton fans have yet to see the best of Nick Barmby, but there is no doubt the young forward is one of the most talented players of his generation.

As a kid, Hull-born Barmby's talent was spotted early on and he was one of the first to graduate from the FA School of Excellence at Lilleshall. Tottenham beat off a host of clubs to sign Barmby in February 1991 and he made his League debut against Sheffield Wednesday in September 1992. The former Tottenham Hotspur manager, Terry Venables, gave Barmby an international debut in March 1995. His career may have been progressing well, but the homesick forward never made any secret of his desire to move back North.

Middlesbrough manager Bryan Robson came to Barmby's rescue, signing him in August 1995 for £5.25 million, and he scored on his debut against Arsenal. However, the arrival of Juninho and Ravanelli restricted Barmby's development at Boro and he made the move to Everton in October 1996 for £5.75 million.

Duncan Ferguson

Everton's top scorer last season has been dogged by disciplinary problems during his short career, but is determined to be recognised for what he does best – scoring goals.

The big striker, who stands 6ft 4in tall, scored 10 times in what was a disappointing League campaign for Everton. It was his first full season since his conviction and imprisonment for headbutting Raith Rovers defender John McStay while playing for Rangers in a Scottish Premier League match in April 1994. He spent 44 days in Glasgow's tough Barlinnie jail during the 1995–96 season as a result.

Stirling-born Ferguson has never been far from the headlines. He was still at Dundee United, his first club, when he made his full international debut for Scotland, against the United States in 1992. He already had a reputation as a player who was difficult to handle, but Rangers beat off a host of other clubs to sign Ferguson in the summer of 1993, for a then record British transfer fee of £4 million.

The big man was plagued by a serious knee injury during his time in Glasgow and made just 14 League appearances in two seasons. But Everton manager Joe Royle offered Ferguson a chance to resurrect his career over the border in England and after an initial loan period Everton signed the big Scot for a then club record £4 million.

Despite his off-the-pitch problems Ferguson has given Everton's attack a focus which few teams can match, and his height and heading ability cause problems for the Premier League's finest defenders. The danger for Everton is that they may have become too dependent on their Scottish striker for goals.

Slaven Bilic

Everton's big summer signing is no ordinary centre-back. Croatian international Slaven Bilic, who moved to Merseyside in a £4.5 million transfer from West Ham, is one of Europe's most accomplished defenders.

Bilic joined West Ham from German club Karlsruhe less than two years ago for a knockdown price of £1.5 million. He had been voted into the Bundesliga "Team of the Season"

Goodison Regular: England international Andy Hinchcliffe

Big Is Best: Scottish striker Duncan Ferguson

Player Records

	BORN	NATIONALITY	HEIGHT	WEIGHT	APPS	GOALS	PREVIOUS TEAMS
GOALKEEPERS							
Paul Gerrard	22.1.73 Heywood	English	6-2	13-1	122	1	Oldham Ath.
Neville Southall	16.9.58 Llandudno	Welsh	6-0	14-0	614	0	Bury, Port Vale.
DEFENDERS							
Earl Barrett	28.4.67 Rochdale	English	5-9	11-7	378	8	Manchester C, Oldham Ath, Aston Villa
Slaven Bilic	11.9.68 Croatia	Croatian	6-2	13-6	48	0	Hajduk Split (Cro), Karlsruhe (Ger), West Ham U.
Gareth Farrelly	28.8.75 Dublin	Irish	6-1	12-7	8	0	Aston Villa, Rotherham.
Andy Hinchcliffe	5.2.69 Manchester	English	5-10	13-7	277	15	Manchester C.
Terry Phelan	16.3.67 Manchester	Irish	5-7	9-0	348	2	Leeds U, Swansea C, Wimbledon.
Craig Short	25.6.68 Bridlington	English	6-3	13-8	355	26	Scarborough, Notts Co, Derby Co.
Tony Thomas	12.7.71 Liverpool	English	5-11	12-5	257	12	Tranmere Rovers
Dave Watson	20.1.61 Liverpool	English	6-0	13-7	581	34	Liverpool, Norwich C., Manchester C, Chelsea.
Danny Williamson	5.12.73 West Ham	English	5-10	11-6	64	6	Doncaster Rovers, West Ham United.
MIDFIELDERS							
Graham Allen	8.4.77 Bolton	English	6-1	11-12	1	0	none
Tony Grant	14.11.74 Liverpool	English	5-9	10-0	38	2	Swindon T.
Jon O'Connor	29.10.76 Darlington	English	6-0	11-0	4	0	none
Joe Parkinson	11.6.71 Eccles	English	6-1	13-0	239	10	Wigan Ath, Bournemouth.
Gary Speed	8.9.69 Hawarden	Welsh	5-9	12-10	285	48	Leeds U.
Graham Stuart	24.10.70 London	English	5-9	11-9	208	34	Chelsea.
Claus Thomsen	31.5.70 Aarhus	Danish	6-3	13-6	86	7	Aarhus (Den), Ipswich T.
FORWARDS							
Nick Barmby	11.2.74 Hull	English	5-7	11-4	144	31	Tottenham H, Middlesbrough.
Michael Branch	18.10.78 Liverpool	English	5-9	11-0	28	3	none
Duncan Ferguson	27.12.71 Stirling	Scottish	6-4	13-8	164	52	Dundee U, Rangers.
John Oster	1978 Skegness	Welsh	5-10	11-9	0	0	Grimsby T.
Paul Rideout	14.8.64 Bournemouth	English	5-11	12-0	466	133	Swindon T, Aston Villa, Bari (Ita), Southampton, Swindon T, Notts Co, Rangers.

during his time in Germany and his performances for West Ham and the Croatian national side quickly pushed his price tag up.

Last season, Bilic signed a new contract with West Ham which included a clause allowing him to transfer to any club which offered more than £4 million for his services. Joe Royle fought off competition from Tottenham and weighed in with a bid, but Bilic's move to Merseyside was delayed until the summer to allow him to take part in West Ham's campaign against relegation.

University graduate Bilic is now one of the highest-paid defenders in the Premier League – and is a qualified lawyer to boot.

Gary Speed

Gary Speed is one of the most complete midfielders in the Premier League, a strong, versatile campaigner who pulls no punches

Welsh Wizard: midfielder Gary Speed

for club or country.

While at Leeds, where he came through the youth system, Speed filled in for defenders Mel Sterland and Tony Dorigo. That was during the 1991–92 season, when Leeds won the old first division title. By then, Speed was already established at international level, having made his debut for Wales against Costa Rica in May 1990. In addition to his combative defensive qualities, Speed regularly scores goals. He was Leeds' third top-scorer in 1993–94, but became disillusioned with a lack of success at Elland Road after the 1992 championship success.

In a bid to kick-start his career, Speed signed a five-year contract with Everton in the summer of 1996 following a £3.5 million transfer. The Welsh international supported Everton as a boy and once delivered newspapers to former Everton captain Kevin Ratcliffe.

Leeds United

"We'll score again, don't know where, don't know when!"* was the cry of Leeds fans last season. Under George Graham, goals became a scarce commodity as the new manager sought to introduce the sort of defensive discipline that had won him two League titles with Arsenal.*

For the Elland Road faithful, Graham's tactics were not pretty, but they were effective. Leeds finished the season in a mid-table position, having avoided the relegation battle that had seemed a strong possibility early on in the campaign.

The new manager arrived at the club in September 1996 to replace Howard Wilkinson, who had paid the price for a 4–0 home thrashing by Manchester United. Wilkinson had been at the club since October 1988 when they were languishing in the old second division.

Wilkinson quickly steered United back to the top flight and within two years of promotion had won the League title, at the expense of Manchester United. It was Leeds' first championship since the 1970s, when Don Revie built a great side who won the title in 1974 and finished runners-up on no less than five occasions.

Leeds struggled after Revie left to manage England and it was only under Wilkinson that they came close to emulating the successes of the side that featured the likes of Billy Bremner, Peter Lorimer, Allan Clarke, Norman Hunter and Jackie Charlton. Wilkinson, a shrewd tactician but also a fierce disciplinarian, assembled a side in the early 1990s with an impressive midfield quartet: David Batty, Gary Speed, Gary McAllister and Gordon Strachan. Wilkinson was also responsible for introducing a Frenchman called Eric Cantona to English football, but was unable to sustain Leeds' success, either at home or in the European Cup. Cantona was sold to Manchester United, and Leeds finished 17th in the inaugural season of the Premier League.

The arrival of Ghanaian striker Tony Yeboah revived Leeds' fortunes, and the

Young Pretender: England Under-21 midfielder Lee Bowyer

LEEDS UNITED

Formed: 1919.
Nickname: United.
Stadium: Elland Road.
Capacity: 40,000.
Address: Elland Road, Leeds
LS11 0ES.
Telephone: 0113 2716037.
Clubcall: 0891 121180.
Fax: 0113 2720370.
Website: www.fa-carling/com/club/lu.fc
Manager: George Graham.

COLOURS

RECORDS

Record Premier League victory:
5–0 (v Tottenham H, Aug 25, 1992; v
Swindon Town, May 7, 1994).
Record Premier League defeat:
5–0 (v Liverpool, Jan 20, 1996).
Record transfer fee received:
£3.5 million from Everton for Gary Speed,
June 1996.
Record transfer fee paid: £4.5 million
to Manchester U for Lee Sharpe, July 1997.
Record attendance:
57,892, v Sunderland, FA Cup 5th round
replay, Mar 15, 1967.

HONOURS

League (3): 1968–69, 1973–74,
1991–92.
FA Cup (1): 1972.
League Cup (1): 1968.
Fairs Cup (2): 1969, 1971.

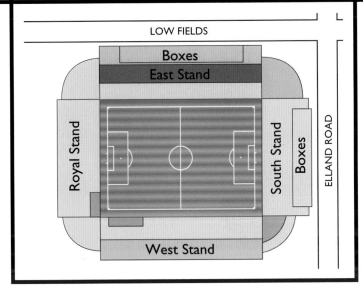

FIXTURES 1997–98

9 AUG	ARSENAL	H	____ : ____
13 AUG	SHEFFIELD WEDNESDAY	A	____ : ____
23 AUG	CRYSTAL PALACE	H	____ : ____
26 AUG	LIVERPOOL	H	____ : ____
30 AUG	ASTON VILLA	A	____ : ____
14 SEPT	BLACKBURN ROVERS	A	____ : ____
20 SEPT	LEICESTER CITY	H	____ : ____
24 SEPT	SOUTHAMPTON	A	____ : ____
27 SEPT	MANCHESTER UNITED	H	____ : ____
4 OCT	COVENTRY CITY	A	____ : ____
18 OCT	NEWCASTLE UNITED	H	____ : ____
25 OCT	WIMBLEDON	A	____ : ____
1 NOV	TOTTENHAM HOTSPUR	A	____ : ____
8 NOV	DERBY COUNTY	H	____ : ____
23 NOV	WEST HAM UNITED	H	____ : ____
29 NOV	BARNSLEY	A	____ : ____
6 DEC	EVERTON	H	____ : ____
13 DEC	CHELSEA	A	____ : ____
20 DEC	BOLTON	H	____ : ____
26 DEC	LIVERPOOL	A	____ : ____
28 DEC	ASTON VILLA	H	____ : ____
10 JAN	ARSENAL	A	____ : ____
17 JAN	SHEFFIELD WEDNESDAY	H	____ : ____
31 JAN	CRYSTAL PALACE	A	____ : ____
7 FEB	LEICESTER CITY	A	____ : ____
14 FEB	BLACKBURN ROVERS	H	____ : ____
21 FEB	NEWCASTLE UNITED	A	____ : ____
28 FEB	SOUTHAMPTON	H	____ : ____
7 MAR	TOTTENHAM HOTSPUR	H	____ : ____
14 MAR	DERBY COUNTY	A	____ : ____
28 MAR	WEST HAM UNITED	A	____ : ____
4 APR	BARNSLEY	H	____ : ____
11 APR	EVERTON	A	____ : ____
13 APR	CHELSEA	H	____ : ____
18 APR	BOLTON	A	____ : ____
25 APR	COVENTRY CITY	H	____ : ____
2 MAY	MANCHESTER UNITED	A	____ : ____
10 MAY	WIMBLEDON	H	____ : ____

signing of Swedish World Cup star Tomas Brolin promised great things. United made the 1996 Coca-Cola Cup Final but flopped at Wembley, losing 3–0 to Aston Villa.

Even before the sacking of Wilkinson, last season's priority was rebuilding. The departures from Elland Road of McAllister and Speed meant a big shake-up was on the cards and the new arrivals, goalkeeper Nigel Martyn and young midfielder Lee Bowyer, offered a useful basis for the future.

George Graham had been out of work for over a year following his worldwide suspension for allegedly receiving a transfer bung. He had received other offers, but had waited for what he thought was a big enough club. Leeds fitted the bill.

The manager has since said he did not realize just how many changes were needed at Elland Road. His priority last season was to sort out the defence, reflected in his first signings – defenders Gunnar Halle, Robert Molenaar and David Robertson and Norwegian midfielder Alf-Inge Haaland. This season, Graham is looking further forward as Leeds seek to improve on the wretched goal tally (28) of the last campaign. Striker Jimmy Floyd Hasselbaink, signed from Portuguese side Boavista for £1.75 million, promises to add punch to an Elland Road frontline that suffered the departure of Brian Deane to Sheffield United during the close season.

It was not all doom and gloom last season, however. Leeds won the FA Youth Cup, beating Crystal Palace in the final, and giving an indication that there is some useful talent coming through the ranks.

PREMIER LEAGUE TABLES

SEASON	POS.	P	W	D	L	F	A	PTS	TOP SCORER	AV. GATE
1992–93	17th	42	12	15	15	57	62	51	Chapman 14	29,250
1993–94	5th	42	18	16	8	65	39	70	Wallace 17	34,493
1994–95	5th	42	20	13	9	59	38	73	Yeboah 12	32,925
1995–96	13th	38	12	7	19	40	57	43	Yeboah 12	32,580
1996–97	11th	38	11	13	14	28	38	46	Deane/Sharpe 5	32,117

Squad Info

KEY PLAYERS TO WATCH

Lee Bowyer

It says something about Leeds' goalscoring record last season that young midfielder Lee Bowyer finished as United's second highest scorer – with four goals – behind Lee Sharpe and Brian Deane (who both hit five).

That's not to say the 20-year-old Londoner had a bad first season for Leeds. He scored on his debut against Derby on the opening day of the season and was also called up by Glenn Hoddle to the full England squad, although he did not play.

The England call-up was a sign that Bowyer has a very big future in front of him, despite problems off the pitch that have affected him during his short career. Leeds spotted his potential early on, fighting off interest from other Premier League clubs to sign him from First Division Charlton Athletic during the summer of 1996 for £2.6 million.

Nigel Martyn

Goalkeeper Nigel Martyn was all set to join Everton last summer from Crystal Palace, but had a last-minute change of heart and switched his allegiances to Elland Road, signing in a £2.25 million deal.

Martyn is no stranger to million-pound deals. He became Britain's first million-pound goalkeeper when he joined Crystal Palace from Bristol Rovers in November 1989. He spent almost six seasons at Selhurst Park, where his performances earned him a call-up to the full England squad. He made his international debut against Germany in the 1993 US Cup, but was unable to dislodge David Seaman or Tim Flowers from the number one goalkeeping spot.

His move from First Division Palace in the summer of 1996 was a clear sign that Martyn wanted to be part of the England set-up again. The transfer to Leeds quickly paid off as his performances in the Premier League brought him to the attention of England coach Glenn Hoddle. Martyn got the call-up from Hoddle for his squad for the World Cup qualifier against Italy in February and was a member of the England squad for the summer tournament in France.

Unflappable under pressure and a superb shot-stopper, Martyn is now at the age (he turned 30 last August) when goalkeepers often reach their peak. Leeds manager George Graham, who says he has the best goalkeeper in the country, would certainly agree.

In From Oldham: Gunnar Halle, George Graham's first signing for Leeds

Gunnar Halle

When Gunnar Halle's on-off transfer from Oldham Athletic finally went through last December, the Norwegian defender became George Graham's first signing as Leeds manager.

Leeds fans weren't particularly impressed by the signing of Halle for £400,000. They had been expecting the arrival of centre-back John Scales from Liverpool, but Scales turned down United at the 11th hour in favour of a move south to Tottenham. So Halle it was. Halle had joined Oldham from Lillestrom in 1991 for £280,000 and become a firm favourite at Boundary Park. He is an established international, with more than 50 caps for Norway, and a versatile defender to boot, although his preferred position is wide on the right.

Halle quickly established himself at Elland Road, making 20 Premier League appearances as Graham tightened up Leeds' defence. With Halle alongside new signing David Robertson, Leeds are unlikely to leak many goals this season.

England's Number One: Nigel Martyn's form for Leeds earned him an international call-up

Player Records

	BORN	NATIONALITY	HEIGHT	WEIGHT	APPS	GOALS	PREVIOUS TEAMS
GOALKEEPERS							
Mark Beeney	30.12.67 Pembury	English	6-3	15-8	162	0	Gillingham, Maidstone U, Aldershot, Brighton & HA.
Nigel Martyn	11.8.66 St Austell	English	6-2	14-7	410	0	Bristol R, Crystal Palace.
DEFENDERS							
Tony Dorigo	31.12.65 Melbourne	English	5-8	11-0	428	17	Aston Villa, Chelsea.
Gunnar Halle	11.8.65 Oslo	Norwegian	5-11	11-2	188	14	Lillestrom (Nor), Oldham Ath.
Mark Jackson	30.9.77 Leeds	English	6-1	11-13	18	0	none
Richard Jobson	9.5.63 Hull	English	6-2	13-6	460	32	Watford, Hull C, Oldham Ath.
Gary Kelly	9.7.74 Drogheda	Irish	5-9	11-0	156	1	Home Farm (Ire).
Robert Molenaar	27.2.69 Holland	Dutch	5-10	11-5	13	1	Volendam (Hol).
Carlton Palmer	5.12.65 Oldbury	English	6-3	12-13	428	23	West Brom, Sheffield W.
Lucas Radebe	12.4.69 Johannesburg	South African	6-0	11-9	57	0	Kaiser Chiefs (SA).
David Robertson	17.10.68 Aberdeen	Scottish	5-11	12-7	318	17	Aberdeen, Rangers.
David Wetherall	14.3.71 Sheffield	English	6-3	13-11	146	9	Sheffield W.
MIDFIELDERS							
Jason Blunt	16.8.77 Penzance	English	5-8	11-7	4	0	none
Lee Bowyer	3.1.77 London	English	5-9	9-9	80	12	Charlton Ath.
Tomas Brolin	29.11.69 Hudiksvall	Swedish	5-8	11-4	19	4	Sundsvall, Norrkoping (Swe), Parma (Ita)
Andy Gray	15.11.77 Harrogate	English	6-1	14-6	21	1	none
Alf-Inge Haaland	23.11.72 Stavanger	Norwegian	5-10	12-12	75	7	Young Boys (Swi), Nottingham F.
David Hopkin	21.8.70 Greenock	Scottish	5-9	10-3	141	23	Greenock Morton, Chelsea Crystal P.
Pierre Laurent	13.12.70 Tulle	French	5-9	11-2	4	0	Brive (Fra), Bastia (Fra).
Lee Sharpe	27.5.71 Halesowen	English	6-0	12-6	235	29	Torquay U, Manchester U.
FORWARDS							
Jimmy Floyd Hasselbaink	27.3.72 Surinam	Dutch	6-0	13-6	0	0	Boavista (Por).
Derek Lilley	27.3.97	Scottish	5-11	12-7	170	78	Greenock Morton.
Ian Rush	20.10.61 St Asaph	Welsh	6-0	12-6	568	253	Chester C, Liverpool, Juventus (Ita), Liverpool.
Rod Wallace	2.10.69 Lewisham	English	5-7	11-7	309	85	Southampton.
Tony Yeboah	6.6.66 Kumasi	Ghanaian	5-11	14-9	47	24	Okwanu U (Gha), Saarbrucken (Ger), Eintracht Frankfurt (Ger).
Bruno Ribeiro	1976 Portugal	Portugese	-	-	0	0	Vitoria Setubal (Por)

Gary Kelly

Republic of Ireland international defender Gary Kelly is one of Leeds United's most consistent performers, having made his debut for Leeds as a teenager in the 1991–92 season following his move from Dublin side Home Park. Only Nigel Martyn played more Premiership games for Leeds last season and Kelly also weighed in with his first League goal for the club, a stunning volley against West Ham at Upton Park. Kelly demonstrated his versatility, performing in positions other than his favoured right-back when required.

Kelly is in the strange position of playing in the same team as his nephew Ian Harte, three years his junior and also a full-back.

Double Act: Assistant Manager David O'Leary with Leeds boss George Graham

Leicester City
The Foxes

When Leicester captain Steve Walsh lifted the Coca-Cola League Cup at Hillsborough after his team's 1–0 victory over Middlesbrough last April, the progress Leicester have made under manager Martin O'Neill was there for all to see. The feeling of complete and utter jubilation that Foxes fans had felt when Steve Claridge "shinned" that winning goal with seconds to go in the 1996 Wembley Play-off Final had quickly turned to anxiety and worry over the summer as they prepared themselves for a battle for survival back in the Premier League.

They need not have worried. Under Martin O'Neill, Leicester have been moulded in their manager's own image: feisty, determined battlers with more than a little skill thrown in for good measure. That Leicester have a talented young manager who is committed to the cause is a relief for the fans. Recent experiences with Brian Little and Mark McGhee have taught the Leicester faithful to take oaths of loyalty from their manager with a pinch of salt.

Brian Little was a Leicester hero until he turned his back on the club during their first Premier League season to take charge at Aston Villa, the club where he had been a favourite as a player. Under Mark McGhee, the young Scottish manager who had done such a good job at Reading and who replaced Little,

Leicester failed to avoid the drop. In December 1995 he walked out of Filbert Street for Wolves.

Leicester sent for Martin O'Neill, the former Nottingham Forest player who had taken Wycombe Wanderers from the Vauxhall Conference up to the second division. Under O'Neill, Leicester embarked on a late promotion push which culminated in that dramatic Play-off Final win at Wembley.

Matchwinner: Striker Steve Claridge, whose goal won the League Cup last season

New arrivals

O'Neill was given £5 million to spend on new players, and he spent it wisely. Muzzy Izzet, who had been on loan from Chelsea, signed on a permanent basis. American international goalkeeper Kasey Keller arrived from Millwall. They joined a group of promising players that included midfielders Neil Lennon and Scott Taylor and strikers Steve Claridge and Emile Heskey. There were some old heads in the squad too, notably Garry Parker and club captain Steve Walsh, and even some Continental influence in Swedish defender Pontus Kaamark.

LEICESTER CITY

Formed: 1884.
Nickname: The Foxes.
Stadium: Filbert Street.
Capacity: 21,500.
Address: City Stadium, Filbert Street, Leicester LE3 7FL.
Telephone: 0116 2555000.
Clubcall: 0891 121185.
Fax: 0116 2470585.
Website: www.fa-carling.com/club/lc.fc
Manager: Martin O'Neill.

COLOURS

RECORDS

Record Premier League victory:
4–2 (v Blackburn R, May 11, 1997).
Record Premier League defeat:
4–0 (v Manchester U, April 15, 1996).
Record transfer fee received:
£3.25 million from Aston Villa for Mark Draper, July 1995.
Record transfer fee paid: £1.6 million to Oxford U for Matt Elliott, January 1997.
Record attendance: 47,298, v Tottenham H, FA Cup 5th round, February 18, 1928.

HONOURS

League: Runners-up, Division One, 1928–29.
FA Cup: Runners-up 1949, 1961, 1963, 1969.
League Cup (2): 1969, 1997.

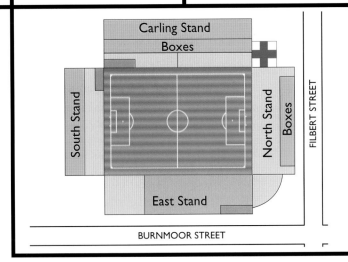

FIXTURES 1997–98

Date	Opponent	H/A	Score
9 AUG	ASTON VILLA	H	____ : ____
13 AUG	LIVERPOOL	A	____ : ____
23 AUG	MANCHESTER UNITED	H	____ : ____
27 AUG	ARSENAL	H	____ : ____
30 AUG	SHEFFIELD WEDNESDAY	A	____ : ____
13 SEPT	TOTTENHAM HOTSPUR	H	____ : ____
20 SEPT	LEEDS UNITED	A	____ : ____
24 SEPT	BLACKBURN ROVERS	H	____ : ____
27 SEPT	BARNSLEY	A	____ : ____
4 OCT	DERBY COUNTY	H	____ : ____
18 OCT	CHELSEA	A	____ : ____
27 OCT	WEST HAM UNITED	H	____ : ____
1 NOV	NEWCASTLE UNITED	A	____ : ____
10 NOV	WIMBLEDON	H	____ : ____
22 NOV	BOLTON	H	____ : ____
29 NOV	COVENTRY CITY	A	____ : ____
6 DEC	CRYSTAL PALACE	H	____ : ____
13 DEC	SOUTHAMPTON	A	____ : ____
20 DEC	EVERTON	H	____ : ____
26 DEC	ARSENAL	A	____ : ____
28 DEC	SHEFFIELD WEDNESDAY	H	____ : ____
10 JAN	ASTON VILLA	A	____ : ____
17 JAN	LIVERPOOL	H	____ : ____
31 JAN	MANCHESTER UNITED	A	____ : ____
7 FEB	LEEDS UNITED	H	____ : ____
14 FEB	TOTTENHAM HOTSPUR	A	____ : ____
21 FEB	CHELSEA	H	____ : ____
28 FEB	BLACKBURN ROVERS	A	____ : ____
7 MAR	NEWCASTLE UNITED	H	____ : ____
14 MAR	WIMBLEDON	A	____ : ____
28 MAR	BOLTON	A	____ : ____
4 APR	COVENTRY CITY	H	____ : ____
11 APR	CRYSTAL PALACE	A	____ : ____
13 APR	SOUTHAMPTON	H	____ : ____
18 APR	EVERTON	A	____ : ____
25 APR	DERBY COUNTY	A	____ : ____
2 MAY	BARNSLEY	H	____ : ____
10 MAY	WEST HAM UNITED	A	____ : ____

Despite the new faces, though, players and fans knew they would be fighting for their lives in the Premier League. Good team spirit was going to be vital. Fortunately, Leicester had that in abundance.

By the New Year, it was clear that Leicester were no pushovers. Newcastle (2–0 losers at Filbert Street), Aston Villa (turned over at home 3–1) and Wimbledon (beaten 1–0 at Filbert Street) would testify to that.

In the cups, O'Neill's men gave as good as they got. In the League Cup, Manchester United were beaten 2–0 on a memorable night at Filbert Street. In the FA Cup, victories over Southend and Norwich set up a fifth round tie at home to favourites Chelsea, who won the replay, after a 2–2 draw at Filbert Street, with a controversial goal.

Premier survival ensured

As it was, O'Neill's side were able to concentrate on success in the Coca-Cola Cup and maintaining Premier League status. There were a few jittery moments during the final run-in, but a 1–0 win over Sheffield Wednesday ensured City's top-flight status and a 4–2 victory at Blackburn ended the season in style.

Europe now beckons for Leicester in the UEFA Cup. Anybody who doubts whether the Leicester success story can continue should remember the example of O'Neill's former club Nottingham Forest, another Midlands outfit with modest means who, under Brian Clough, became champions of Europe.

PREMIER LEAGUE TABLES

SEASON	POS.	P	W	D	L	F	A	PTS	TOP SCORER	AV. GATE
1994–95	21st	42	6	11	25	45	80	29	Roberts 9	19,532
1996–97	9th	38	12	11	15	46	54	47	Claridge 12	20,184

Steve Claridge

There can be few players with more stories to tell about life on the wrong side of football's tracks than Steve Claridge. The 31-year-old striker is finally experiencing life at the top after spending the bulk of his career in the lower reaches of the Football League, and beyond.

Claridge's CV is not a distinguished one. Bournemouth, non-League Weymouth, Crystal Palace, Aldershot, Cambridge United, Luton Town and Cambridge (again) were the height of his achievements until he joined Birmingham in 1993. Even so, a few eyebrows were raised when Claridge joined Leicester in March 1996 from Birmingham in a £1.2 million deal. He soon silenced the critics with his goal in the Wembley Play-off Final, even if the ball did come off his shin!

Steve Claridge is guaranteed a place in the history books of Leicester City Football Club after his winning goal in last season's Coca-Cola Cup Final. Now, with Europe beckoning, there are more than a few Foxes fans dreaming of Stevie "Wonder" Claridge, socks rolled down, scoring at the San Siro stadium in Milan.

Emile Heskey

Last season, Emile Heskey made the big breakthrough. This term, he will be out to prove that he is no one-season wonder.

Although still a teenager, Heskey has all the qualities to be a striker of the highest order: pace, strength, technique and an eye for goal. No wonder people are talking about him as the best striker Leicester has produced since Gary Lineker.

It was a measure of Martin O'Neill's belief in Leicester-born Heskey's potential that last summer the manager was prepared to sanction the sale of Iwan Roberts to Wolves even though Leicester needed all the firepower they could muster as they prepared for life back in the Premier League.

The England Under-21 striker, dubbed Bruno by his team-mates, did not let O'Neill down, scoring vital goals for Leicester, including the scrambled equaliser against Middlesbrough at Wembley in the Coca-Cola Cup Final.

Local Boy: Young striker Emile Heskey

Kasey Keller

American goalkeeper Kasey Keller was one of the stars of last season for Leicester, more than justifying his £900,000 transfer fee.

The 28-year-old, who hails from Washington, USA, had spent five seasons with Millwall, making over 175 appearances for the South London club. However, Millwall's relegation to the second division in 1996 caused a rethink for Keller. He was keen to keep his place in the USA national squad, especially with the World Cup finals in 1998.

Kasey Keller still has a long way to go to match Leicester's greatest ever goalkeeper, Gordon Banks, but he has already made his mark at Filbert Street.

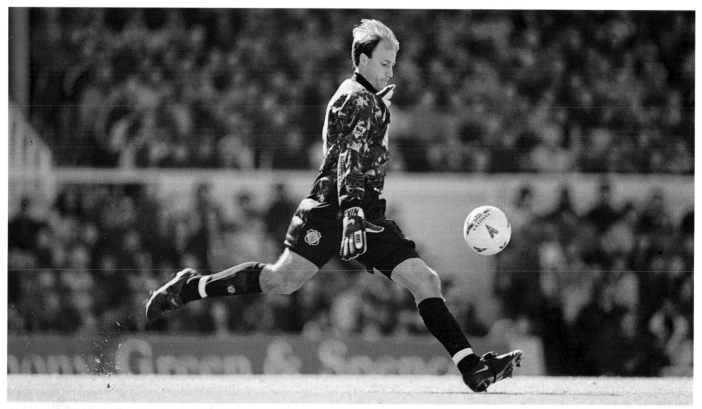

On Guard: American goalkeeper Kasey Keller

Player Records

	BORN	NATIONALITY	HEIGHT	WEIGHT	APPS	GOALS	PREVIOUS TEAMS
GOALKEEPERS							
Kasey Keller	27.1.69 Washington	American	6-1	12-7	207	0	Portland Univ (USA), Millwall.
DEFENDERS							
Matt Elliott	1.11.68 Epsom	English	6-3	14-10	323	44	Charlton Ath, Torquay U, Scunthorpe U, Oxford U.
Pontus Kaamark	5.4.69 Sweden	Swedish	5-10	12-3	10	0	IFK Gothenburg (Swe).
Spencer Prior	22.4.71 Rochford	English	6--3	12-12	243	4	Southend U, Norwich C.
Steve Walsh	3.11.64 Fulwood	English	6-3	14-6	437	51	Wigan Ath.
Julian Watts	17.3.71 Sheffield	English	6-3	13-7	80	3	Rotherham U, Sheffield W, Shrewsbury T.
Mike Whitlow	13.1.68 Northwich	English	6-0	13-3	224	12	Leeds U
MIDFIELDERS							
Steve Guppy	29.3.69 Winchester	English	5-11	10-10	125	14	Wycombe W, Newcastle U, Port Vale.
Muzzy Izzet	31.10.74 Mile End	English	5-10	10-12	44	4	Chelsea
Neil Lennon	25.6.71 Lurgan	Northern Irish	5-10	12-12	198	17	Manchester C, Crewe Alex.
Sam McMahon	10.2.76 Newark	English	5-10	11-6	4	1	none
Garry Parker	7.9.65 Oxford	English	6-0	13-2	409	48	Luton, Hull C, Nottingham F, Aston Villa.
Scott Taylor	28.11.70 Portsmouth	English	5-9	11-0	271	30	Reading
Robert Ullathorne	11.10.71 Wakefield	English	5-8	11-3	94	7	Norwich C, Osasuna (Spa).
FORWARDS							
Steve Claridge	10.4.66 Portsmouth	English	6-0	12-10	350	119	Luton, Cambridge, Birmingham C.
Emile Heskey	11.1.78 Leicester	English	6-2	13-2	66	17	none
Ian Marshall	20.3.66 Liverpool	English	6-1	12-12	294	77	Everton, Oldham Ath, Ipswich T.
Mark Robins	22.12.69 Ashton under Lyne	English	5-8	11-8	171	43	Manchester U, Norwich C.
Rob Savage	18.10.74 Wrexham	Welsh	6-0	10-1	77	10	Crewe Alexandra
Graham Fenton	22.5.74 Wallsend	English	5-10	12-10	66	13	Aston Villa, WBA, Blackburn R
Tony Cottee	11.7.65 London	English	5-8	11-5	245	186	West Ham, Everton, Selangor (Mal)

Garry Parker

Martin O'Neill has managed to bring the best out of Garry Parker, one of football's great underachievers. Manager O'Neill and midfielder Parker did not see eye to eye when O'Neill took over at Filbert Street and Parker found himself stuck in the reserves. But the 32-year-old soon won the respect of his new boss and played a key role in Leicester's successes last season back in the Premier League.

Parker started his career at Luton, but made a name for himself under Brian Clough at Nottingham Forest, when he reached four Wembley finals. He then spent more than three years at Aston Villa under Ron Atkinson before Leicester decided to take a chance on his talent, snapping him up for a bargain £250,000. He remains a gifted playmaker and his passing proved invaluable to Leicester in their Coca-Cola Cup success last season.

Midfield Playmate: Gary Parker

Liverpool

The Reds

This is Anfield. Three words that command respect from footballers and football fans everywhere. Although other clubs cast envious glances in the direction of Anfield and its proud and successful history, Liverpool feel the pressure to succeed more than any other club in the Premier League.

Liverpool are the most successful club in the history of English football. The roll of honours is impressive: 18 League titles (a record), runners-up on 10 occasions, five FA Cups, five League Cups, two UEFA cups and four European Cups. It's some record, and current Liverpool manager Roy Evans is aware of the expectations that come with such a record.

Anfield has not celebrated a League title since 1990. That in itself is cause for serious concern. But when four of the last five championships have gone to deadly rivals Manchester United, it's easy to understand why feelings on Merseyside have reached fever pitch.

Last season was a failure for Liverpool, not so much because of what happened as much as how it happened. Evans' side topped the Premier League table for much of the season, only to finish the campaign in fourth position with not even the consolation of a place in the UEFA Champions' League. Worse still, United, as their fans' banner declared at Anfield "won the championship on Merseyside". United's 3–1 defeat of Liverpool virtually guaranteed Alex Ferguson's men the title.

Evans' men fared no better in the Cups. After being 2–0 up and apparently cruising to victory in the fourth round of the FA Cup at Stamford Bridge, Liverpool somehow contrived to lose 4–2 to Ruud Gullit's Chelsea. Middlesbrough had already seen Liverpool out of the Coca-Cola Cup, so Liverpool's ambitions rested on success in the Cup-winners' Cup. They reached the semi-finals with relative ease, but crashed 3–0 away to Paris St Germain in the first leg, from which there was no return.

Pressure on Evans

Evans is aware of the pressure on him to deliver success. "We've set the standards ourselves and we've got to live up to them," he

Fowler the Prowler: Liverpool's young hitman is always in the goals

LIVERPOOL

Formed: 1892.
Nickname: Reds or Pool.
Stadium: Anfield.
Capacity: 41,352.
Address: Anfield Road,
Liverpool L4 0TH.
Telephone: 0151 263 2361
Clubcall: 0891 121184.
Fax: 0151 260 8813.
Website: www.fa-carling.com/club.l.fc
Manager: Roy Evans.

COLOURS

RECORDS

Record Premier League victory:
6–0 (v Manchester C, Oct 28, 1995).
Record Premier League defeat:
5–1 (v Coventry C, Dec 9, 1992).
Record transfer fee received:
£7 million from Aston Villa for Stan
Collymore, May 1997.
Record transfer fee paid:
£8.5 million to Nottingham F for Stan
Collymore, June 1995.
Record attendance:
61,905, v Wolves, FA Cup 4th round,
Feb 2, 1952.

HONOURS

League (18): 1900–01, 1905–06,
1921–22, 1922–23, 1946–47, 1963–64,
1965–66, 1972–73, 1975–76, 1976–77,
1978–79, 1979–80, 1981–82, 1982–83,
1983–84, 1985–86, 1987–88, 1989–90.
FA Cup (5): 1965, 1974, 1986, 1989,
1992.
League Cup (5): 1981, 1982, 1983,
1984, 1995.
European Cup (4): 1977, 1978, 1981,
1984.
UEFA Cup (2): 1973, 1976.
European Super Cup: 1977.

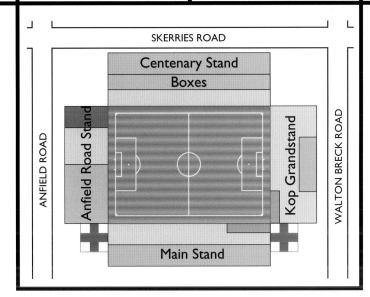

said last season. "I don't think any manager of a club this size is going to get five years and not win major trophies."

Liverpool's sale of talented but troublesome striker Stan Collymore to Aston Villa gave Evans the money to reorganize things at Anfield. However, the manager was keen to stress he was not going to buy foreign stars just for the sake of it. "We're not buying players to put bums on seats. I'm not one who wants to fill the place with foreigners. I'd like to think that there's a fair amount of talent in this country."

The biggest criticism of Liverpool last season was that they lacked an "enforcer" to win possession in midfield. John Barnes said: "The old Liverpool sides all had ball-winners, whereas we didn't. You could say that we lacked a ball-winner, but you could also say that if we got a ball-winner we might lose that Liverpool fluency." The signing of Paul Ince will test that.

Tactical changes

Evans may well switch to playing a flat back four in a bid to give Liverpool more options in midfield this season. He made such a change against Paris St Germain in the return leg of last season's Cup-winners' Cup semi-final, and very nearly pulled things around. However, for all the talk of tactics and transfers, the biggest change at Anfield over the summer took place behind the scenes with the retirement of first-team coach Ronnie Moran, a boot room legend and Evans' right-hand man.

FIXTURES 1997–98

Date	Opponent	H/A	Score
9 AUG	WIMBLEDON	A	___ : ___
13 AUG	LEICESTER CITY	H	___ : ___
23 AUG	BLACKBURN ROVERS	A	___ : ___
26 AUG	LEEDS UNITED	A	___ : ___
31 AUG	NEWCASTLE UNITED	H	___ : ___
13 SEPT	SHEFFIELD WEDNESDAY	H	___ : ___
22 SEPT	SOUTHAMPTON	A	___ : ___
24 SEPT	ASTON VILLA	H	___ : ___
27 SEPT	WEST HAM UNITED	A	___ : ___
5 OCT	CHELSEA	H	___ : ___
18 OCT	EVERTON	A	___ : ___
25 OCT	DERBY COUNTY	H	___ : ___
1 NOV	BOLTON	A	___ : ___
8 NOV	TOTTENHAM HOTSPUR	H	___ : ___
22 NOV	BARNSLEY	H	___ : ___
29 NOV	ARSENAL	A	___ : ___
6 DEC	MANCHESTER UNITED	H	___ : ___
13 DEC	CRYSTAL PALACE	A	___ : ___
20 DEC	COVENTRY CITY	H	___ : ___
26 DEC	LEEDS UNITED	H	___ : ___
28 DEC	NEWCASTLE UNITED	A	___ : ___
10 JAN	WIMBLEDON	H	___ : ___
17 JAN	LEICESTER CITY	A	___ : ___
31 JAN	BLACKBURN ROVERS	H	___ : ___
7 FEB	SOUTHAMPTON	H	___ : ___
14 FEB	SHEFFIELD WEDNESDAY	A	___ : ___
21 FEB	EVERTON	H	___ : ___
28 FEB	ASTON VILLA	A	___ : ___
7 MAR	BOLTON	H	___ : ___
14 MAR	TOTTENHAM HOTSPUR	A	___ : ___
28 MAR	BARNSLEY	A	___ : ___
4 APR	ARSENAL	H	___ : ___
11 APR	MANCHESTER UNITED	A	___ : ___
13 APR	CRYSTAL PALACE	H	___ : ___
18 APR	COVENTRY CITY	A	___ : ___
25 APR	CHELSEA	A	___ : ___
2 MAY	WEST HAM UNITED	H	___ : ___
11 MAY	DERBY COUNTY	A	___ : ___

PREMIER LEAGUE TABLES

SEASON	POS.	P	W	D	L	F	A	PTS	TOP SCORER	AV. GATE
1992–93	6th	42	16	11	15	62	55	59	Rush 14	37,004
1993–94	8th	42	17	9	16	59	55	60	Rush 14	38,503
1994–95	4th	42	21	11	10	65	37	74	Fowler 25	34,176
1995–96	3rd	38	20	11	7	70	34	71	Fowler 28	39,553
1996–97	4th	38	19	11	8	62	37	68	Fowler 18	39,776

Squad Info

KEY PLAYERS TO WATCH

Robbie Fowler

Robbie Fowler certainly knows how to make a name for himself. Liverpool-born Fowler, an Everton fan as a boy, scored on his debut for Liverpool, a Coca-Cola Cup game at Fulham in September 1993, and then scored all five Liverpool goals in the return leg at Anfield. He has not stopped scoring since and surely seems destined for a glittering career at the highest level.

Fowler, still only 22, has finished as Liverpool's top scorer for the past three seasons and has been hailed as the best striker in Britain. He scored his first goal for the full England side last season against Mexico after a prolific career with the Under-21s.

Fowler's goal-scoring style has been compared to the master goal-poacher, Jimmy Greaves, and there is something uncanny about the way Fowler makes it look so easy. The comparisons with Greaves and Ian Rush, the Liverpool legend Fowler has now replaced, would be enough to knock many strikers off their stride, but goals just come naturally to Robbie Fowler.

Oyvind Leonhardsen

Liverpool were quick to spend some of the £7 million they received from Aston Villa for Stan Collymore on Norwegian Oyvind Leonhardsen. The midfielder joined his fellow countrymen Stig Inge Bjornebye and Bjorn Tore Kvarme at Anfield after nearly three seasons with Wimbledon.

Leonhardsen joined the Dons after performing for Norway at the 1994 World Cup finals in the USA. At Selhurst Park, he quickly repaid the £600,000 Wimbledon paid Norwegian champions Rosenborg.

With his creative skills, shooting ability and tackling strength, it could be argued that Leonhardsen is the best of the many Norwegians now earning a living in the Premier League. He gives Liverpool new options in midfield, following the criticism that last season's first-choice midfielders – John Barnes, Jamie Redknapp and Michael Thomas – were too similar.

Jason McAteer

Republic of Ireland international Jason McAteer has made the right-wing-back position his own since joining Liverpool from Bolton Wanderers in a £4.5 million deal in September 1995.

Birkenhead-born McAteer first came to prominence during Bolton's Cup runs, which included an FA Cup win at Anfield and defeat at the hands of Liverpool in the 1995 Coca-Cola Cup Final. McAteer, who played in the 1994 World Cup finals in the USA for Jack Charlton's Ireland side, fulfilled a life-long ambition when he joined Liverpool, having supported the club from the Kop as a boy. His first goal for Liverpool came in the 1996–97 season.

His commitment to the Liverpool cause sometimes boils over into frustration – "He's Liverpool daft," manager Roy Evans said last season – but his attacking runs and phenomenal work-rate make him one of the best wing-backs in the Premier League.

Liverpool Daft: right wing-back Jason McAteer

Michael Owen

Robbie Fowler has had to live with the label "the new Ian Rush", but teenager Michael Owen is already having to live down predictions that he is "the new Robbie Fowler".

The young striker had been scoring goals at such a prolific rate in Liverpool's youth and reserve sides that throughout last season manager Roy Evans was under pressure to introduce him to first-team action. Evans bowed to the inevitable with two games of the season to go. With Fowler suspended, Owen was given his chance against Wimbledon at Selhurst Park. The youngster made a dramatic impact, scoring his first League goal, although Liverpool's failings blew their title chances that night.

New Sensation: big things are predicted for teenage striker Michael Owen

Player Records

	BORN	NATIONALITY	HEIGHT	WEIGHT	APPS	GOALS	PREVIOUS TEAMS
GOALKEEPERS							
David James	1.8.70 Welwyn	English	6-5	14-2	150	0	Watford.
Tony Warner	11.5.74 Liverpool	English	6-4	13-9	0	0	none
DEFENDERS							
Phil Babb	30.11.70 Lambeth	English	6-0	12-3	241	18	Millwall, Bradford C, Coventry C.
Stig Inge Bjornebye	11.12.69 Norway	Norwegian	5-10	11-9	91	2	Rosenborg (Nor).
Jamie Carragher	28.1.78 Liverpool	English	6-0	11-3	2	1	none
Steve Harkness	27.8.71 Carlisle	English	5-10	11-2	95	2	Carlisle U, Huddersfield T, Southend U.
Rob Jones	5.11.71 Wrexham	English	5-8	11-0	237	2	Crewe Alex.
Bjorn Tore Kvarme	17.7.72 Trondheim	Norwegian	6-1	12-3	15	0	Elverum (Nor), Kongsvinger (Nor), Rosenborg (Nor).
Dominic Matteo	24.4.74 Dumfries	English	6-1	11-10	50	0	Sunderland.
Danny Murphy	18.3.77 Chester	English	5-9	10-8	0	0	Crewe A
Neil Ruddock	9.5.68 London	English	6-2	12-12	269	24	Millwall, Tottenham H, Millwall, Southampton, Tottenham H.
David Thompson	12.9.77 Liverpool	English	5-7	10-0	1	0	none
Mark Wright	1.8.63 Dorchester	English	6-2	13-3	476	22	Oxford U, Southampton, Derby Co.
MIDFIELDERS							
Paul Ince	21.10.67 Ilford	English	5-10	12-2	277	35	West Ham, Manchester U, Inter (Ita).
Mark Kennedy	15.5.76 Dublin	Irish	5-11	11-0	58	9	Millwall.
Oyvind Leonhardsen	17.8.70 Norway	Norwegian	5-10	11-13	76	12	Rosenborg (Nor), Wimbledon.
Jason McAteer	18.6.71 Birkenhead	English	5-11	11-10	180	9	Bolton W.
Steve McManaman	11.2.72 Liverpool	English	6-0	10-6	208	31	none
Jamie Redknapp	25.6.73 Barton on Sea	English	6-0	12-10	170	16	Bournemouth.
Michael Thomas	24.8.67 Lambeth	English	5-9	12-6	277	32	Arsenal, Portsmouth.
FORWARDS							
Patrik Berger	10.11.73 Czech Rep	Czech	6-1	12-10	23	6	Slavia Prague (Cze), Sparta Prague (Cze), Borussia Dortmund (Ger).
Robbie Fowler	9.4.75 Liverpool	English	5-11	11-10	140	83	none
Michael Owen	14.12.79 Liverpool	English	5-7	10-4	2	1	none
Karlheinz Reidle	16.9.65 Simmerberg-Weiler	German	6-0	11-2	0	0	Werder Bremen (Ger), Lazio (Ita), Borussia Dortmund (Ger).

Steve McManaman

For all the excitement foreign stars bring to the Premier League, it's worth remembering that in Steve McManaman, Liverpool have one of the brightest prospects in European football.

Like his team-mate Robbie Fowler, Bootle-born McManaman originally supported Everton. He attended Campion High, a school with a reputation for producing professional footballers situated close to both Anfield and Goodison Park, and signed as a professional with Liverpool on his birthday in February 1990.

McManaman played for England Under-21s, in December 1990, before he made his first-team debut for Liverpool 10 days later against Sheffield Wednesday. Since then, he has become one of the most accomplished attacking midfielders in the Premier League. He became an England regular under Terry Venables and was one of the stars of England's Euro 96 campaign.

Known As Shaggy: Steve McManaman, former Everton fan

Manchester United
The Red Devils

Under manager Alex Ferguson, Manchester United have become the undisputed heavyweight champions of the Premier League. Last season's title triumph, United's fourth in five seasons, was achieved with such ease that the biggest question in the final weeks of the campaign was who was going to finish second.

Despite the amazing success of recent seasons, it's easy to forget that Ferguson was nearly forced out of Old Trafford in 1990. Only a late Mark Robins goal against Nottingham Forest kept United in the FA Cup third round. Later that year, Lee Martin scored the winner as United beat Crystal Palace at Wembley to secure Ferguson's first trophy.

While many fans turned against Fergie, Bobby Charlton and the other United directors did not. They knew something that few were aware of – that Ferguson was completely overhauling the youth team at Old Trafford, sowing the seeds of future success. In 1992, two years after the FA Cup triumph and a year after winning the European Cup-winners' Cup in Rotterdam, United won the FA Youth Cup. Ryan Giggs, already a first-team regular at the age of 17, turned out for the winning side, which also contained David Beckham, Nicky Butt and Gary Neville.

Those players now form the backbone of the United first team which has won so much in such a short space of time. They will take on even greater responsibility now that Frenchman Eric Cantona, United's lucky charm of recent years, has shocked everybody in English football by announcing his retirement. Ferguson is keen to credit his home-grown youngsters, notably David Beckham, and he believes the best is yet to come from them. "We are still a young club," he says. "The players are still learning and have still got their hunger. With that hunger you can achieve things."

For all the League and Cup triumphs, one prize still eludes Ferguson's United – the European Cup. United's finest hour came in 1968, when they beat Benfica at Wembley in the European Cup Final. It was a personal triumph for manager

Home-grown Hero: England midfielder David Beckham is the new star at Old Trafford

MANCHESTER UTD

Formed: 1878.
Nickname: The Red Devils.
Stadium: Old Trafford.
Capacity: 55,500.
Address: Sir Matt Busby Way,
Old Trafford, Manchester
M16 0RA.
Telephone: 0161 872 1661/
0161 930 1968.
Clubcall: 0891 121161.
Fax: 0161 876 5502.
Website: www.fa-carling/club/com/mu.fc
Manager: Alex Ferguson.

COLOURS

RECORDS

Record Premier League victory:
9–0 (v Ipswich T, Mar 4, 1995).
Record Premier League defeat:
5–0 (v Newcastle U, Oct 20, 1996).
Record transfer fee received:
£7 million from Internazionale for Paul
Ince, June 1995.
Record transfer fee paid: £6 million
plus Keith Gillespie (worth £1 million) to
Newcastle U for Andy Cole, Jan 1995.
Record attendance: 70,504, v Aston
Villa, Division 1, Dec 27, 1920.

HONOURS

League (11): 1907–08, 1910–11,
1951–52, 1955–56, 1956–57, 1964–65,
1966–67, 1992–93, 1993–94, 1995–96,
1996–97.
FA Cup (9): 1909, 1948, 1963, 1977,
1983, 1985, 1990, 1994, 1996.
League Cup (1): 1992.
European Cup (1): 1968.
European Cup-winners' Cup (1):
1991.

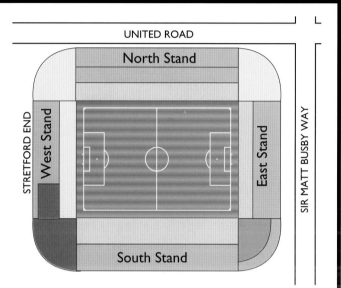

UNITED ROAD

North Stand

STRETFORD END | West Stand | East Stand | SIR MATT BUSBY WAY

South Stand

FIXTURES 1997–98

10 AUG	TOTTENHAM HOTSPUR	A	___	:	___
13 AUG	SOUTHAMPTON	H	___	:	___
23 AUG	LEICESTER CITY	A	___	:	___
27 AUG	EVERTON	A	___	:	___
30 AUG	COVENTRY CITY	H	___	:	___
13 SEPT	WEST HAM UNITED	H	___	:	___
20 SEPT	BOLTON	A	___	:	___
24 SEPT	CHELSEA	H	___	:	___
27 SEPT	LEEDS UNITED	A	___	:	___
4 OCT	CRYSTAL PALACE	H	___	:	___
18 OCT	DERBY COUNTY	A	___	:	___
25 OCT	BARNSLEY	H	___	:	___
1 NOV	SHEFFIELD WEDNESDAY	H	___	:	___
9 NOV	ARSENAL	A	___	:	___
22 NOV	WIMBLEDON	A	___	:	___
29 NOV	BLACKBURN ROVERS	H	___	:	___
6 DEC	LIVERPOOL	A	___	:	___
15 DEC	ASTON VILLA	H	___	:	___
21 DEC	NEWCASTLE UNITED	A	___	:	___
26 DEC	EVERTON	H	___	:	___
28 DEC	COVENTRY CITY	A	___	:	___
10 JAN	TOTTENHAM HOTSPUR	H	___	:	___
17 JAN	SOUTHAMPTON	A	___	:	___
31 JAN	LEICESTER CITY	H	___	:	___
7 FEB	BOLTON	H	___	:	___
14 FEB	WEST HAM UNITED	A	___	:	___
21 FEB	DERBY COUNTY	H	___	:	___
28 FEB	CHELSEA	A	___	:	___
7 MAR	SHEFFIELD WEDNESDAY	A	___	:	___
14 MAR	ARSENAL	H	___	:	___
28 MAR	WIMBLEDON	H	___	:	___
4 APR	BLACKBURN ROVERS	A	___	:	___
11 APR	LIVERPOOL	H	___	:	___
13 APR	ASTON VILLA	A	___	:	___
18 APR	NEWCASTLE UNITED	H	___	:	___
25 APR	CRYSTAL PALACE	A	___	:	___
2 MAY	LEEDS UNITED	H	___	:	___
10 MAY	BARNSLEY	A	___	:	___

Matt Busby, a survivor of the 1958 Munich air disaster. Busby remains the most successful manager in United's history. Ferguson is not far behind, with four Leagues, three Cups (including two doubles) and the European Cup-winners' Cup, but until he guides United to the European Cup, comparisons are pointless. United came close last season, losing to Borussia Dortmund in the Champions Cup semi-finals, and Ferguson's young players can only have benefited from the experience.

Despite early jitters in the League (losing 5–0 to Newcastle and 6–3 to Southampton), they bounced back to win the Premier League title with ease. Beckham and Norwegian striker Ole Gunnar Solskjaer were the stars of the campaign, while seasoned United veterans Cantona, Peter Schmeichel, Roy Keane and Ryan Giggs again proved more than a match for their Premier League rivals.

This season's campaign may well be closer, but Ferguson knows just how hard his team are to beat at Old Trafford, the biggest stadium in the Premier League. And England striker Teddy Sheringham could prove a more than adequate replacement for Cantona.

"People ask me what motivates me," Ferguson said after his players had showed off the Premiership trophy to the fans at Old Trafford. "Well, you only had to see what winning the League means to those fans. They keep me going. I'm supposed to motivate the staff and the players, but it's the fans who motivate me."

PREMIER LEAGUE TABLES

SEASON	POS.	P	W	D	L	F	A	PTS	TOP SCORER	AV. GATE
1992–93	1st	42	24	12	6	67	31	84	Hughes 15	35,152
1993–94	1st	42	27	11	4	80	38	92	Cantona 18	44,244
1994–95	2nd	42	26	10	6	77	28	88	Kanchelskis 14	43,681
1995–96	1st	38	25	7	6	73	35	82	Cantona 14	41,700

Squad Info

KEY PLAYERS TO WATCH

David Beckham

With his stunning lobbed goal on the opening day of last season against Wimbledon, David Beckham confirmed what many at Old Trafford already knew – that he is one of the most gifted midfielders English football has produced for ages.

Beckham has come a long way in a short space of time. A "Cockney Red" who supported United as a boy, Beckham initially found first-team opportunities hard to come by at Old Trafford after his elevation from United's youth team. He went on loan to Preston North End towards the end of the 1994–95 season and returned a changed man, winning a regular place in United's double-winning team of 1995–96.

Last season the spectacular goals just kept on coming and Beckham made his full England debut against Moldova in the World Cup qualifiers. His tough tackling, quickstep dribbling and thoughtful passing make Beckham the perfect long-term replacement for Paul Gascoigne at the heart of England's midfield. And he's still only 22!

Roy Keane

Republic of Ireland midfielder Roy Keane is the unsung hero of the United team – his drive and determination inspire his team-mates and scare the living daylights out of opponents.

Keane cost United a then British record £3.75 million in the summer of 1993 when they signed him from Nottingham Forest. Since then, along with Peter Schmeichel and Gary Pallister, Keane has formed the backbone of United's League- and Cup-winning teams.

One Hundred Per Cent: Irishman Roy Keane has been a rock in United's midfield

Ole Gunnar Solskjaer

Beckham may have been the revelation of last season, but young Norwegian striker Ole Gunnar Solskjaer was not far behind, finishing as United's top scorer with 18 League goals – something no one would have predicted at the start of the campaign.

Solskjaer joined United during the summer of 1996 from Norwegian side Molde. Little was known about him and he was expected to spend the season learning the ropes at Old Trafford. But an injury to Andy Cole gave Solskjaer his chance in the first-team, and he has not looked back. He scored crucial goals for United in the title race and the Champions League and established himself in Norway's national side.

Ryan Giggs

With all the attention being paid to David Beckham and Ole Solskjaer, it is easy to forget just what an important player Ryan Giggs is to Alex Ferguson's team. The Welsh international showed some of his best

Player Records

	BORN	NATIONALITY	HEIGHT	WEIGHT	APPS	GOALS	PREVIOUS TEAMS
GOALKEEPERS							
Peter Schmeichel	18.11.63 Gladsaxe	Danish	6-4	15-13	226	0	Hvidore (Den), Brondby (Den).
Raimond Van Der Gouw	24.3.63 Odenzaal	Dutch	6-5	13-0	2	0	Go Ahead Eagles (Hol), Vitesse Arnhem (Hol).
DEFENDERS							
Chris Casper	28.4.75 Burnley	English	6-0	11-11	18	1	Bournemouth.
Michael Clegg	3.7.77 Tameside	English	5-8	11-8	4	0	none
Dennis Irwin	31.10.65 Cork	Irish	5-8	10-8	495	20	Leeds U, Oldham Ath.
Ronnie Johnsen	10.6.69 Norway	Norwegian	6-1	13-0	31	0	Lillestrom (Nor), Besiktas (Tur).
David May	24.6.70 Oldham	English	6-0	12-10	187	8	Blackburn R.
Gary Neville	18.2.75 Bury	English	5-10	11-11	81	1	none
Philip Neville	21.1.77 Bury	English	5-10	11-10	44	0	none
John O'Kane	15.11.74 Nottingham	English	5-10	12-2	2	0	Wimbledon.
Gary Pallister	30.6.65 Ramsgate	English	6-4	14-13	449	17	Middlesbrough, Darlington.
Henning Berg	1.9.68 Eidsvoll	Norwegian	6-0	12-4	159	4	Lillestrom, Blackburn R.
MIDFIELDERS							
Michael Appleton	4.12.75 Salford	English	5-9	11-13	4	0	Lincoln C.
David Beckham	2.5.75 Leytonstone	English	6-0	11-2	78	17	Preston NE.
Nicky Butt	21.5.75 Manchester	English	5-10	11-3	84	8	none
Ryan Giggs	29.11.73 Cardiff	Welsh	5-11	10-7	207	42	none
Roy Keane	10.8.71 Cork	Irish	5-10	12-10	228	37	Cobh Ramblers (Ire), Nottingham F.
Brian McClair	8.12.63 Airdrie	Scottish	5-10	12-12	526	202	Aston Villa, Motherwell, Celtic.
Karel Poborsky	30.3.72 Jindrichuv Hradec	Czech	5-9	11-2	22	4	Ceske Budejovice (Cze), Slavia Prague (Cze).
Ben Thornley	21.4.75 Bury	English	5-9	11-12	26	3	Stockport C, Huddersfield T.
FORWARDS							
Andy Cole	15.10.71 Nottingham	English	5-11	11-2	197	108	Arsenal, Fulham, Bristol C, Newcastle U
Jordi Cruyff	9.2.74 Barcelona	Dutch	6-0	11-0	16	3	Barcelona (Spa).
Erik Nevland	10.11.77 Norway	Norwegian	5-10	11-10	0	0	Viking Stavangar (Nor).
Paul Scholes	16.11.74 Salford	English	5-7	11-0	67	18	none
Ole Gunnar Solskjaer	26.2.73 Norway	Norwegian	5-10	11-10	31	18	Molde (Nor).
Teddy Sheringham	2.4.66 Highams Park	English	6-0	12-5	433	183	Millwall, Nottingham F, Tottenham H.

last season, especially against Porto in the Champions League quarter-final at Old Trafford.

Giggs seems to have been around forever, but he is still only 23. He was on the books of Manchester City as a schoolboy but made his debut for United at the age of 17. He was the star of the United team which won the 1991 FA Youth Cup Final and has since clocked up more than 200 League appearances.

The inevitable comparisons with George Best which surfaced early in Giggs' career have not hindered his progress. The emergence of other young stars in United's first team last season helped to take the pressure off Giggs. We are already seeing a more mature Ryan Giggs, and the best could be yet to come.

Life of Ryan: Giggs is already a legend at Old Trafford

Newcastle United
The Magpies

It has taken a while but Newcastle fans are getting to used to life AK – "After Keegan" – and it's not nearly as bad as they thought it might have been when, on that earth-shattering day back in January, Kevin Keegan stepped out of the St James' Park hot-seat.

Keegan's resignation took everybody by surprise. It had been another rollercoaster ride of a season – we had come to expect little different – and the manager was never one to keep his emotions to himself. But nobody could have predicted the manner of Keegan's departure.

Keegan said at the time that he had taken the club as far as he could and that he had little more to offer. It soon emerged that the club had wanted Keegan to sign a new contract so that his name could be included in the prospectus for the club's share issue. But Keegan had already decided that he wanted out at the end of the season – he couldn't commit himself to Newcastle for any longer.

So King Kev quit. Whatever the real reasons for his departure, nobody can deny that Kevin Keegan was not a huge success on Tyneside.

Tyneside Messiah

Perhaps only Keegan, a hero as a player during his short time at St James' Park in the early 1980s, was capable of reviving such a slumbering giant. Because make no mistake, back in early 1992, when Keegan got the call to return to Tyneside, Newcastle were in serious danger of going under. They were slipping slowly but surely into the old Third Division. Attendances were down, morale was at rock bottom, and things couldn't get much worse.

Keegan performed a miracle in rescuing the Magpies from relegation, the purchase of Arsenal reject Andy Cole from Bristol City proving inspired. Next season, a combination of Keegan's leadership, chairman Sir John Hall's money and Cole's goals fired Newcastle in the Premier League as Division One champions.

Keegan had always said he did not want to be a manager, preferring life in retirement in sunny Spain. But after his instant success in management on Tyneside, he was already being talked about as a future manager of England. It seemed Keegan could do no wrong – he took Newcastle into the UEFA Cup in their first season back in the top flight.

The 1995–96 season promised great things at St James' Park. Andy Cole had been sold to Manchester United in a staggering £7 million deal that brought young Northern Ireland winger Keith Gillespie to St James'. The Cole deal upset a lot of people on Tyneside, but Keegan had two words for the fans outside St James' Park when he explained why he had sold his prolific striker: trust me.

The Cole cash and a little more besides was spent in the summer of 1995 on Les Ferdinand (QPR), French winger David Ginola (from Paris St Germain), Warren Barton (Wimbledon) and Shaka Hislop (Reading). The previous two seasons had seen Newcastle challenging at the right end of the League table, but not quite good enough for the final push. This season promised to be different. And so it almost was.

With Gillespie and Ginola supplying the bullets, Ferdinand and Peter Beardsley fired Newcastle into what, by the spring, seemed like an unbeatable lead. Unfortunately Keegan let his attacking instincts get the better of him, signing Colombian striker Faustino Asprilla from Italy for another Newcastle record: £6.7 million. Asprilla's arrival seemed to knock Keegan's side out of their stride, and they finished the season in second place to Manchester United.

The warning signs were there in the title run-in that Keegan was feeling the strain. A thrilling match at Anfield had ended 4–3 to Liverpool and tested the nerves of everybody involved. Then, as the title seemed to be slipping away from Newcastle, Keegan lost his rag. He "would love it, just love it," he screamed in a post-match TV interview if Newcastle beat Manchester United. That never happened and Keegan was left to contemplate his missed opportunities.

Worth Every Penny: Alan Shearer was top scorer for 1996–97

Formed: 1881
Nickname: The Magpies
Stadium: St. James' Park
Capacity: 36,610
Address: St James' Park, Newcastle-upon-Tyne, NE1 4ST
Telephone: 0191 201 8400
Clubcall: 0891 121 190
Fax: 0191 201 8600
Email: nufc@dila.pipex.com
Manager: Kenny Dalglish

Premier League victory:
6–0 v Manchester City, 28 October 1995
Premier League defeat:
5–1 v Coventry City, 19 December 1992
Transfer fee received: £6,000,000 from Manchester Utd for Andy Cole, January 1995 (plus Keith Gillespie valued at £1,000,000)
Transfer fee paid: £15,000,000 to Blackburn Rovers for Alan Shearer, July 1996
Attendance: 68,386 v Chelsea, Division 1, 3 September 1930.

FA Premier League: 1993–94; runners-up 1995–96
Football League: Champions 1904–05, 1906–07, 1908–09, 1926–27
Division 2: Champions 1964–65, 1992–93 (as Division 1); runners-up 1897–98, 1947–48.
FA Cup: Winners 1910, 1924, 1932, 1951, 1952, 1955; runners-up 1905, 1906, 1908, 1911, 1974.
Football League Cup: Runners-up 1976
Fairs (UEFA) Cup: Winners 1969

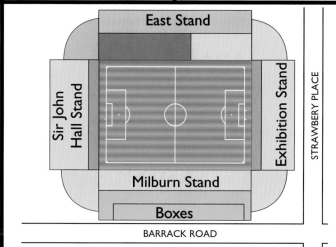

FIXTURES 1997–98

9 AUG	SHEFFIELD WEDNESDAY	H	____	:	____
23 AUG	ASTON VILLA	H	____	:	____
31 AUG	LIVERPOOL	A	____	:	____
13 SEPT	WIMBLEDON	H	____	:	____
20 SEPT	WEST HAM UNITED	A	____	:	____
24 SEPT	EVERTON	H	____	:	____
27 SEPT	CHELSEA	A	____	:	____
4 OCT	TOTTENHAM HOTSPUR	H	____	:	____
18 OCT	LEEDS UNITED	A	____	:	____
25 OCT	BLACKBURN ROVERS	H	____	:	____
1 NOV	LEICESTER CITY	H	____	:	____
8 NOV	COVENTRY CITY	A	____	:	____
22 NOV	SOUTHAMPTON	H	____	:	____
29 NOV	CRYSTAL PALACE	A	____	:	____
1 DEC	BOLTON	A	____	:	____
6 DEC	ARSENAL	H	____	:	____
13 DEC	BARNSLEY	A	____	:	____
17 DEC	DERBY COUNTY	H	____	:	____
21 DEC	MANCHESTER UNITED	H	____	:	____
26 DEC	DERBY COUNTY	A	____	:	____
28 DEC	LIVERPOOL	H	____	:	____
10 JAN	SHEFFIELD WEDNESDAY	A	____	:	____
17 JAN	BOLTON	H	____	:	____
31 JAN	ASTON VILLA	A	____	:	____
7 FEB	WEST HAM UNITED	H	____	:	____
14 FEB	WIMBLEDON	A	____	:	____
21 FEB	LEEDS UNITED	H	____	:	____
28 FEB	EVERTON	A	____	:	____
7 MAR	LEICESTER CITY	A	____	:	____
14 MAR	COVENTRY CITY	H	____	:	____
28 MAR	SOUTHAMPTON	A	____	:	____
4 APR	CRYSTAL PALACE	H	____	:	____
11 APR	ARSENAL	A	____	:	____
13 APR	BARNSLEY	H	____	:	____
18 APR	MANCHESTER UNITED	A	____	:	____
25 APR	TOTTENHAM HOTSPUR	A	____	:	____
2 MAY	CHELSEA	H	____	:	____
10 MAY	BLACKBURN ROVERS	A	____	:	____

Perhaps that summer Keegan decided he had done all he could for the Magpies. Not even the world record signing of Alan Shearer could prevent Keegan from calling it quits. With the twin strike force of Shearer and Ferdinand, Keegan's side notched up notable victories last season – the 5–0 thrashing of Manchester United, a 7–1 demolition of Tottenham – but the end was in sight.

Long live King Kenny

Keegan's departure was a major milestone in the history of Newcastle United Football Club, but it could turn out to have been one of the best things ever to happen to the club. Kevin Keegan was and will always be a Geordie hero and will receive a hero's welcome whenever he returns. But in Kenny Dalglish, Newcastle have a world-class manager and one of just three men (the others are Herbert Chapman and Brian Clough) to have won the English League title with two different clubs.

Kenny carried on where Kevin left off, even managing to lose 4–3 to his old club Liverpool after another remarkable game at Anfield! Newcastle's battle for the second Champions League spot behind Manchester United showed the determination that the new boss has quickly instilled into side.

Dalglish has stamped his mark on Tyneside, with the departure of David Ginola the most obvious sign that Kenny is his own man. His restoration of the reserve team and plan to develop a youth policy along the lines of the famous Ajax academy. There will be millions from the share issue to spend on players and plans for the new stadium are taking shape. Newcastle are still a force to be reckoned with.

PREMIER LEAGUE TABLES

SEASON	POS.	P	W	D	L	F	A	PTS	TOP SCORER	AV. GATE
1993-94	3rd	42	23	8	11	82	41	77	Cole (34)	33,679
1994-95	6th	42	20	12	10	67	47	72	Beardsley (13)	34,690
1995-96	2nd	38	24	6	8	68	37	78	Ferdinand (25)	36,507
1996-97	4th	38	19	10	9	70	42	67	Shearer (25)	36,578

Alan Shearer

Jackie Milburn, Malcolm MacDonald, Andy Cole, Alan Shearer. The number nine shirt at Newcastle United has always been special, but for many on Tyneside Alan Shearer is the best centre-forward ever to have worn the black-and-white stripes.

When Newcastle paid Blackburn Rovers a then world record £15 million in the summer of 1996 to bring Alan Shearer to Tyneside, they knew they were buying a world-class striker. Shearer had just finished as top scorer at Euro 96 and had been wanted by some of the world's top clubs, including Barcelona and Juventus.

The move to Newcastle was a move back home to his roots for Shearer. The England striker had stood on the terraces at St James' Park as a boy and cheered on his heroes, including one Kevin Keegan. Ironically, Shearer had to go all the way down south to Southampton to make a name as a professional footballer after being rejected by Newcastle as a youngster.

Last season, Shearer wasted no time in making himself at home at St James' Park. Despite two spells out through injury, he still finished as the Premiership's top scorer.

However, an horrific ankle injury sustained in a July pre–season friendly has sidelined Shearer for months, damaging both Newcastle's and England's prospects of success.

David Batty

When Leeds United decided to sell midfielder David Batty to Blackburn Rovers, fans at Elland Road were so incensed that they displayed a banner at home games with the slogan "Batty is God" in protest at the transfer.

The move to Blackburn provoked strong feelings at Leeds, and it was easy to see why. David Batty is a passionate, committed player and fans have always been quick to respond to his dedication to the cause.

It was a wrench for Batty to leave Leeds, the team he had supported as a boy and with whom

Gone But Not Forgotten: Robbie Elliott did great things for United before leaving to join Bolton

he had won the League title in 1992, but at Blackburn, under Kenny Dalglish, Batty continued to collect silverware, winning the Premier League in 1995.

Kevin Keegan was quick to recognize Batty's battling qualities in midfield and brought him to Newcastle in the spring of 1996. Batty quickly settled in at St James' where he began to be seen as more

England Regular: midfielder Robert Lee

than just a midfield "enforcer". England coach Glenn Hoddle, like Terry Venables before him, has recognized the qualities Batty brings to the national side, and looks certain to include the Newcastle midfielder in England's remaining World Cup qualifying games.

Back at Newcastle, Batty is hoping to win a League Championship medal with a record third club. With his commitment and desire to win, don't rule it out.

Robert Lee

When Kevin Keegan described Robert Lee as the best midfielder in England, there were few on Tyneside who disagreed. Lee was Keegan's first major signing when he took charge in the spring of 1992.

The East Londoner had been playing as a winger at Charlton, the club for which he had made his debut aged 18. But Keegan saw a big role for his new signing in central midfield and Lee quickly established himself at the centre of a St James' Park side that was challenging for the first division title and a golden future in the new Premier League. Lee's performances, and particularly his goals (10 in his first season), caught the eye of many, including England coach Terry Venables.

With barely a season of top division football under his belt, Lee made his debut for England against Romania at Wembley. It proved to be a sensational start with the Newcastle midfielder scoring just before half-time. The match ended 1–1 but Lee had done more than enough to secure another chance with England. Further appearances followed , and Lee was desperately unlucky to be left out of England's Euro 96 squad. He bounced back from that disappointment, though, and under new manager Glenn Hoddle has regained his place in the side. He was particularly effective against Mexico in a right-wing-back role, although he still likes getting forward and scoring goals. Kenny Dalglish, who has used Lee as an emergency striker, will testify to that.

Player Records

	BORN	NATIONALITY	HEIGHT	WEIGHT	APPS	GOALS	PREVIOUS TEAMS
GOALKEEPERS							
Shay Given	20.4.76 Lifford	Irish	6-1	12-10	24	0	Blackburn R, Sunderland.
Shaka Hislop	22.2.69 London	Trinidad & Tobago	6-3	14-4	144	0	Howard Univ (USA), Reading.
Pavel Srnicek	10.3.68 Ostrava	Czech	6-2	14-7	148	0	Banik Ostrava (Cze).
DEFENDERS							
Philippe Albert	10.8.67 Bouillon	Belgian	6-3	13-0	70	8	Charleroi (Bel), Mechelen (Bel), Anderlecht (Bel).
Warren Barton	19.3.69 Stoke Newington	English	5-11	12-00	270	11	Maidstone U, Wimbledon.
John Beresford	4.9.66 Sheffield	English	5-5	10-12	356	14	Manchester C, Barnsley, Portsmouth.
Steve Howey	26.10.71 Sunderland	English	6-1	11-12	154	6	none
Darren Peacock	3.2.68 Bristol	English	6-1	12-12	326	12	Newport Co, Hereford U, QPR.
Stuart Pearce	24.4.62 Hammersmith	English	5-10	13-0	359	57	Coventry C, Nottingham F.
Alessandro Pistone	27.7.75 Milan	Italian	5-11	12-2	0	0	Inter Milan.
Steve Watson	1.4.74 North Shields	English	6-1	12-7	172	11	none
MIDFIELDERS							
David Batty	2.12.68 Leeds	English	5-8	12-0	308	7	Leeds U, Blackburn R.
Peter Beardsley	18.1.61 Newcastle	English	5-8	11-7	592	200	Carlisle U, Vancouver Whitecaps (Can), Manchester U, Vancouver Whitecaps, (Can), Newcastle U, Liverpool, Everton.
Keith Gillespie	18.2.75 Larne	Northern Irish	5-9	11-5	94	12	Manchester U, Wigan Ath.
Des Hamilton	15.8.76 Bradford	English	5-11	12-9	88	5	Bradford C.
Temuri Ketsbaia	18.3.68 Georgia	Georgian	5-11	11-12	0	0	AEK Athens (Gre).
Robert Lee	1.2.66 West Ham	English	5-10	11-13	378	98	Charlton Ath.
Jon Dahl Tomasson	19.8.76 Denmark	Danish	5-11	11-8	0	0	Koge BK (Den), Heerenveen (Hol)
John Barnes	7.11.63 Jamaica	English	5-11	12-07	547	149	Watford, Liverpool.
FORWARDS							
Faustino Asprilla	10.11.69 Tulua	Colombian	5-9	11-3	37	7	Deportivo Cucuta (Col), Atletico Nacional (Col), Parma (Ita).
Alan Shearer	13.8.70 Newcastle	English	5-11	12-6	287	160	Southampton, Blackburn R.
Bjarni Gudjonsson	26.2.79 Iceland	Icelandic	5-10	12-0	0	0	IA Arkanes (Ice).

Steve Watson and Jon Dahl Tomasson

For all the millions spent on the likes of Shearer, Asprilla, Ferdinand, Ginola and Cole in recent years, one of Newcastle's brightest stars, Steve Watson, did not cost the club a penny.

Watson, a local lad from North Shields, is only 23 but has already made more than 150 appearances for the Magpies – in a variety of positions. He's been used as a striker and in midfield, but looks most comfortable as an attacking full-back.

Kenny Dalglish signed one of Europe's most wanted men when he collected the signature of Jon Dahl Tomasson last summer. The Dane had just finished as one of the top scorers in the Dutch first division – an impressive feat considering he was playing for the unfashionable club Heerenveen.

The 21-year-old, who plays in a deep position behind the main striker, scored more than 30 League goals in two seasons in Holland, which brought him to the attention of a host of top European clubs and Denmark national manager Bo Johansen, who called up Tomasson to the Danish squad for the World Cup qualifier against Croatia.

If his whirlwind career so far is anything to go by, the young Tomasson could be playing a big part in the Danish plans for the 1998 World Cup Finals in France. And Newcastle look to have landed a real catch.

Full Of Promise: home-grown all-rounder Steve Watson

Sheffield Wednesday

The Owls

Sheffield Wednesday have all the qualities needed to be one of England's leading clubs: strong support, a famous stadium and top quality players, but no silverware. However under manager David Pleat, a talented team is being assembled at Hillsborough that could start to challenge for honours.

Wednesday have not won the League for 67 years, when they collected back-to-back titles in 1929 and 1930; the last time they won the FA Cup was in 1935. In fact, the only major honour Wednesday have won since the Second World War was the League Cup, in 1991. They lived a yo-yo existence in the 1950s, being relegated three times and promoted on four occasions. The 1960s were spent in division one, but with limited success; the high point was reaching the 1966 FA Cup Final, which they lost to Everton.

Things took a turn for the worse in the 1970s with relegation to the second division and worse still, in 1975, division three. However, under the management of Jack Charlton and then Howard Wilkinson, Wednesday climbed back towards the big time. Promotion to the top division was secured in 1984.

League Cup success

Wilkinson had moved on to Leeds United in 1988 and Ron Atkinson moved in at Hillsborough. Wednesday lost their top-flight status in 1990 on goal difference, but bounced back after just one season while also winning the League Cup following a Wembley win over Atkinson's former club Manchester United.

Atkinson was succeeded in 1991 by Trevor Francis who took Wednesday to third place in the League in his first season in charge. The following year Francis's men reached two Wembley finals, but lost both to Arsenal.

Regi, Steady, Go: Regi Blinker added Continental flair last season

Formed: 1905.
Nickname: The Owls.
Stadium: Hillsborough.
Capacity: 39,814.
Address: Hillsborough,
Sheffield S6 1SW.
Telephone: 0114 2343122.
Clubcall: 0891 121186.
Fax: 0114 2337145.
Website: www.fa-carling.com/club/sw.fc
Manager: David Pleat.

COLOURS

RECORDS

Record Premier League victory:
5–0 (v West Ham U, December 18, 1993;
v Ipswich T, April 24, 1994).
Record Premier League defeat:
7–1 (v Nottingham F, April 1, 1995).
Record transfer fee received:
£2.65 million from Blackburn R for Paul
Warhurst, Sept 1993.
Record transfer fee paid: £3 million
to Internazionale for Benito Carbone,
Oct 1996.
Record attendance: 72,841, v
Manchester C, FA Cup 5th round,
17 Feb 1934.

HONOURS

League (4): 1903, 1904, 1929, 1930.
FA Cup (3): 1896, 1907, 1935.
League Cup (1): 1991.

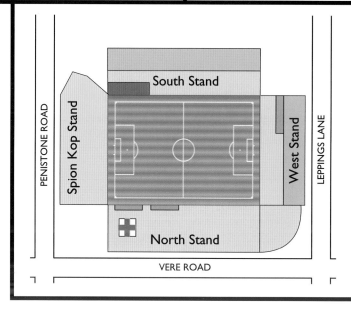

FIXTURES 1997–98

9 AUG	NEWCASTLE UNITED	A	____ : ____
13 AUG	LEEDS UNITED	H	____ : ____
23 AUG	WIMBLEDON	A	____ : ____
25 AUG	BLACKBURN ROVERS	A	____ : ____
30 AUG	LEICESTER CITY	H	____ : ____
13 SEPT	LIVERPOOL	A	____ : ____
20 SEPT	COVENTRY CITY	H	____ : ____
24 SEPT	DERBY COUNTY	H	____ : ____
27 SEPT	ASTON VILLA	A	____ : ____
4 OCT	EVERTON	H	____ : ____
19 OCT	TOTTENHAM HOTSPUR	A	____ : ____
25 OCT	CRYSTAL PALACE	H	____ : ____
1 NOV	MANCHESTER UNITED	A	____ : ____
8 NOV	BOLTON	H	____ : ____
22 NOV	ARSENAL	H	____ : ____
29 NOV	SOUTHAMPTON	A	____ : ____
8 DEC	BARNSLEY	H	____ : ____
13 DEC	WEST HAM UNITED	A	____ : ____
20 DEC	CHELSEA	H	____ : ____
26 DEC	BLACKBURN ROVERS	H	____ : ____
28 DEC	LEICESTER CITY	A	____ : ____
10 JAN	NEWCASTLE UNITED	H	____ : ____
17 JAN	LEEDS UNITED	A	____ : ____
31 JAN	WIMBLEDON	H	____ : ____
7 FEB	COVENTRY CITY	A	____ : ____
14 FEB	LIVERPOOL	H	____ : ____
21 FEB	TOTTENHAM HOTSPUR	H	____ : ____
28 FEB	DERBY COUNTY	A	____ : ____
7 MAR	MANCHESTER UNITED	H	____ : ____
14 MAR	BOLTON	A	____ : ____
28 MAR	ARSENAL	A	____ : ____
4 APR	SOUTHAMPTON	H	____ : ____
11 APR	BARNSLEY	A	____ : ____
13 APR	WEST HAM UNITED	H	____ : ____
18 APR	CHELSEA	A	____ : ____
25 APR	EVERTON	A	____ : ____
2 MAY	ASTON VILLA	H	____ : ____
10 MAY	CRYSTAL PALACE	A	____ : ____

Francis was building an impressive side, with Chris Waddle joined by fellow England internationals Des Walker and Andy Sinton in 1994, along with Romanian Dan Petrescu and Swede Klas Ingesson. But the expensively assembled side could finish the 1994–95 season in only 13th place, and Francis was sacked.

Wednesday then turned to former Tottenham manager David Pleat, who experienced mixed fortunes with the foreign legion. Ingesson and Petrescu soon left and Yugoslav Darko Kovacevic and Belgian Marc Degryse barely lasted the 1995–96 season, which ended with Wednesday needing a point on the last day to be sure of avoiding relegation.

Home improvements

Last season a mixture of foreign flair and English grit saw Wednesday as the early leaders of the Premier League. Andy Booth, a £2.8 million capture from Huddersfield, and Italian midfielder Benito Carbone, a club record buy from Internazionale, were the outstanding performers as Pleat's side finished seventh.

A lack of strength in depth probably cost Wednesday a place in Europe, but manager Pleat feels that his team did not get the recognition they deserved for a vastly improved performance. Pleat strengthened his squad during the summer with the purchase of French defender Patrick Blondeau and is determined that, this time around, Wednesday pick up the plaudits – and some silverware.

PREMIER LEAGUE TABLES

SEASON	POS.	P	W	D	L	F	A	PTS	TOP SCORER	AV. GATE
1992–93	7th	42	15	14	13	55	51	59	Bright/Hirst 11	27,264
1993–94	7th	42	16	16	10	76	54	64	Bright 19	27,191
1994–95	13th	42	13	12	17	49	57	51	Bright 11	26,570
1995–96	15th	38	10	10	18	48	61	40	Hirst 13	24,577

Squad Info

KEY PLAYERS TO WATCH

Andy Booth

England Under-21 striker Andy Booth arrived at Hillsborough in July 1996 with a reputation for scoring goals. He had managed a goal every other game for his home-town club Huddersfield, hence the fee – a then-club record £2.8 million.

Wednesday had won the race with a number of other Premier League clubs for Booth's signature and the 24-year-old forward did not disappoint, finishing the season as Wednesday's top scorer.

Young Gun: last season's top scorer Andy Booth

Mark Pembridge

For all the foreign stars Sheffield Wednesday have had among their ranks in recent years, one of the Owls' most effective midfield performers has been British. Welsh international Mark Pembridge is now well established on the left side of Wednesday's midfield following his £900,000 move in July 1995 from Derby County.

The switch to Sheffield reunited Pembridge with his old Luton manager David Pleat, who had signed the Merthyr Tydfil-born player as a 14-year-old. Pembridge gained international recognition while at Luton, making his Wales debut in 1991 against Brazil. Within a year he had joined Derby County in a £1.3 million deal.

Welsh Wizard: midfielder Mark Pembridge

Benito Carbone

Italian Benito Carbone proved to be Sheffield Wednesday's player of last season following his transfer from Internazionale in October 1996 for a club record £3 million.

Carbone had been surplus to requirements at Inter under English coach Roy Hodgson, now manager of Blackburn Rovers, but quickly established himself in the Wednesday first team. He announced his arrival in England to a live TV audience when he scored one of the goals of the season against Nottingham Forest at Hillsborough.

Carbone started his career with Torino, and played for six different clubs in eight years in Italy. The former Italian Under-21 international is seen by David Pleat as a natural successor to Chris Waddle. Carbone himself says: "I think my best position is on the right side of midfield, but really I just want to play. It doesn't matter where."

Pleat also believes that if Carbone had been playing for a more prominent club, he would have come close to challenging Chelsea's Gianfranco Zola for last season's Footballer of the Year award.

Top Man: Benito Carbone was Wednesday's player of last season

Player Records

	BORN	NATIONALITY	HEIGHT	WEIGHT	APPS	GOALS	PREVIOUS TEAMS
GOALKEEPERS							
Matt Clarke	3.11.73 Sheffield	English	6-3	11-7	125	0	Rotherham U.
Kevin Pressman	6.11.67 Fareham	English	6-1	14-13	196	0	Stoke C.
DEFENDERS							
Peter Atherton	6.4.70 Wigan	English	5-7	13-7	377	4	Wigan Ath, Coventry C.
Patrick Blondeau	27.1.68 Marseille	French	5-8	11-6	0	0	Martigues (Fra), Monaco (Fra).
Lee Briscoe	30.9.75 Pontefract	English	5-11	11-5	39	0	none
Jon Newsome	6.9.70 Sheffield	English	6-3	13-10	163	12	Sheffield W, Leeds U, Norwich C.
Steve Nicol	11.12.61 Irvine	Scottish	5-10	12-6	487	45	Ayr U, Liverpool, Notts Co.
Ian Nolan	9.7.70 Liverpool	Northern Irish	5-11	11-11	197	5	Tranmere R.
Dejan Stefanovic	28.10.74 Yugoslavia	Yugoslav	6-2	12-10	35	2	Red Star Belgrade (Yug).
Des Walker	26.11.65 Hackney	English	5-11	11-11	446	1	Nottingham F, Sampdoria (Ita).
MIDFIELDERS							
Benito Carbone	14.8.71 Bagnara Calabra	Italian	5-6	1-7	25	6	Torino (Ita), Reggina (Ita), Casertara (Ita), Ascoli (Ita), Torino (Ita), Napoli (Ita), Internazionale (Ita).
Wayne Collins	4.3.69 Manchester	English	6-0	12-0	129	15	Crewe Alex.
Graham Hyde	10.11.70 Doncaster	English	5-8	11-11	149	10	none
Ryan Jones	23.7.73 Sheffield	Welsh	6-3	13-8	52	9	Scunthorpe U.
Scott Oakes	5.8.72 Leicester	English	5-11	11-11	193	29	Leicester C, Luton T.
Mark Pembridge	29.11.70 Merthyr Tydfil	Welsh	5-7	11-11	233	41	Luton T, Derby Co.
Orlando Trustfull	4.8.70 Holland	Dutch	5-11	11-6	19	3	Haarlem (Hol), SVV (Hol), SVV/Dordrecht 90 (Hol), Twente (Hol), Feyenoord (Hol).
Guy Whittingham	10.11.64 Evesham	English	5-10	12-0	280	118	Portsmouth, Aston Villa, Wolverhampton W.
FORWARDS							
Andy Booth	17.3.73 Huddersfield	English	6-1	12-6	158	64	Huddersfield T.
O'Neill Donaldson	24.11.69 Birmingham	English	5-11	11-7	49	15	Shrewsbury T, Doncaster R, Mansfield T
David Hirst	7.12.67 Barnsley	English	6-0	13-8	316	115	Barnsley.
Richie Humphreys	30.11.77 Sheffield	English	5-10	11-3	34	3	none
Paolo Di Canio	14.4.69 Italy	Italian	5-10	12-5	0	0	Celtic

Peter Atherton

Sheffield Wednesday's high League placing last season (they finished 7th) owed more than a little to their defensive strength. Wednesday conceded just 41 goals, three fewer than champions Manchester United, and captain Peter Atherton played a crucial role in ensuring Wednesday's meanness at the back.

Atherton made his League debut for Wigan at the age of 17, and went on to make 177 appearances before moving to Coventry City in August 1991 for £300,000. He became an established Premier League performer at Highfield Road, and made the move to Hillsborough in June 1994 for a tribunal-decided fee of £800,000.

Wednesday fans were quick to appreciate Atherton's talents, voting him Player of the Year in 1995, and he took over the captain's armband in the 1995–96 season.

Patrick Blondeau

French defender Patrick Blondeau is the latest addition to Wednesday's growing foreign legion. Blondeau has signed a three-year deal following his move from French champions Monaco and believes he has made the right choice.

He rejected offers from Internazionale, Benito Carbone's old club, and Scottish champions Rangers in favour of a move to Sheffield. The 29-year-old says: "I love England, I've always had the feeling. On meeting the Sheffield directors that feeling was reinforced. Sheffield is an industrial city, a people of workers. They are aware of the real values of football."

Blondeau spent eight seasons with Monaco, after starting his career with Martigues, and gained rave reviews for his consistent displays at right-back. He was a key component in Monaco's French League title win last season.

Southampton
The Saints

Southampton are living proof that small clubs can survive in the Premier League. They have been in the top division since 1978 and last season again survived a relegation scare. The Saints went into the final match of last season, against Aston Villa at Villa Park, with relegation still a possibility. They lost 1–0, but Middlesbrough's failure to beat Leeds and Sunderland's defeat by Wimbledon ensured Premier League football on the South Coast for another season.

Rocket Power: Le Tissier enjoyed another good season at the Dell, ending as the Saints' top scorer

For much of last season, Southampton were favourites to go down. They slipped into the bottom three in January and only moved out of the danger zone with a handful of games to go. The season had offered so much for the Saints at the start. Many fans felt disappointment about the close-season sacking of manager Dave Merrington, but there was a new mood of cautious optimism about his replacement, Graeme Souness.

Early defeats by Leicester City, West Ham United and Liverpool suggested the campaign would be a struggle, but a 4–0 rout of Middlesbrough at the end of September was followed weeks later by a 6–3 thrashing of Manchester United. The champions were looking to bounce back from their 5–0 defeat by Newcastle a week earlier, but the Saints had other ideas. The club's newly-arrived foreign contingent, Israeli midfielder Eyal Berkovic and Norwegian striker Egil Ostenstad, were in terrific form and the victory was capped by a spectacular goal from Matthew Le Tissier in which the Saints' number seven chipped United keeper

Peter Schmeichel.

In the previous season's meeting at The Dell, United had resorted to changing their shirts at half-time, claiming they couldn't see each other in their new grey strip, but there could be no excuses this time around: the Saints had completely outclassed the champions.

The victory promised to kick-start Southampton's season, but within weeks the Saints crashed 7–1 to Everton at Goodison Park and a long hard winter lay ahead. That Southampton survived was a tribute to Souness's power of motivation and a battling spirit that has been hardened over the years of relegation battles.

SOUTHAMPTON

Formed: 1885.
Nickname: The Saints.
Stadium: The Dell.
Capacity: 15,000.
Address: Milton Road,
Southampton SO15 2XH.
Telephone: 01703 220505.
Clubcall: 0891121178.
Fax: 01703 330360.
Website: www.fa-carling.com/club.s.fc
Manager: Dave Jones.

COLOURS

RECORDS

Record Premier League victory:
6–3 (v Manchester U, Oct 26, 1996).
Record Premier League defeat:
7–1 (v Everton, Nov 16, 1996).
Record transfer fee received:
£3.3 million from Blackburn Rovers for
Alan Shearer, July 1992.
Record transfer fee paid:
£1.3 million to Galatasaray for Ulrich Van
Gobbel, Oct 1996.
Record attendance:
31,044, v Manchester United, Division 1, 8
October, 1969.

HONOURS

League: Runners-up, 1983-84.
FA Cup (1): 1976.
League Cup: Runners-up, 1979.

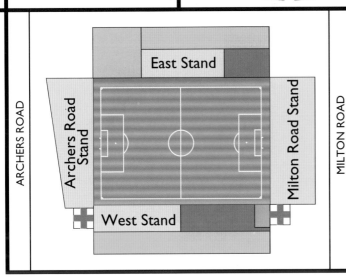

FIXTURES 1997–98

Date	Opponent	H/A	Score	
9 AUG	BOLTON	H	____	: ____
13 AUG	MANCHESTER UNITED	A	____	: ____
23 AUG	ARSENAL	H	____	: ____
27 AUG	CRYSTAL PALACE	H	____	: ____
30 AUG	CHELSEA	A	____	: ____
13 SEPT	COVENTRY CITY	A	____	: ____
20 SEPT	LIVERPOOL	H	____	: ____
24 SEPT	LEEDS UNITED	H	____	: ____
27 SEPT	DERBY COUNTY	A	____	: ____
4 OCT	WEST HAM UNITED	H	____	: ____
18 OCT	BLACKBURN ROVERS	A	____	: ____
25 OCT	TOTTENHAM HOTSPUR	H	____	: ____
1 NOV	EVERTON	A	____	: ____
10 NOV	BARNSLEY	H	____	: ____
22 NOV	NEWCASTLE UNITED	A	____	: ____
29 NOV	SHEFFIELD WEDNESDAY	H	____	: ____
6 DEC	WIMBLEDON	A	____	: ____
13 DEC	LEICESTER CITY	H	____	: ____
20 DEC	ASTON VILLA	A	____	: ____
26 DEC	CRYSTAL PALACE	A	____	: ____
28 DEC	CHELSEA	H	____	: ____
10 JAN	BOLTON	A	____	: ____
17 JAN	MANCHESTER UNITED	H	____	: ____
31 JAN	ARSENAL	A	____	: ____
7 FEB	LIVERPOOL	A	____	: ____
14 FEB	COVENTRY CITY	H	____	: ____
21 FEB	BLACKBURN ROVERS	H	____	: ____
28 FEB	LEEDS UNITED	A	____	: ____
7 MAR	EVERTON	H	____	: ____
14 MAR	BARNSLEY	A	____	: ____
28 MAR	NEWCASTLE UNITED	H	____	: ____
4 APR	SHEFFIELD WEDNESDAY	A	____	: ____
11 APR	WIMBLEDON	H	____	: ____
13 APR	LEICESTER CITY	A	____	: ____
18 APR	ASTON VILLA	H	____	: ____
25 APR	WEST HAM UNITED	A	____	: ____
2 MAY	DERBY COUNTY	H	____	: ____
10 MAY	TOTTENHAM HOTSPUR	A	____	: ____

The delight at avoiding relegation turned to frustration last summer following the resignation of Souness and, worse still, of Director of Football Lawrie McMenemy, the most successful manager in the club's history. It was under McMenemy that Southampton won their only major honour to date when, as second-division underdogs, the Saints beat Manchester United 1–0 to win the 1976 FA Cup Final. McMenemy steered Southampton to promotion two years later and in 1983–84 guided the club through their best-ever season. They finished a close second behind Liverpool in the League and reached the semi-finals of the FA Cup.

Under successive managers Chris Nicholl, Ian Branfoot and Alan Ball, Southampton flirted with success in the Cups, but struggled to make an impression in the top division. In the 1990s, only the goals of Alan Shearer (before his £3.3 million move to Blackburn) and Matthew Le Tissier have saved the Saints from relegation. The Channel Islander remains crucial to their future, although the club continues to scour the lower leagues for talent.

New manager Dave Jones, a big hit with Stockport, knows all about achieving success on a small budget. The Dell may be the smallest Premier League ground, but it can still offer top-flight football. Kevin Davies, one of the stars of Chesterfield's FA Cup run last season, was the latest to be lured by the bright lights of the Premier League. The Saints signed him despite interest from a host of other top clubs.

PREMIER LEAGUE TABLES

SEASON	POS.	P	W	D	L	F	A	PTS	TOP SCORER	AV. GATE
1992-93	18th	42	13	11	18	54	61	50	Le Tissier (15)	15,382
1993-94	18th	42	12	7	23	49	66	43	Le Tissier (25)	14,751
1994-95	10th	42	12	18	12	61	63	54	Le Tissier (19)	14,685
1995-96	17th	38	9	11	18	34	52	38	Le Tissier/Shipperley (7)	14,819
1996-97	16th	38	10	11	17	50	56	41	Le Tissier (13)	15,105

Matthew Le Tissier

There have been some great players who have graced The Dell over the years – Alan Ball, Mick Channon, Kevin Keegan, Alan Shearer – but none has been more talented than Matthew Le Tissier. Saints fans were compensated for the loss of Graeme Souness and Lawrie McMenemy over the summer by news that the Channel Islander had signed a new four-year contract with the club.

No other player comes close to Le Tissier in the eyes of Saints supporters. Le Tissier's defence-splitting passes, breathtaking goals and match-winning free-kicks make him one of the most gifted players of his generation. For many it is a mystery why Le Tissier has never moved to a bigger club, but for Southampton fans it is a cause for celebration. His goals – 140 in 357 League games – are the main reason the Saints are still in the Premier League.

As a professional, Guernsey-born Le Tissier has always been a one-club man, but as a boy he played for Guernsey side Vale Recreation. He began his association with Southampton more than 13 years ago, signing schoolboy forms in 1984 and becoming an apprentice a year later. He made his debut in August 1986, two months before turning fully professional. Le Tissier scored six goals in 24 games during his first season, but then suffered through injuries during 1987–88 and failed to score in 19 outings. He returned to form and fitness the following year and in 1989–90, his 20 goals in 35 games earned him the PFA Young Player of the Season award.

Since then, Le Tissier's form and goals have been crucial to Southampton's survival in the top flight. Nineteen League goals in 1990–91, 15 in 1992–93, 25 in 1993–94, 20 in 1994–95 – and no ordinary goals either. His spectacular long-range effort against Blackburn was goal of the 1994–95 season and renewed calls for his inclusion in the England squad.

As a Channel Islander, Le Tissier was eligible to play for any of the home countries – England, Wales, Scotland and

Bargain Buy: keeper Maik Taylor

Northern Ireland – as well as France. He turned down an offer to play for the French as his dream was always to play for England. He made his debut for England as a substitute against Denmark in Terry Venables' first game as England coach, but failed to make the squad for Euro 96.

Glenn Hoddle has made it clear Le Tissier still has a future in international football, despite a barrage of criticism for his performance against Italy in England's World Cup qualifier at Wembley last season.

Egil Ostenstad

Matthew Le Tissier may be the Saints' most gifted player, but Egil Ostenstad was the most popular last season. The Norwegian striker collected the Saints' Player of the Season award after an impressive first season on the South Coast. Ostenstad joined Southampton for £900,000 in October 1996 after scoring 23 goals in 24 games for Norwegian side Viking Stavanger. He made his debut against Coventry and soon established a good relationship with another new arrival from abroad, Eyal Berkovic. The two foreigners combined with devastating effect in the Saints' 6–3 humiliation of Manchester United.

Ostenstad was a busy man this sum-

Scandinavian Hitman: Norwegian striker Egil Ostenstad

Player Records

	BORN	NATIONALITY	HEIGHT	WEIGHT	APPS	GOALS	PREVIOUS TEAMS
GOALKEEPERS							
Dave Beasant	20.3.59 Ealing	English	6-4	14-3	517	0	Wimbledon, Newcastle U, Chelsea, Grimsby T, Wolverhampton W.
Maik Taylor	4.9.71 Germany	English	6-5	13-8	63	0	Barnet.
DEFENDERS							
Francis Benali	30.12.68 Southampton	English	5-10	10-13	220	0	none
Frankie Bennett	3.1.69 Birmingham	English	5-7	12-1	19	1	none
Simon Charlton	25.10.71 Huddersfield	English	5-8	11-10	234	3	Huddersfield T.
Jason Dodd	2.11.70 Bath	English	5-11	12-3	195	6	none
Richard Dryden	14.6.69 Stroud	English	6-0	13-0	214	11	Bristol R, Exeter C, Manchester C, Notts Co, Plymouth Argyle, Birmingham C, Bristol C.
Claus Lundekvam	22.2.73 Norway	Norwegian	6-1	13-6	29	0	SK Brann (Nor).
Ken Monkou	29.11.64 Surinam	Dutch	6-3	14-5	238	10	Feyenoord (Hol), Chelsea.
Alan Neilson	26.9.72 Wegburg	Welsh	5-11	12-9	89	1	Newcastle U.
Ulrich Van Gobbel	16.1.71 Surinam	Dutch	6-0	13-7	25	1	Galatasaray (Tur).
Barry Venison	16.8.64 Consett	English	5-10	12-3	416	4	Sunderland, Liverpool, Newcastle U, Galatasaray (Tur).
MIDFIELDERS							
David Hughes	30.12.72 St Albans	English	5-10	11-8	30	3	none
Neil Maddison	2.10.69 Darlington	English	5-11	11-6	162	18	none
Jim Magilton	6.5.69 Belfast	Northern Irish	6-1	14-2	273	47	Liverpool, Oxford U.
Matt Oakley	17.8.77 Peterborough	English	5-10	12-1	39	3	none
Robbie Slater	26.11.64 Ormskirk	Australian	5-11	12-5	71	5	Lens (Fra), Blackburn R, West Ham U.
Paul Tisdale	14.1.73 Malta	English	5-9	11-13	21	1	Northampton T.
Christopher Warren	10.10.74 Bournemouth	English	5-10	11-4	8	0	none
FORWARDS							
Kevin Davies	26.3.77 Sheffield	English	6-0	13-5	109	29	Chesterfield.
Micky Evans	1.1.73 Plymouth	English	6-0	13-4	142	30	Plymouth Argyle, Blackburn R.
Matt Le Tissier	14.10.68 Guernsey	English	6-1	13-8	357	140	none
Egil Ostenstad	2.10.66 Haugesund	Norwegian	6-0	12-8	30	10	Viking Stavanger (Nor).

mer. He joined up with his national team-mates for a friendly against world champions Brazil. The Norwegians pulled off one of the shocks of the year, beating the Brazilians 4–2, with Ostenstad scoring the final goal.

Maik Taylor and Kevin Davies

Although Southampton do not have the resources of most other Premier League clubs, they do have a talent for unearthing talent from the lower reaches of the Football League. Maik Taylor and Kevin Davies are two such examples.

The Saints signed Taylor from Barnet in January for £500,000 and the German-born goalkeeper quickly proved why he was one of the most-highly rated players in the lower leagues.

Kevin Davies made a name for himself in Chesterfield's giant-killing FA Cup run last season. He scored a hat-trick against Bolton and was trailed by a host of top clubs before the Saints signed him just before the end of last season. Only 20, Davies is definitely one to watch.

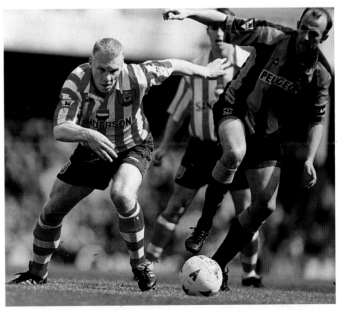

Midfield Battler: Robbie Slater

Tottenham
Hotspur Spurs

Tottenham Hotspur are one of English football's most high-profile clubs but have won only one trophy, the 1991 FA Cup, in the past 13 years. Despite that lack of recent success, Spurs are rarely out of the headlines for long.

Last season Spurs finished tenth in the Premier League after a campaign destroyed by injuries to key players. With many of his best players missing for much of the season, manager Gerry Francis was forced to give debuts to inexperienced teenagers from the youth team. With a third-round FA Cup exit at the hands of Manchester United and a League Cup humiliation by Bolton Wanderers, it was a season for Spurs fans to forget.

They have come to expect success – and stylish football, too. The club have won the League twice, in 1951 and 1961, when the team managed by Bill Nicholson and featuring such talented players as Danny Blanchflower, John White and Dave Mackay did the League and FA Cup double. They retained the FA Cup a year later and then, with striker Jimmy Greaves in the ranks, they won the 1963 Cup-winners' Cup, making Spurs the first British team to win a European trophy.

Cup-winning tradition

Since then, Spurs' finest hours have been in the Cups. In 1967, they were FA Cup-winners again, launching the club into a successful new era. With a side that featured the likes of Pat Jennings, Mike England, Alan Gilzean and Alan Mullery, Tottenham won two League Cups (1971 and 1973) and a second European prize, the 1972 UEFA Cup.

The Cup tradition continued in the 1980s with a side built by manager Keith Burkinshaw around the current England manager Glenn Hoddle. Foreign players were rare in England at the time, so Tottenham's signing of two World Cup-winners, the Argentinians Ossie Ardiles and Ricardo Villa, made the team which won the 1981 and 1982 FA Cups a special side for many reasons.

The club fell into decline in the late 1980s, but remained headline news as a battle took place for control of Tottenham's finances, with businessman Alan Sugar eventually winning. No sooner had Terry Venables guided a side featuring Gary Lineker

Missing from the Action: Darren Anderton was injured for much of last season

TOTTENHAM HOTSPUR

Formed: 1882.
Nickname: Spurs.
Stadium: White Hart Lane.
Capacity: 33,083.
Address: 748 High Rd,
London N17 0AP.
Telephone: 0181 365 5000.
Clubcall: 0891 335555.
Fax: 0181 365 5005.
Website: www.fa-carling.com/club/th.fc
Manager: Gerry Francis.

COLOURS

RECORDS

Record Premier League victory:
5–0 (v Oldham Athl Sept 18, 1993).
Record Premier League defeat:
7–1 (v Newcastle U, Dec 28, 1996).
Record transfer fee received:
£5.5 million from Lazio for Paul
Gascoigne, May 1992.
Record transfer fee paid:
£4.5 million to Crystal Palace for Chris
Armstrong, June 1995.
Record attendance:
75,038, v Sunderland, FA Cup 6th round,
Mar 5, 1938.

HONOURS

League (2): 1951, 1961.
FA Cup (8): 1901, 1921, 1961, 1962,
1967, 1981, 1982, 1991.
League Cup (2): 1971, 1973.
European Cup-winners' Cup (1):
1963.
Fairs Cup (2): 1972, 1984.

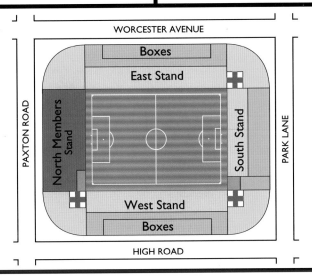

FIXTURES 1997–98

10 AUG	MANCHESTER UNITED	H	___ : ___
13 AUG	WEST HAM UNITED	A	___ : ___
23 AUG	DERBY COUNTY	H	___ : ___
27 AUG	ASTON VILLA	H	___ : ___
30 AUG	ARSENAL	A	___ : ___
13 SEPT	LEICESTER CITY	A	___ : ___
20 SEPT	BLACKBURN ROVERS	H	___ : ___
23 SEPT	BOLTON	A	___ : ___
27 SEPT	WIMBLEDON	H	___ : ___
4 OCT	NEWCASTLE UNITED	A	___ : ___
19 OCT	SHEFFIELD WEDNESDAY	H	___ : ___
25 OCT	SOUTHAMPTON	A	___ : ___
1 NOV	LEEDS UNITED	H	___ : ___
8 NOV	LIVERPOOL	A	___ : ___
24 NOV	CRYSTAL PALACE	H	___ : ___
29 NOV	EVERTON	A	___ : ___
6 DEC	CHELSEA	H	___ : ___
13 DEC	COVENTRY CITY	A	___ : ___
20 DEC	BARNSLEY	H	___ : ___
26 DEC	ASTON VILLA	A	___ : ___
28 DEC	ARSENAL	H	___ : ___
10 JAN	MANCHESTER UNITED	A	___ : ___
17 JAN	WEST HAM UNITED	H	___ : ___
31 JAN	DERBY COUNTY	A	___ : ___
7 FEB	BLACKBURN ROVERS	A	___ : ___
14 FEB	LEICESTER CITY	H	___ : ___
21 FEB	SHEFFIELD WEDNESDAY	A	___ : ___
28 FEB	BOLTON	H	___ : ___
7 MAR	LEEDS UNITED	A	___ : ___
14 MAR	LIVERPOOL	H	___ : ___
28 MAR	CRYSTAL PALACE	A	___ : ___
4 APR	EVERTON	H	___ : ___
11 APR	CHELSEA	A	___ : ___
13 APR	COVENTRY CITY	H	___ : ___
18 APR	BARNSLEY	A	___ : ___
25 APR	NEWCASTLE UNITED	H	___ : ___
2 MAY	WIMBLEDON	A	___ : ___
10 MAY	SOUTHAMPTON	H	___ : ___

and Paul Gascoigne to a then-record eighth FA Cup in 1991 than everything fell apart. An acrimonious dispute with Sugar led to Venables' departure and his eventual replacement by Ossie Ardiles.

Under Ardiles, the Spurs tradition of stylish attacking football continued. But not even the shock signing of German World Cup striker Jurgen Klinsmann could prevent Ardiles from getting the sack as Spurs' "famous five" attack scored goals by the bucketful, but conceded just as many.

Francis arrives

Gerry Francis replaced the sacked Ardiles in November 1994 and adopted a more pragmatic approach. Klinsmann scored 20 League goals, but by the summer the German had left for Bayern Munich. In a matter of months Spurs also lost homesick youngster Nicky Barmby to Middlesbrough, and two other foreign stars, Romanians Gica Popescu and Ilie Dumitrescu.

In came Chris Armstrong and Ruel Fox, but injuries to key midfielder Darren Anderton hampered Spurs' progress. The injury jinx worsened last season: Gary Mabbutt, Anderton, Armstrong and new signings John Scales (from Liverpool), Steffen Iversen (Rosenborg) and Ramon Vega (Cagliari) all spent more time on the treatment table than on the pitch.

The summer signings of Les Ferdinand and David Ginola should boost the morale of the fans, but the squad lacks the strength in depth needed for when the inevitable injury list begins to take its toll.

PREMIER LEAGUE TABLES

SEASON	POS.	P	W	D	L	F	A	PTS	TOP SCORER	AV. GATE
1992–93	8th	42	16	11	15	60	66	59	Sheringham 21	27,740
1993–94	15th	42	11	12	19	54	59	45	Sheringham 14	27,150
1994–95	7th	42	16	14	12	66	58	62	Klinsmann 20	27,259
1995–96	8th	38	16	13	9	50	38	61	Sheringham 16	30,510

It is as a centre-back that Campbell has become established as an England international. Terry Venables called Campbell into the national squad for Euro 96 and current England coach Glenn Hoddle is a big fan. "I've been watching him a lot," said Hoddle. "He's played extremely well. What I really like about him is that he has never adopted that 'I've made it now' attitude. Apart from his excellent defending, he's a super lad with a fresh attitude."

Darren Anderton

Last season, midfielder Darren Anderton was the forgotten man of English football. He returned from injury in the late spring of 1996 to reclaim his place in the England side. but no sooner had he helped his country to reach the semi-finals of Euro 96 than Anderton suffered from the recurrence of a long-term hernia injury. He made just 15 appearances last term and Spurs struggled to find consistency without him.

Tricky winger Anderton has never been one to grab the limelight. He reportedly burst out laughing when he heard how much the then Tottenham manager Terry Venables was going to pay for him in May 1992 – £1.75 million. He had come to everybody's attention during Portsmouth's 1992 run to the semi-finals of the FA Cup. Since then, despite all the injuries, he has become an established international.

Steffen Iversen

Norwegian Steffen Iversen was one of Europe's most wanted men last year. Spurs fought off reported interest from PSV Eindhoven, Barcelona, Ajax, Liverpool and Manchester United to sign the young striker from Norwegian champions Rosenborg.

Iversen may only be 21, but he already has more European experience than most of the rest of the Spurs squad put together. Last autumn, Iversen led Rosenborg's forward line in the Champions League, when they shocked Europe by knocking Italian champions Milan out of the competition.

Spurs boss Gerry Francis sees Iversen as the replacement for Teddy Sheringham at White Hart Lane, even though at 6ft 2in the Norwegian is more effective when playing as a target man. With 17 Under-21 caps for Norway, Iversen is one to watch for the future.

Sol Power: Campbell has signed for four more years at Spurs

Sol Campbell

The best news for Spurs fans last summer was that defender Sol Campbell signed a new four-year contract which will keep him at White Hart Lane until 2001. Campbell says it was "a gut feeling" which led him to agree the new deal, despite reported interest from Manchester United and Liverpool.

A move north never seemed attractive for Londoner Sol, who is now a regular in the England squad. Campbell, who has been at Spurs since the age of 14, is still only 22 and said: "Because I've been around so long people think I'm 26 or 27, but I'm not. I'll only be that age when I come out of the new contract, and that's not old these days."

Campbell first came to prominence in the 1993–94 season when injuries forced the then manager Ossie Ardiles to use the youngster as an emergency striker. Campbell was also playing as a full-back, but said at the time that his favourite position was in central midfield. However, current Spurs boss Gerry Francis was quick to spot that Campbell's qualities would be best used in central defence.

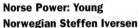

Norse Power: Young Norwegian Steffen Iversen

Player Records

	BORN	NATIONALITY	HEIGHT	WEIGHT	APPS	GOALS	PREVIOUS TEAMS
GOALKEEPERS							
Espen Baardsen	7.12.77 Norway	Norwegian	6-1	13-2	2	0	Major league soccer (USA).
Ian Walker	31.10.71 Watford	English	6-1	12-9	165	0	Oxford U, Ipswich T.
DEFENDERS							
Dean Austin	26.4.70 Hemel Hempstead	English	6-0	11-6	120	2	Southend U.
Colin Calderwood	20.1.65 Glasgow	Scottish	6-0	12-12	555	23	Mansfield T, Swindon T.
Sol Campbell	18.9.74 Newham	English	6-1	14-1	134	2	none
Stephen Carr	29.8.76 Dublin	Irish	5-7	12-2	27	0	none
Justin Edinburgh	18.12.69 Brentwood	English	5-10	11-8	210	1	Southend U.
Gary Mabbutt	23.8.61 Bristol	English	5-10	12-9	597	37	Bristol R.
Stuart Nethercott	21.3.73 Chadwell Heath	English	5-11	13-8	70	1	Maidstone U, Barnet.
John Scales	4.7.66 Harrogate	English	6-2	13-5	389	15	Bristol R, Wimbledon, Liverpool.
Ramon Vega	14.6.71 Olten	Swiss	6-2	13-6	8	1	Trimbach (Swi), Olten (Swi), Grasshopper (Swi), Cagliari (Ita).
Clive Wilson	13.11.62 Manchester	English	5-7	10-0	445	29	Manchester C, Chester, Chelsea, Manchester C, QPR.
MIDFIELDERS							
Darren Anderton	3.3.72 Southampton	English	6-1	12-0	191	29	Portsmouth.
Jason Dozzell	9.12.67 Ipswich	English	6-1	13-8	416	65	Ipswich T.
Ruel Fox	14.1.68 Ipswich	English	5-6	10-0	281	41	Norwich C, Newcastle U.
David Ginola	25.1.67 Gossin	French	6-0	11-10	54	4	Brest (Fra), Paris SG (Fra) Newcastle U.
David Howells	15.12.67 Guildford	English	5-11	12-4	257	22	none
Allan Nielsen	13.3.71 Denmark	Danish	5-10	11-6	29	6	Brondby (Den).
Andy Sinton	19.3.66 Newcastle	English	5-8	11-5	504	72	Cambs. U, Brentford, QPR, Sheffield W.
FORWARDS							
Rory Allen	17.10.77 Beckenham	English			12	2	none
Chris Armstrong	19.6.71 Newcastle	English	6-0	13-3	254	83	Wrexham, Millwall, Crystal Palace.
Neale Fenn	18.1.77 Edmonton	English	5-10	11-6	4	0	none
Les Ferdinand	18.12.66 Acton	English	5-11	13-5	234	121	QPR, Brentford, Besiktas, Newcastle U
Steffen Iversen	13.7.75 Trondheim	Norwegian	6-2	13-6	16	6	Rosenborg (Nor).
Jose Dominguez	Portugal	Portugese	-	-	0	0	Sporting Lisbon (Por)

Ramon Vega

Spurs have not had much success with foreign players lately. White Hart Lane fell in love with Jurgen Klinsmann during the 1994–95 season, but the German striker was soon on his way back home, leaving chairman Alan Sugar fuming about the uselessness of "Carlos Kickaball". Fans are hoping for better things from Swiss defender Ramon Vega, who arrived last season after an abortive spell with Italian Serie A side Cagliari.

Injuries (the story of Spurs' season) kept him out of the side initially, but Vega has formed a promising three-man central defence with John Scales and Sol Campbell.

Ian Walker

Goalkeeper Ian Walker made his League debut in April 1991 away to Norwich, having joined as a fresh-faced 18-year-old in late 1989. He quickly established himself as first choice at White Hart Lane, edging out Norwegian keeper Erik Thorstvedt. It was not long before Walker's performances for Spurs earned him an international call-up, and he went on to play nine times for England Under-21s, conceding only five goals. Walker's full England debut came when he was brought on as a second-half substitute for David Seaman in England's Euro 96 match against Hungary. He made a second substitute appearance against China before making his first and so far only start, against Italy at Wembley. Walker was criticised at the time for failing to save Gianfranco Zola's shot (the only goal of the game) but it has since emerged that he was not fully fit.

Tottenham's Number One: Spurs and England goalkeeper Ian Walker

West Ham United
The Hammers

West Ham United may be small when compared with the likes of Liverpool and Manchester United, but they continue to play skilful, attractive soccer in the great tradition of the East End "Academy" of football.

Tradition remains important in E13. West Ham have had only eight managers in their history (six since the war), fewer than any other Premier League club. The current boss, Harry Redknapp, was a former player, as was his predecessor Billy Bonds.

Under Redknapp, West Ham have struggled to maintain their top-flight status at times, but last season the Hammers survived again, largely thanks to Redknapp's dealings in the transfer market. West Ham broke the bank in a bid for goals, signing strikers John Hartson (from Arsenal) and Paul Kitson (Newcastle) for a combined total of more than £7 million. Redknapp was criticized for paying so much money for two reserve team players, but the gamble paid off, and West Ham lived to fight another day in the Premier League.

The most successful period in the club's history came in the 1960s when, under manager Ron Greenwood, they won the FA Cup for the first time in 1964, followed a year later by the European Cup-winners' Cup. By beating German side 1860 Munich the Hammers became only the second British club to win a European trophy.

Much in demand: Hammers' youngster Danny Williamson joined Everton in August 1997

At that time three West Ham players – Bobby Moore, Geoff Hurst and Martin Peters – were established members of the English national team, and they were Wembley winners again in 1966 when England won the World Cup after famously beating West Germany 4–2 in extra time.

Greenwood became general manager in 1974, before going on to manage England, and was succeeded by John Lyall. In Lyall's first season in charge the Hammers reached the FA Cup Final, where they beat second division Fulham 2–0. A year later Lyall's side reached the Cup-winners' Cup Final, but could not repeat the heroics of 1965, losing to Belgian side Anderlecht.

Up and down

West Ham were relegated from the old first division in 1978, but reached the FA Cup Final as a second-division side in 1980, beating Arsenal 1–0. Promotion back to the top flight followed in 1981, along with a League Cup Final appearance (they lost the replay to Liverpool) and in 1985–86 the Hammers had their best season yet, finishing third in the League behind Everton and champions Liverpool.

Lyall stayed in charge until 1989, when West Ham were relegated. Lou Macari spent a short, unpopular time as manager before the club turned to the services of former captain Billy Bonds. Under Bonds, the Hammers won promotion but were relegated again in 1992 and spent a season outside the new Premier League before returning a year later.

WEST HAM UNITED

Formed: 1895.
Nickname: The Hammers.
Stadium: Boleyn Ground.
Capacity: 25,985.
Address: Green Street, Upton Park, London E13 9AZ.
Phone: 0181 548 2748.
Clubcall: 0891 121165.
Fax: 0181 548 2758.
Website: www.fa-carling.com/club.wh.fc
Manager: Harry Redknapp.

COLOURS

RECORDS

Record Premier League victory:
5–1 (v Sheffield Wednesday, May 3, 1997)
Record Premier League defeat:
5–0 (v Sheffield Wednesday, Dec 18, 1993)
Record transfer fee received:
£4.5 million from Everton for Slaven Bilic, May 1997.
Record transfer fee paid:
£5 million to Arsenal for John Hartson, Feb 1997.
Record attendance:
42,322, v Tottenham Hotspur, Division 1, Oct 17, 1970.

HONOURS

League: 3rd place 1985-86.
FA Cup (3): 1964, 1975, 1980.
League Cup: runners-up 1966, 1981.
European Cup-winners' Cup (1): 1965.

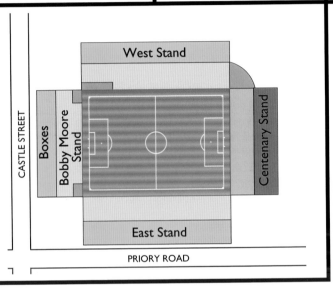

FIXTURES 1997–98

9 AUG	BARNSLEY	A	___ : ___
13 AUG	TOTTENHAM HOTSPUR	H	___ : ___
23 AUG	EVERTON	A	___ : ___
27 AUG	COVENTRY CITY	A	___ : ___
30 AUG	WIMBLEDON	H	___ : ___
13 SEPT	MANCHESTER UNITED	A	___ : ___
20 SEPT	NEWCASTLE UNITED	H	___ : ___
23 SEPT	ARSENAL	A	___ : ___
27 SEPT	LIVERPOOL	H	___ : ___
4 OCT	SOUTHAMPTON	A	___ : ___
18 OCT	BOLTON	H	___ : ___
27 OCT	LEICESTER CITY	A	___ : ___
3 NOV	CRYSTAL PALACE	H	___ : ___
8 NOV	CHELSEA	A	___ : ___
23 NOV	LEEDS UNITED	A	___ : ___
29 NOV	ASTON VILLA	H	___ : ___
6 DEC	DERBY COUNTY	A	___ : ___
13 DEC	SHEFFIELD WEDNESDAY	H	___ : ___
20 DEC	BLACKBURN ROVERS	A	___ : ___
26 DEC	COVENTRY CITY	H	___ : ___
28 DEC	WIMBLEDON	A	___ : ___
10 JAN	BARNSLEY	H	___ : ___
17 JAN	TOTTENHAM HOTSPUR	A	___ : ___
31 JAN	EVERTON	H	___ : ___
7 FEB	NEWCASTLE UNITED	A	___ : ___
14 FEB	MANCHESTER UNITED	H	___ : ___
21 FEB	BOLTON	A	___ : ___
28 FEB	ARSENAL	H	___ : ___
7 MAR	CRYSTAL PALACE	A	___ : ___
14 MAR	CHELSEA	H	___ : ___
28 MAR	LEEDS UNITED	H	___ : ___
4 APR	ASTON VILLA	A	___ : ___
11 APR	DERBY COUNTY	H	___ : ___
13 APR	SHEFFIELD WEDNESDAY	A	___ : ___
18 APR	BLACKBURN ROVERS	H	___ : ___
25 APR	SOUTHAMPTON	H	___ : ___
2 MAY	LIVERPOOL	A	___ : ___
10 MAY	LEICESTER CITY	A	___ : ___

Redknapp moves in

Bonds gave way to his assistant and former team-mate Harry Redknapp in August 1994. Redknapp has been a sharp operator in the transfer market, particularly overseas. Croatian defender Slaven Bilic arrived from Germany and formed a solid partnership with Danish defender Marc Rieper, and midfielder John Moncur brought his passing ability from Swindon. Julian Dicks returned from his short spell at Liverpool and another former Hammers favourite, Tony Cottee, arrived from Everton.

Other signings were not so successful. Don Hutchison, a record £1.5 million buy from Liverpool, was sold to Sheffield United after failing to settle, and the money was used to buy Romanian World Cup star Ilie Dumitrescu. Fellow Romanian Florin Raducioiu arrived last summer from Spain but fell out with Redknapp. With Portuguese stars Paulo Futre and Hugo Porfirio, Northern Ireland's Michael Hughes and Australians Robbie Slater and Stan Lazaridis joining veteran Czech goalkeeper Ludek Miklosko, the Hammers had a seriously cosmopolitan feel to them last season.

However, the foreign influence failed to yield the desired results, especially on the goalscoring front, and by Christmas Redknapp had offloaded a number of his foreign legion and later splashed out on two British forwards Hartson and Kitson. With the money from Slaven Bilic's £4.5 million move to Everton available, more arrivals, such as Israeli Eyal Berkovic, are guaranteed at Upton Park.

PREMIER LEAGUE TABLES

SEASON	POS.	P	W	D	L	F	A	PTS	TOP SCORER	AV. GATE
1993-94	13th	42	13	13	16	47	58	52	Morley (13)	20,572
1994-95	14th	42	13	11	18	44	48	50	Cottee (13)	20,118
1995-96	10th	38	14	9	15	48	52	51	Cottee/Dicks (10)	22,340
1996-97	14th	38	10	12	16	39	48	42	Kitson (8)	36,578

Frank Lampard (Junior)

West Ham have always had a knack for producing talented young players. Some of England's finest – Bobby Moore, Geoff Hurst, Trevor Brooking – have graduated from West Ham's Academy down the years. However, in recent times West Ham have lost out to North London rivals Arsenal and Tottenham in the race to recruit local schoolboy talent. Frank Lampard, Danny Williamson (now at Everton) and Rio Ferdinand are proof that the production line is up and running again.

Midfielder Lampard was born in Romford, and is the son of the former Hammers' full–back of the same name, and also the nephew of Harry Redknapp. Frank notched up 13 appearances for West Ham last season, a figure that would have been higher but for a broken leg sustained against Aston Villa in March. However, in the opening game of the 1997–98 season, Frank erased that unhappy memory by scoring the winner against Barnsley.

Paul Kitson

Just as John Hartson was edged out of Highbury by Dennis Bergkamp, so the arrival of Alan Shearer and Faustino Asprilla at St James' Park reduced Paul Kitson's first-team opportunities at Newcastle United. In almost two-and-a-half years in the north-east, Kitson made just 26 first-team starts.

Top Scorer: striker Paul Kitson

Kitson was signed by Kevin Keegan from Derby County for £2.25 million in September 1994, having started his career with Leicester City. But with Shearer, Asprilla and Les Ferdinand ahead of him in the pecking order, 26-year-old Kitson found himself on the bench...if he was lucky. New manager Kenny Dalglish even dropped him from the first-team squad.

So the £2.3 million move south to London made sense for Kitson, who quickly established an effective partnership with Hartson, and Newcastle were later to rue his departure when they lost strikers through injury. With Hartson acting as a more traditional target man, Kitson grabbed eight League goals to finish the season as the Hammers' top scorer.

John Hartson

More than a few eyebrows were raised last February when Harry Redknapp smashed West Ham's transfer record to sign striker John Hartson from Arsenal. Yet the £5 million turned out to be money well spent. West Ham were stuck in the relegation zone before Hartson arrived, but his five goals, and those of Paul Kitson, helped the Hammers to finish the season comfortably clear of trouble.

The 22-year-old Welshman was languishing in Arsenal's reserves following the arrival of Dennis Bergkamp. New manager Arsène Wenger had given him few first-team opportunities, so he jumped at the chance to revive his career in East London.

Hartson has always been a promising player. He was Britain's most expensive teenager when George Graham signed him from Luton Town for £2.5 million in January 1995. The move to West Ham has also revived ginger-haired Hartson's international career – he scored the only goal in Wales' friendly win over Scotland last May.

Julian Dicks

West Ham captain Julian Dicks is not entirely happy with his image as one of the hardest men in English football. Dicks played four times for England Under-21s, but was sent off in one of those games, and he has found it hard to shake off the 'hard man'

Money Well Spent: John Hartson's goals kept West Ham up

Player Records

	BORN	NATIONALITY	HEIGHT	WEIGHT	APPS	GOALS	PREVIOUS TEAMS
GOALKEEPERS							
Ludek Miklosko	9.12.61 Ostrava	Czech	6-5	14-0	302	0	Banik Ostrava (Cze).
Craig Forrest	20.9.67 Vancouver	Canadian	6-4	14-4	0	0	Ipswich T, Colchester U.
DEFENDERS							
Mark Bowen	7.12.63 Neath	Welsh	5-8	11-7	340	1	Tottenham H, Norwich C.
Tim Breacker	2.7.65 Bicester	English	5-11	13-0	428	11	Luton T.
Julian Dicks	8.8.68 Bristol	English	5-10	13-0	366	54	Birmingham C, West Ham U, Liverpool.
Rio Ferdinand	7.11.78 London	English	6-2	12-0	16	2	none
Richard Hall	14.3.72 Ipswich	English	6-2	13-11	155	15	Scunthorpe U, Southampton.
Steve Potts	7.5.67 Hartford, Connecticut	English	5-7	10-11	354	27	none
Marc Rieper	5.6.68 Denmark	Danish	6-3	14-0	85	4	Brondby (Den).
MIDFIELDERS							
Eyal Berkovic	2.4.72 Haifa	Israeli	5-8	10-6	28	4	Southampton.
Ian Bishop	29.5.65 Liverpool	English	5-9	10-12	452	30	Everton, Crewe Alex, Carlisle U, Bournemouth, Manchester C.
Michael Hughes	2.8.71 Larne	Northern Irish	5-7	10-13	104	6	Manchester C, Strasbourg (Fra)
Andrew Impey	13.9.71 London	English	5-8	11-2	187	13	Queens Park Rangers.
John Moncur	22.9.66 Stepney	English	5-7	9-10	181	11	Tottenham H.
Frank Lampard	21.6.78 Romford	English	6-0	13-7	24	1	Swansea C.
Stan Lazaridis	16.8.72 Perth	Australian	5-9	11-12	26	1	West Adelaide (Aus).
Steve Lomas	18.1.74 Hanover	Northern Irish	6-0	11-9	118	8	Manchester C.
Keith Rowland	1.9.71 Portadown	Northern Irish	5-10	10-0	146	3	Bournemouth, Coventry C.
David Terrier	4.8.73 Verdun	French	5-11	11-8	0	0	Metz.
David Unsworth	16.10.73 Chorley	English	6-0	13-0	116	11	Everton
FORWARDS							
Iain Dowie	9.1.65 Hatfield	Northern Irish	6-1	13-7	280	65	Luton T, Fulham, West Ham U. Southampton, Crystal Palace.
John Hartson	5.4.75 Swansea	Welsh	6-1	14-6	118	30	Luton T, Arsenal.
Paul Kitson	9.1.71 Murton	English	5-10	10-12	205	60	Leicester C, Derby Co, Newcastle U.

tag. He still has serious ambitions to play for England and his performances for the Hammers last season will have done his international prospects nothing but good. Although he will miss the start of the new season because of a knee operation, when he returns expect him to be as effective as he was in 1996–97.

The OPTA index, as used by Sky Sports and *The Observer*, rated Dicks the best defender in last year's Premier League, a remarkable achievement considering his team finished the campaign in 14th place. His forward play, as well as his defensive work, is a vital part of West Ham's play – Dicks finished the season as the Hammers' second-highest scorer. What's more, since his sending-off against Arsenal in September 1995, the eighth red card of his career, he has not been sent off.

Dicks is now happy back at West Ham after an unsuccessful spell at Liverpool. He was signed by Graeme Souness but soon fell out with new boss Roy Evans, who criticized him for being overweight and out of condition. The full-back played just 24 League games for the Anfield side before Harry Redknapp stepped in and set up a return to Upton Park.

Captain's Example: Julian Dicks celebrates with Mark Bowen

Wimbledon
The Dons

Wimbledon are one of the most dramatic success stories to have gripped English football in the past 20 years. Since they entered the Football League in 1977, the South London side have surpassed all the wildest dreams of their supporters, winning the FA Cup in 1988 and surviving in the top division for more than a decade.

Despite their humble beginnings, Wimbledon's history goes back more than 100 years to the days of the Wimbledon Old Centrals, who played their home games on Wimbledon Common. For 75 years Wimbledon were one of London's top amateur sides. They beat Sutton United at Wembley to win the 1962 Amateur Cup and came to national prominence in 1975 when they beat first division Burnley in the third round of the FA Cup and took Leeds United to a replay in the fourth round.

Following three straight Southern League titles, the Dons gained election to the Football League in 1977 and entered the old fourth division. Under manager Dario Gradi, Wimbledon won promotion to the third division in 1979, only to be relegated immediately. The same fate awaited new manager Dave "Harry" Bassett, as the Dons went up in 1981, down in 1982, but then, crucially, up again in 1983. Since then, there has been no stopping them.

Bassett's men won promotion to the second division in 1984, and by 1986 they had made it to the top flight. From non-League to first division in nine years was a remarkable achievement which will probably never be equalled.

Bassett moved on in 1987, by which time Lebanese businessman Sam Hammam was the club's chairman. It was love at first sight for Hammam, who had not been interested in football before he visited Plough Lane. Under Bassett, Wimbledon's long-ball style attracted more than its fair share of critics, but the "Crazy Gang" tag which replaced the Wombles image only spurred the club on to greater things. New manager Bobby Gould led the Dons to their proudest moment, the 1988 FA Cup Final. At Wembley, the Crazy Gang famously overcame Liverpool's Culture Club thanks to Lawrie Sanchez, who scored the only goal of the game, and goalkeeper and captain Dave Beasant, who saved a penalty from John Aldridge.

Gould was succeeded by Ray Harford, Peter Withe and then Joe Kinnear, but Wimbledon continued to hold their own in the top flight, despite a move from their cramped Plough Lane home to share Selhurst Park with Crystal Palace in 1991. However, attendances at their temporary home are such that money was often tight. Dennis Wise, Vinnie Jones, Dave Beasant, Terry Phelan, John Scales, Keith Curle and Warren Barton were just some of the players sold to make ends meet. In came cut-price replacements like Robbie Earle, Oyvind Leonhardsen and Marcus Gayle, as well as such home-grown talent as defender Chris Perry.

Last season was a watershed for the Dons. The club did not

Bargain Buy: Marcus Gayle was signed for a song from Brentford

WIMBLEDON

Formed: 1889.
Nickname: The Dons.
Stadium: Selhurst Park.
Address: Selhurst Park,
South Norwood,
London SE25 6PY.
Telephone: 0181 771 2233.
Clubcall: 0891 121175.
Fax: 0181 768 0640.
Email: www.fa-carling.com/club.w.fc
Manager: Joe Kinnear.

COLOURS

RECORDS

Record Premier League victory:
4–0 (v Crystal Palace, April 9, 1993; v Everton, Sept 7, 1996).
Record Premier League defeat:
7–1 (v Aston Villa, Feb 11, 1995).
Record transfer fee received:
£4 million from Newcastle for Warren Barton, June 1995.
Record transfer fee paid:
£2 million to Millwall for Ben Thatcher, June 1996.
Record attendance:
30,115 v Manchester United, FA Premier League, May 9, 1993.

HONOURS

League: best season 6th, 1993-94.
FA Cup (1): 1988.
League Cup: semi-finalists 1997.

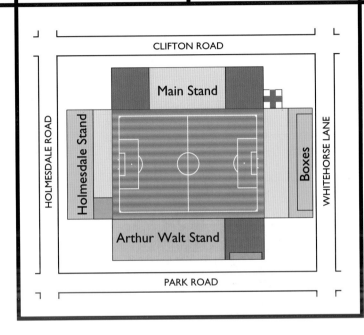

FIXTURES 1997–98

Date	Opponent	H/A	Score
9 AUG	LIVERPOOL	H	___ : ___
13 AUG	DERBY COUNTY	A	___ : ___
23 AUG	SHEFFIELD WEDNESDAY	H	___ : ___
26 AUG	CHELSEA	H	___ : ___
30 AUG	WEST HAM UNITED	A	___ : ___
13 SEPT	NEWCASTLE UNITED	A	___ : ___
20 SEPT	CRYSTAL PALACE	H	___ : ___
23 SEPT	BARNSLEY	H	___ : ___
27 SEPT	TOTTENHAM HOTSPUR	A	___ : ___
4 OCT	BLACKBURN ROVERS	H	___ : ___
18 OCT	ASTON VILLA	A	___ : ___
25 OCT	LEEDS UNITED	H	___ : ___
1 NOV	COVENTRY CITY	H	___ : ___
10 NOV	LEICESTER CITY	A	___ : ___
22 NOV	MANCHESTER UNITED	H	___ : ___
29 NOV	BOLTON	A	___ : ___
7 DEC	SOUTHAMPTON	H	___ : ___
13 DEC	EVERTON	A	___ : ___
22 DEC	ARSENAL	H	___ : ___
26 DEC	CHELSEA	A	___ : ___
28 DEC	WEST HAM UNITED	H	___ : ___
10 JAN	LIVERPOOL	A	___ : ___
17 JAN	DERBY COUNTY	H	___ : ___
31 JAN	SHEFFIELD WEDNESDAY	A	___ : ___
7 FEB	CRYSTAL PALACE	A	___ : ___
14 FEB	NEWCASTLE UNITED	H	___ : ___
21 FEB	ASTON VILLA	H	___ : ___
28 FEB	BARNSLEY	A	___ : ___
7 MAR	COVENTRY CITY	A	___ : ___
14 MAR	LEICESTER CITY	H	___ : ___
28 MAR	MANCHESTER UNITED	A	___ : ___
4 APR	BOLTON	H	___ : ___
11 APR	SOUTHAMPTON	A	___ : ___
13 APR	EVERTON	H	___ : ___
18 APR	ARSENAL	A	___ : ___
25 APR	BLACKBURN ROVERS	A	___ : ___
2 MAY	TOTTENHAM HOTSPUR	H	___ : ___
10 MAY	LEEDS UNITED	A	___ : ___

have to sell any players in the summer of 1996 and instead splashed out a record £1.84 million on Ben Thatcher. Defeats in their opening three League games had the critics claiming that this would be the season that Wimbledon would be found out, but Joe Kinnear's men surprised everyone and by Christmas it was clear that they would be challenging for honours come the end of the season.

Kinnear's men finished eighth in the League, a remarkable achievement for a club with such limited resources. The Dons reached two Cup semi-finals (beating holders Aston Villa on the way in the Coca-Cola Cup and Manchester United in the FA Cup) but were swamped by fixtures and their good chance of a first European campaign through a high League placing or a Cup win was missed after looking probable for much of the season. The fighting spirit is still there, but the direct route football has been replaced by a more thoughtful, passing game.

Oyvind Leonhardsen was the latest player to be sold to make ends meet, moving to Liverpool for £3.5 million, but could be the last to be put on the market after two Norwegian businessmen promised to invest heavily in the club. Wimbledon insist they would still like to move back to the London Borough of Merton, and it is unlikely that Sam Hammam's plan to move the Dons to Dublin will ever see the light of day.

PREMIER LEAGUE TABLES

SEASON	POS.	P	W	D	L	F	A	PTS	TOP SCORER	AV. GATE
1992–93	12th	42	14	12	16	56	55	54	Holdsworth 19	8,405
1993–94	6th	42	18	11	13	56	53	65	Holdsworth 17	10,474
1994–95	9th	42	15	11	16	48	65	56	Ekoku 9	10,230
1995–96	14th	38	10	11	17	55	70	41	Earle 11	13,246
1996–97	8th	38	15	11	12	49	46	56	Ekoku 11	15,141

Robbie Earle

By today's prices, the £775,000 Wimbledon paid Port Vale to sign Robbie Earle in July 1991 seems like an absolute bargain. The attacking midfielder was one of the most impressive performers in Wimbledon's League and Cup exploits last season and it was a mystery to many why Glenn Hoddle did not call Earle up to the England squad.

It is possible that if he was playing for a more glamorous club, Robbie Earle would have received the international call-up long ago. He looked all set to move to a bigger club in 1994, but injury wiped out the 1994–95 season and he was restricted to just nine appearances.

He returned to form the following season, scoring 11 League goals from midfield. Goals are one of 32-year-old Earle's major strengths – he finished his first season with the Dons as top scorer and his powerful, well-timed runs from midfield have been a major source of goals for Wimbledon ever since. Earle looks set to stay at Wimbledon for the rest of his playing career, and he is busy carving out a future for himself as a media pundit.

Chris Perry

Over the years Wimbledon have had to sell their best players to wealthier clubs just to make ends meet. But their survival in the top flight has owed as much to their unnerving ability to unearth stars in their own ranks. Defender Chris Perry is one such case.

Perry, a local lad from nearby Carshalton, supported the Dons as a boy and chose to train with them as an associated schoolboy in 1987 despite interest from other, bigger clubs. He became a trainee in 1989 and signed as a professional in 1991. Perry broke into the first team towards the end of the 1993–94 season and soon became a regular choice for manager Joe Kinnear.

Last season, Perry attracted praise from all quarters for his performances for the Dons. There were calls for him to be included in the England squad, and he capped a fine season by being shortlisted for the PFA Young Player of the Year award.

Young Talent: defender Chris Perry was a regular for the Dons in the 1996–97 season

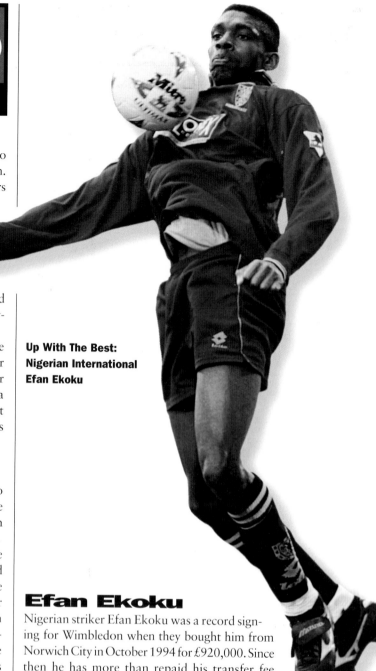

Up With The Best: Nigerian International Efan Ekoku

Efan Ekoku

Nigerian striker Efan Ekoku was a record signing for Wimbledon when they bought him from Norwich City in October 1994 for £920,000. Since then he has more than repaid his transfer fee with some crucial goals and last season Ekoku was the Dons' top scorer with 11 League goals.

The big forward, who was a member of Nigeria's 1994 World Cup squad, started his professional career with Bournemouth, before moving to Norwich in 1993 for £500,000.

Marcus Gayle

Wimbledon have made a habit of taking players from the lower leagues and turning them into accomplished Premier League performers. Forward Marcus Gayle is the latest to get the Wimbledon career-enhancing treatment.

Hammersmith-born Gayle, a former England youth international, spent six seasons with Brentford before joining Wimbledon for £250,000 in March 1994. At first the Dons used 26-year-old Gayle as a winger without any great success, but last season he came into his own as a striker. He scored a memorable goal against Chelsea and played well enough to keep first-choice forward Dean Holdsworth out of the side.

Player Records

	BORN	NATIONALITY	HEIGHT	WEIGHT	APPS	GOALS	PREVIOUS TEAMS
GOALKEEPERS							
Paul Heald	20.9.68 Wath on Dearne	English	6-2	12-5	200	0	Sheffield U, Leyton Orient, Coventry C, Crystal Palace, Swindon T.
Neil Sullivan	24.2.70 Sutton	Scottish	6-0	12-1	69	0	Crystal Palace.
DEFENDERS							
Dean Blackwell	5.12.69 Camden	English	6-1	12-10	126	1	Plymouth Argyle.
Kenny Cunningham	28.6.71 Dublin	Irish	5-11	11-2	233	1	Millwall.
Gary Elkins	4.5.66 Wallingford	English	5-9	11-13	219	5	Fulham, Exeter C.
Duncan Jupp	25.1.75 Guildford	English	6-0	12-11	111	2	Fulham.
Alan Kimble	6.8.66 Poole	English	5-10	12-4	408	24	Charlton Ath, Exeter C, Cambridge U.
Brian McAllister	30.11.70 Glasgow	Scottish	5-11	12-5	99	1	Plymouth Argyle, Crewe Alex.
Chris Perry	26.4.73 London	English	5-8	10-8	98	1	none
Alan Reeves	19.11.67 Birkenhead	English	6-0	12-0	236	15	Norwich C, Gillingham, Chester C, Rochdale.
Ben Thatcher	30.11.75 Swindon	English	5-11	12-7	99	1	Millwall.
MIDFIELDERS							
Neil Ardley	1.9.72 Epsom	English	5-11	11-9	106	8	none
Stewart Castledine	22.1.73 Wandsworth	English	6-1	12-13	28	7	Wycombe W.
Andy Clarke	22.7.67 Islington	English	5-10	11-7	154	17	Barnet
Robbie Earle	27.1.65 Newcastle-under-Lyme	English	5-9	10-10	396	125	Port Vale
Jason Euell	6.2.77 South London	English	5-11	11-2	16	4	none
Peter Fear	10.9.73 London	English	5-10	11-7	62	2	none
Ceri Hughes	26.2.71 Pontypridd	Welsh	5-10	11-6	0	0	Luton T.
Vinnie Jones	5.1.65 Watford	Welsh	6-0	11-12	353	32	Wimbledon, Leeds U, Sheffield U, Chelsea.
FORWARDS							
Efan Ekoku	8.6.67 Manchester	Nigerian	6-1	12-0	183	63	Bournemouth, Norwich C.
Marcus Gayle	27.9.70 Hammersmith	English	6-1	12-9	258	37	Brentford.
Jon Goodman	2.6.71 Walthamstow	English	6-0	12-3	168	46	Millwall.
Mick Harford	12.2.59 Sunderland	English	6-3	14-5	582	186	Lincoln C, Newcastle U, Bristol C, Birmingham C, Luton T, Derby Co, Luton T, Chelsea, Sunderland, Coventry C.
Dean Holdsworth	8.11.68 Walthamstow	English	5-11	11-13	312	119	Watford, Carlisle U, Port Vale, Swansea C, Brentford.

Vinnie Jones

There is more to Wimbledon than their "Crazy Gang" image suggests, just as there is more to Vinnie Jones than his "hard man" tag. At the end of last season, the Dons' captain signed a new contract to stay at the club, ending speculation that he would launch a legal challenge to bring down English football's transfer system.

Vinnie Jones has always been happier on a football pitch than in a court room, even if opposing teams are never too pleased to see him. Jones says referees target him because of his reputation, but his style

Over The Top: Wimbledon Regular Vinnie Jones

has always been aggressive and intimidating. He has been sent off 12 times in his career, and was even shown the red card while playing for Wales, his adopted country.

Jones joined the Dons from non-League Wealdstone in November 1986 and was a key member of the side which won the FA Cup in 1988. Jones had spells with Leeds United, where he helped win promotion to the old first division, Sheffield United and Chelsea, before returning to Wimbledon in September 1992.

Premier League Records

Not surprisingly, Manchester United are the most successful club in the history of the Premier League. United, champions four times in five Premier League seasons, also hold the record for most points in a season, most wins, fewest goals conceded, biggest win and most goals for.

Single Season Records

MOST GOALS FOR:	Newcastle United (1993–94): 82
FEWEST GOALS FOR:	Leeds United (1996–97): 28
MOST GOALS AGAINST:	Swindon Town (1993–94): 100
FEWEST GOALS AGAINST:	Arsenal (1993–94), Manchester United (1994–95): 28
MOST POINTS:	Manchester United (1993–94): 92
FEWEST POINTS:	Ipswich Town (1994–95): 27
BEST START:	Nottingham Forest (1995–96): 12 games undefeated
WORST START:	Swindon Town (1993–94): 15 games without a win
MOST WINS:	Manchester United (1993–94), Blackburn Rovers (1994–95): 27
FEWEST WINS:	Swindon Town (1993–94): 5
MOST DEFEATS:	Ipswich Town (1994–95): 29
FEWEST DEFEATS:	Manchester United (1993–94): 4
MOST CLEAN SHEETS:	Manchester United (1994–95): 24
FEWEST CLEAN SHEETS:	Ipswich Town (1994–95): 3
BEST AVERAGE ATTENDANCE:	Manchester United (1996–97): 55,081
WORST AVERAGE ATTENDANCE:	Wimbledon (1992–93): 8,405
FIRST SIDE TO FINISH SEASON UNBEATEN AT HOME:	Manchester United (1995–96)

Overall Records

BIGGEST WIN:	Manchester United v Ipswich Town (March 4, 1995): 9–0
BIGGEST AWAY WIN:	Sheffield Wednesday v Blackburn Rovers (March 2, 1995): 1–7
MOST GOALS FOR:	Manchester United: 373
FEWEST GOALS FOR:	Bolton Wanderers: 39
MOST GOALS AGAINST:	Southampton: 298
MOST POINTS:	Manchester United: 421
FEWEST POINTS:	Bolton: 29
MOST WINS:	Manchester United: 123
MOST DRAWS:	Coventry City: 69
MOST DEFEATS:	Southampton: 88
LONGEST UNBEATEN RUN:	Nottingham Forest (February 21, 1995 – November 18, 1995): 25 games
LONGEST UNBEATEN HOME RUN:	Manchester United (December 17, 1994 – November 2, 1996): 36 games
LONGEST UNBEATEN AWAY RUN:	Manchester United (October 8, 1994 – February 25, 1995): 10 games
HIGHEST AVERAGE ATTENDANCE:	Manchester United: 43,971
LOWEST AVERAGE ATTENDANCE:	Wimbledon: 11,499
HIGHEST ATTENDANCE:	Manchester United v Middlesbrough (May 5, 1997): 55,489
LOWEST ATTENDANCE:	Wimbledon v Coventry (November 11, 1995): 4,578

Individual Records

MOST GOALS:	Alan Shearer (Blackburn Rovers and Newcastle United): 137
MOST HAT-TRICKS:	Alan Shearer (Blackburn Rovers and Newcastle United): 7
MOST GOALS IN ONE GAME:	Andy Cole (Manchester United v Ipswich Town, March 4, 1995): 5
MOST GOALS IN ONE AWAY GAME:	Efan Ekoku (Norwich City, at Everton September 25, 1993): 4
MOST GOALS IN ONE SEASON:	Andy Cole (1993–94), Alan Shearer (1994–95): 34
YOUNGEST PLAYER:	Andy Turner (Tottenham Hotspur): 17 years, 145 days
YOUNGEST SCORER:	Andy Turner (Tottenham Hotspur): 17 years, 166 days

Season-by-season – Premier League average attendances

Team	1992–93	1993–94	1994–95	1995–96	1996–97	Ave
ARSENAL	24,403	30,563	35,330	37,568	37,821	33,137
ASTON VILLA	29,594	29,015	29,756	32,614	36,027	31,401
BLACKBURN ROVERS	16,246	17,721	25,272	27,716	24,947	22,380
BOLTON WANDERERS				18,822		18,822
CHELSEA	18,787	19,416	21,057	25,486	27,617	22,469
COVENTRY CITY	14,951	13,352	15,980	18,507	19,608	16,480
CRYSTAL PALACE	15,748		14,922			15,370
DERBY COUNTY					17,888	17,888
EVERTON	20,447	22,876	31,291	35,435	36,188	29,050
IPSWICH TOWN	18,223	16,382	16,818			17,141
LEEDS UNITED	29,250	34,493	32,925	32,528	32,117	32,273
LEICESTER CITY			19,532		20,184	19,858
LIVERPOOL	37,004	38,493	34,176	39,553	39,776	37,796
MANCHESTER CITY	24,698	26,709	22,725	27,869		25,500
MANCHESTER UTD	35,152	44,244	43,681	41,700	55,081	43,971
MIDDLESBROUGH	16,724			29,283	29,871	25,293
NEWCASTLE UNITED		33,679	34,690	36,507	36,467	35,328
NORWICH CITY	16,154	18,164	18,625			17,648
NOTTINGHAM FOR	21,910		23,633	25,916	24,587	24,053
OLDHAM ATHLETIC	12,859	12,563				12,711
QPR	15,015	14,228	14,613	15,683		14,975
SHEFFIELD UNITED	18,801	19,562				19,182
SHEFFIELD WEDS	27,264	27,191	26,572	24,877	25,714	26,264
SOUTHAMPTON	15,382	14,751	14,685	14,819	15,105	14,948
SUNDERLAND					20,973	20,973
SWINDON TOWN		15,274				15,274
TOTTENHAM HOTS	27,740	27,160	27,259	30,510	31,067	28,747
WEST HAM UNITED		20,572	20,118	22,340	23,242	21,568
WIMBLEDON	8,405	10,474	10,230	13,246	15,141	11,499

Overall Premier League Records (1992–93 to 1996–97)

Team	P	W	D	L	F	A	Pts
MANCHESTER UNITED	202	123	52	27	373	176	421
BLACKBURN ROVERS	202	99	50	53	314	211	347
LIVERPOOL	202	93	53	56	318	218	332
ARSENAL	202	82	63	57	256	179	309
ASTON VILLA	202	82	57	63	253	215	303
NEWCASTLE UNITED	160	86	37	37	288	165	295
LEEDS UNITED	202	73	64	65	249	234	283
TOTTENHAM HOTSPUR	202	72	57	73	274	272	273
WIMBLEDON	202	72	56	74	264	289	272
SHEFFIELD WEDNESDAY	202	68	67	67	278	274	271
CHELSEA	202	68	66	68	254	261	270
EVERTON	202	65	55	82	247	270	250
COVENTRY CITY	202	56	69	77	219	278	237
SOUTHAMPTON	202	56	58	88	248	298	226
QUEENS PARK RANGERS	164	59	39	66	224	232	216
NOTTINGHAM FOREST	160	53	50	57	194	218	209
WEST HAM UNITED	160	50	45	65	173	206	195
MANCHESTER CITY	164	45	54	65	180	222	189
NORWICH CITY	126	43	39	44	163	180	168
MIDDLESBROUGH*	118	32	33	53	140	185	126
IPSWICH TOWN	126	28	38	60	121	206	122
CRYSTAL PALACE	84	22	28	34	82	110	94
SHEFFIELD UNITED	84	22	28	34	96	113	94
OLDHAM ATHLETIC	84	22	23	39	105	142	89
LEICESTER CITY	80	18	22	40	91	134	76
DERBY COUNTY	38	11	13	14	45	58	46
SUNDERLAND	38	10	10	18	35	53	40
SWINDON TOWN	42	5	15	22	47	100	30
BOLTON WANDERERS	38	8	5	25	39	71	29

* Three points deducted

Premier League Top Scorers by season

1992–93

	Player	Goals
1	TEDDY SHERINGHAM (Nottingham Forest/Tottenham Hotspur)	22
2	LES FERDINAND (Queens Park Rangers)	20
3	DEAN HOLDSWORTH (Wimbledon)	19
	MICK QUINN (Newcastle Utd/Coventry City)	19
5	ALAN SHEARER (Blackburn Rovers)	16
	DAVID WHITE (Manchester City)	16
7	CHRIS ARMSTRONG (Crystal Palace)	15
	ERIC CANTONA (Leeds Utd/Manchester Utd)	15
	BRIAN DEANE (Sheffield United)	15
	MARK HUGHES (Manchester United)	15
	MATT LE TISSIER (Southampton)	15
	MARK ROBINS (Norwich City)	15
	IAN WRIGHT (Arsenal)	15
	LEE CHAPMAN (Leeds United)	14

1993–94

1	ANDY COLE (Newcastle United)	34
2	ALAN SHEARER (Blackburn Rovers)	31
3	MATTHEW LE TISSIER (Southampton)	25
	CHRIS SUTTON (Norwich)	25
5	IAN WRIGHT (Arsenal)	23
6	PETER BEARDSLEY (Newcastle United)	21
7	MARK BRIGHT (Sheffield Wednesday)	19
8	ERIC CANTONA (Manchester United)	18
9	ROD WALLACE (Leeds United)	17
	DEAN HOLDSWORTH (Wimbledon)	17

1994–95

1	ALAN SHEARER (Blackburn Rovers)	34
2	ROBBIE FOWLER (Liverpool)	25
3	LES FERDINAND (Queens Park Rangers)	24
4	STAN COLLYMORE (Nottingham Forest)	22
5	ANDY COLE (Newcastle United/Manchester United)	21
6	JURGEN KLINSMANN (Tottenham Hotspur)	20
7	MATT LE TISSIER (Southampton)	19
8	TEDDY SHERINGHAM (Tottenham Hotspur)	18
	IAN WRIGHT (Arsenal)	18
10	ASHLEY WARD (Crewe A/Norwich City)	16

1995–96

1	ALAN SHEARER (Blackburn Rovers)	31
2	ROBBIE FOWLER (Liverpool)	28
3	LES FERDINAND (Newcastle United)	25
4	DWIGHT YORKE (Aston Villa)	17
5	ANDREI KANCHELSKIS (Everton)	16
	TEDDY SHERINGHAM (Tottenham Hotspur)	16
7	CHRIS ARMSTRONG (Tottenham Hotspur)	15
8	IAN WRIGHT (Arsenal)	15
9	ERIC CANTONA (Manchester United)	14
	STAN COLLYMORE (Liverpool)	14
	DION DUBLIN (Coventry City)	14

1996–97

1	ALAN SHEARER (Newcastle United)	25
2	IAN WRIGHT (Arsenal)	23
3	ROBBIE FOWLER (Liverpool)	18
	OLE-GUNNAR SOLSKJAER (Manchester United)	18
4	DWIGHT YORKE (Aston Villa)	17
5	LES FERDINAND (Newcastle United)	16
	FABRIZIO RAVANELLI (Middlesbrough)	16
7	DION DUBLIN (Coventry City)	14
8	MATT LE TISSIER (Southampton)	13
9	STAN COLLYMORE (Liverpool)	12
	JUNINHO (Middlesbrough)	12
	DENNIS BERGKAMP (Arsenal)	12
	STEVE CLARIDGE (Leicester City)	12

Record-Holder: Newcastle's Alan Shearer is the Premier League's all-time top scorer

Premier League Tables

The complete standings for the five seasons the Premier League has been in existence. Battling Blackburn Rovers knocked double double winners Manchester United off the top spot – the one and only time they have been off it – in the 1994–95 season, but the Red Devils from Old Trafford remain far and away the most successful of the 27 teams who have competed in the five Premier League competitions to date.

1992-93

		P	W	D	L	F	A	PTS
1	MANCHESTER UNITED	42	24	12	6	67	31	84
2	ASTON VILLA	42	21	11	10	57	40	74
3	NORWICH CITY	42	21	9	12	61	65	72
4	BLACKBURN ROVERS	42	20	11	11	68	46	71
5	QUEENS PARK RANGERS	42	17	12	13	61	55	63
6	LIVERPOOL	42	16	11	15	62	55	59
7	SHEFFIELD WEDNESDAY	42	15	14	13	55	51	59
8	TOTTENHAM HOTSPUR	42	16	11	15	60	46	59
9	MANCHESTER CITY	42	15	12	15	56	51	57
10	ARSENAL	42	15	11	16	40	38	56
11	CHELSEA	42	14	14	14	51	54	56
12	WIMBLEDON	42	14	12	16	56	55	54
13	EVERTON	42	15	8	19	53	55	53
14	SHEFFIELD UNITED	42	14	10	18	54	53	52
15	COVENTRY CITY	42	13	13	16	52	57	52
16	IPSWICH TOWN	42	12	16	14	50	55	52
17	LEEDS UNITED	42	12	15	15	57	62	51
18	SOUTHAMPTON	42	13	11	18	54	61	50
19	OLDHAM ATHLETIC	42	13	10	19	63	74	49
20	CRYSTAL PALACE	42	11	16	15	48	61	49
21	MIDDLESBROUGH	42	11	11	20	54	75	44
22	NOTTINGHAM FOREST	42	10	12	15	41	62	40

1993-94

		P	W	D	L	F	A	PTS
1	MANCHESTER UNITED	42	27	11	4	80	38	92
2	BLACKBURN ROVERS	42	25	9	8	63	36	84
3	NEWCASTLE UNITED	42	23	8	11	82	41	77
4	ARSENAL	42	18	17	7	53	28	71
5	LEEDS UNITED	42	18	16	8	65	39	70
6	WIMBLEDON	42	18	11	13	56	53	65
7	SHEFFIELD WEDNESDAY	42	16	16	10	76	54	64
8	LIVERPOOL	42	17	9	16	59	55	60
9	QUEENS PARK RANGERS	42	16	12	14	62	61	60
10	ASTON VILLA	42	15	12	13	46	50	57
11	COVENTRY CITY	42	14	14	14	43	45	56
12	NORWICH CITY	42	12	17	13	65	61	53
13	WEST HAM UNITED	42	13	13	16	47	58	52
14	CHELSEA	42	13	12	19	49	53	51
15	TOTTENHAM HOTSPUR	42	11	12	19	54	59	45
16	MANCHESTER CITY	42	9	18	15	38	47	45
17	EVERTON	42	12	8	22	42	63	44
18	SOUTHAMPTON	42	12	7	23	49	66	43
19	IPSWICH TOWN	42	9	16	17	35	58	43
20	SHEFFIELD UNITED	42	8	18	16	42	60	42
21	OLDHAM ATHLETIC	42	9	13	20	42	68	40
22	SWINDON TOWN	42	5	15	22	47	100	30

1994-95

		P	W	D	L	F	A	PTS
1	BLACKBURN ROVERS	42	27	8	7	80	39	89
2	MANCHESTER UNITED	42	26	10	6	77	28	88
3	NOTTINGHAM FOREST	42	22	11	9	72	43	77
4	LIVERPOOL	42	21	11	10	65	37	74
5	LEEDS UNITED	42	20	13	9	59	38	73
6	NEWCASTLE UNITED	42	20	12	10	67	47	72
7	TOTTENHAM HOTSPUR	42	16	14	12	66	58	62
8	QUEENS PARK RANGERS	42	17	9	16	61	59	60
9	SOUTHAMPTON	42	12	18	12	61	63	54
10	CHELSEA	42	13	15	14	50	55	54
11	ARSENAL	42	13	12	17	52	49	51
12	SHEFFIELD WEDNESDAY	42	13	12	17	49	57	51
13	WIMBLEDON	42	13	11	18	45	49	50
14	WEST HAM UNITED	42	13	11	18	44	48	50
15	EVERTON	42	11	17	14	44	51	50
16	COVENTRY CITY	42	12	14	16	44	62	50
17	MANCHESTER CITY	42	12	13	17	53	64	49
18	ASTON VILLA	42	11	15	16	51	56	48
19	CRYSTAL PALACE	42	11	12	19	34	49	45
20	NORWICH CITY	42	10	13	19	37	54	43
21	LEICESTER CITY	42	6	11	25	45	80	29
22	IPSWICH TOWN	42	7	6	29	36	93	27

(left) Oh Lucky Man: Liverpool's Jamie Redknapp has been unlucky with injuries for both Liverpool and England

(right) Net Result: Arsenal's top scorer for every season of the Premier League, Ian Wright

Pleased To Be Here: Aston Villa's Australian goalkeeper Mark Bosnich

1995–96

		P	W	D	L	F	A	PTS
1	MANCHESTER UNITED	38	25	7	6	73	35	82
2	NEWCASTLE UNITED	38	24	6	8	66	37	78
3	LIVERPOOL	38	20	11	7	70	34	71
4	ASTON VILLA	38	18	9	11	52	35	63
5	ARSENAL	38	17	12	9	49	32	63
6	EVERTON	38	17	10	11	64	44	61
7	BLACKBURN ROVERS	38	18	7	13	61	47	61
8	TOTTENHAM HOTSPUR	38	16	13	9	50	38	61
9	NOTTINGHAM FOREST	38	15	13	10	50	54	58
10	WEST HAM UNITED	38	14	9	15	43	52	51
11	CHELSEA	38	12	14	12	46	44	50
12	MIDDLESBROUGH	38	11	10	17	35	50	43
13	LEEDS UNITED	38	12	7	19	40	57	43
14	WIMBLEDON	38	10	11	17	55	70	41
15	SHEFFIELD WEDNESDAY	38	10	10	18	48	61	40
16	COVENTRY CITY	38	8	14	16	42	60	38
17	SOUTHAMPTON	38	9	11	18	34	52	38
18	MANCHESTER CITY	38	9	11	18	33	58	38
19	QUEENS PARK RANGERS	38	9	6	23	38	57	38
20	BOLTON WANDERERS	38	8	5	25	39	71	29

1996–97

		P	W	D	L	F	A	PTS
1	MANCHESTER UNITED	38	21	12	5	76	44	75
2	NEWCASTLE UNITED	38	19	11	8	73	40	68
3	ARSENAL	38	19	11	8	62	32	68
4	LIVERPOOL	38	19	11	8	62	37	68
5	ASTON VILLA	38	17	10	11	47	34	61
6	CHELSEA	38	16	11	11	58	55	59
7	SHEFFIELD WEDNESDAY	38	14	15	9	50	51	57
8	WIMBLEDON	38	15	11	12	49	46	56
9	LEICESTER CITY	38	12	11	15	46	54	47
10	TOTTENHAM HOTSPUR	38	13	7	18	44	51	46
11	LEEDS UNITED	38	11	13	14	28	38	46
12	DERBY COUNTY	38	11	13	14	45	58	46
13	BLACKBURN ROVERS	38	9	15	14	42	43	42
14	WEST HAM UNITED	38	10	12	16	39	48	42
15	EVERTON	38	10	12	16	44	57	42
16	SOUTHAMPTON	38	10	11	17	50	56	41
17	COVENTRY CITY	38	9	14	15	38	54	41
18	SUNDERLAND	38	10	10	18	35	53	40
19	MIDDLESBROUGH	38	10	12	16	51	60	39
20	NOTTINGHAM FOREST	38	6	16	16	31	59	34

Fixtures 1997-98

For the sixth successive season, the FA Premier League will be shown exclusively live on Sky Sports. Sky have scheduled more live matches than ever before, with 34 televised games confirmed into the New Year.

By the first week in November every FA Premier League club will have been seen on Sky Sports with each club seen at least twice by Christmas. All three newly promoted clubs – Crystal Palace, Barnsley and Bolton Wanderers– will be seen live within the first week of September. A total of 60 FA Carling Premiership fixtures will be shown on Sky in 1997–98, with a further 26 fixtures yet to be announced, including several scheduled before the New Year. Notable dates include:

• **Liverpool vs. Chelsea on Sunday, 5 October – Roy Evans' Reds and Ruud Gullit's Blues battle it out.**

• **Barnsley vs. Chelsea on Sunday, 24 August – the FA Cup holders take on the Premiership's newest team.**

• **Newcastle United vs. Manchester United on Sunday, 21 December – can the Magpies teach the Red Devils a lesson for a second time?**

• **The festive season fixtures see a London Derby as Arsenal play Wimbledon on 22 December, Newcastle vs Liverpool on 28 December, and Aston Villa playing Spurs on Boxing Day.**

The shaded fixtures are those which will be televised live on Sky Sports. Please note that these dates are subject to change. No television dates have been confirmed for 1998 games.

Reproduced under Copyright Licence No. NCH 11197
Copyright © The FA Premier League Limited 1997

	ARSENAL	ASTON VILLA	BARNSLEY	BLACKBURN ROVERS	BOLTON WANDERERS
ARSENAL		26.10	4.10	13.12	13.9
ASTON VILLA	10.5		14.2	13.8	25.4
BARNSLEY	25.4	13.9		1.11	26.8
BLACKBURN ROVERS	13.4	17.1	7.3		6.12
BOLTON WANDERERS	14.2	4.10	26.12	11.4	
CHELSEA	21.9	7.3	31.1	28.3	10.5
COVENTRY CITY	17.1	11.4	21.2	2.5	23.8
CRYSTAL PALACE	18.10	8.11	12.8	30.8	27.9
DERBY COUNTY	1.11	7.2	30.8	10.1	13.4
EVERTON	27.9	28.3	20.9	14.3	28.12
LEEDS UNITED	9.8	28.12	4.4	14.2	20.12
LEICESTER CITY	27.8	9.8	2.5	24.9	22.11
LIVERPOOL	4.4	22.9	22.11	31.1	7.3
MANCHESTER UNITED	14.3	15.12	25.10	29.11	7.2
NEWCASTLE UNITED	6.12	23.8	13.4	25.10	17.1
SHEFFIELD WEDNESDAY	22.11	2.5	8.12	26.12	8.11
SOUTHAMPTON	23.8	18.4	8.11	21.2	9.8
TOTTENHAM HOTSPUR	28.12	27.8	20.12	20.9	28.2
WEST HAM UNITED	28.2	29.11	10.1	18.4	18.10
WIMBLEDON	22.12	21.2	23.9	4.10	4.4

CHELSEA	COVENTRY CITY	CRYSTAL PALACE	DERBY COUNTY	EVERTON	LEEDS UNITED	LEICESTER CITY	LIVERPOOL	MANCHESTER UNITED	NEWCASTLE UNITED	SHEFFIELD WEDNESDAY	SOUTHAMPTON	TOTTENHAM HOTSPUR	WEST HAM UNITED	WIMBLEDON
7.2	11.8	21.2	7.3	2.5	10.1	26.12	29.11	9.11	11.4	28.3	31.1	30.8	23.9	18.4
1.11	6.12	14.3	20.9	22.11	30.8	10.1	28.2	13.4	31.1	27.9	20.12	26.12	4.4	18.10
24.8	20.10	17.1	28.12	7.2	29.11	27.9	28.3	10.5	13.12	11.4	14.3	18.4	9.8	28.2
22.11	28.9	28.12	9.8	8.11	14.9	28.2	23.8	4.4	10.5	25.8	18.10	7.2	20.12	25.4
25.10	31.1	2.5	14.12	1.9	18.4	28.3	1.11	20.9	1.12	14.3	10.1	23.9	21.2	29.11
	10.1	14.2	29.11	26.11	13.12	18.10	25.4	28.2	27.9	18.4	30.8	11.4	8.11	26.12
9.8		24.9	28.3	25.10	4.10	29.11	18.4	28.12	8.11	7.2	13.9	13.12	27.8	7.3
13.9	28.2		18.4	10.1	31.1	11.4	13.12	25.4	29.11	10.5	26.12	28.3	7.3	7.2
4.4	22.11	20.12		13.9	14.3	25.4	10.5	18.10	26.12	28.2	27.9	31.1	6.12	13.8
17.1	10.5	9.8	14.2		11.4	18.4	18.10	27.8	28.2	25.4	2.11	29.11	23.8	13.12
13.4	25.4	23.8	8.11	6.12		20.9	26.8	27.9	18.10	17.1	28.2	7.3	23.11	10.5
21.2	4.4	6.12	4.10	20.12	7.2		17.1	23.8	7.3	28.12	13.4	13.9	27.10	10.11
5.10	20.12	13.4	25.10	21.2	26.12	13.8		6.12	31.8	13.9	7.2	8.11	2.5	10.1
24.9	30.8	4.10	21.2	26.12	2.5	31.1	11.4		18.4	1.11	13.8	10.1	13.9	28.3
2.5	14.3	4.4	17.12	24.9	21.2	1.11	28.12	21.12		9.8	22.11	4.10	7.2	13.9
20.12	20.9	25.10	24.9	4.10	13.8	30.8	14.2	7.3	10.1		4.4	21.2	13.4	31.1
29.12	14.2	27.8	2.5	7.3	24.9	13.12	20.9	17.1	28.3	29.10		25.10	4.10	11.4
6.12	13.4	24.11	23.8	4.4	1.11	14.2	14.3	10.8	25.4	19.10	10.5		17.1	27.9
14.3	26.12	3.11	11.4	31.1	28.3	10.5	27.9	14.2	20.9	13.12	25.4	13.8		30.8
26.8	1.11	20.9	17.1	13.4	25.10	14.3	9.8	22.11	14.2	23.8	7.12	2.5	28.12	

Photograph references are in italics

A

Adams, Tony 10, 11, 14, 44, *45*
Albert, Philippe 12, *12*
Anderton, Darren *110*, 112
Anelka, Nicolas 19,
Arsenal 8, 9, *10*, 11, 12, 14, *15*, 16, 19, 20, 22, 23, 42–5, *125*
Asanovic, Aljosa 76, *76*
Asprilla, Faustino 16, 17
Aston Villa 8, 10, 13, 15, 46–9, *125*
Atherton, Peter 105
Atkinson, Ron 14

B

Babayaro, Celestine 64–5
Barcelona 32, *32*
Barmby, Nick *78*, 80
Barnsley 50–3
Bassett, Dave 21
Batty, David 100
Beardsley, Peter 14,
Beckham, David 9, *9*, 12, 25, *94*, 96
Berger, Patrick 10, 11, *11*, 20
Bergkamp, Dennis 14, 44, *44*
Bilic, Slaven 80–1
Birmingham City 20
Blackburn Rovers 13, 15, 17, 21, 54–7
Blake, Nathan 60, *60*
Blinker, Regi *102*
Blondeau, Patrick 105
Bolton Wanderers 13, 15, *38–9*, 58–61
Booth, Andy 104, *104*
Borussia Dormund 33, *33*
Bosnich, Mark 13, *125*
Bowyer, Lee *82*, 84
Bradford City 18
Brolin, Tomas 19
Bullock, Martin 53

C

Campbell, Kevin 9
Campbell, Sol 112, *112*
Cantona, Eric *8*, 22, 28, 29, *29*
Carbone, Benito 13, 104, *104*
Champions Cup Final 33, *33*
Charlton Athletic 18
Chelsea 9, 11, 13, *14*, 15, 17, 18, 19, *19*, 20–1, 24, 25, 30–1, *30*, 31, 62–5
Chesterfield 21, 22, 24, *24*, 25
Claridge, Steve 25, *27*, 86, 88
Clark, Frank 16, 17
Coca-Cola Cup 11, 12, 13, 15, 18, 22, 25, *25*, 26–7, *26*, 27, 86
Cole, Andy 13, 24
Coppell, Steve 15, 34
Coventry City 9, 15, 17, 18, 66–9
Crystal Palace 21, 28, 29, 34, 35. *34*, *35*, 70–3
Cup-Winners Cup Final 32, *32*

Curcic, Sasa 9
Curle, Keith *35*

D

Dalglish, Kenny 18
Davies, Kevin 109
De Zeeuw, Arjan 53, *53*
Del Piero, Alessandro 33
Derby County 22, 74–7
Di Matteo, Roberto 30, 31
Dicks, Julian 116–7, *117*
Draper, Mark 48–9, *48*
Dublin, Dion 66, 68
Dyer, Bruce *35*, *70*, 72

E

Earle, Robbie 120
Ehiogu, Ugo 46, 48
Ekoku, Efan 120, *120*
Elliott, Robbie 60, *100*
Emerson 17, *26*, 30, *31*
England 11, 13, *13*, 15, 20, *20*, 21, 22, 28, 29
Eranio, Stefanio 77
Ericksson, Sven-Goran 17, 21
Evans, Roy 11, *11*, 16
Everton 11, 15, 78–81

F

FA Charity Shield 8, *40*
FA Cup 18, 19, 20–1, 22, 23, 24, 25, 28, 29, 30–1, *30*
Ferdinand, Les 13, 15, 111, 113
Ferguson, Alex 14, 16, 19, *19*, 21, 23, 29
Ferguson, Duncan 80, *80*
Fernando Couto 32
Festa, Gianluca *27*
Flo, Tor Andre 65
Flowers, Tim *54*, 56.
Fowler, Robbie 16, *16*, 20, 22, 23, *23*, 24, 40, *90*, 92
Francis, Gerry 18
Freedman, Dougie 73, *73*

G

Gallacher, Kevin 56, *56*
Gayle, Marcus 118, 120
Giggs, Ryan 22, *22*, 96–7, *97*
Ginola, David 13, 111, 113
Gordon, Dean 72, *72*
Graham, George 11, 17, *85*
Green, Scott 58
Gullit, Ruud 13, *14*, 15, 31

H

Halle, Gunnar 17, 84, *84*
Harford, Ray 13
Hartson, John 21, 116, *116*
Hedman, Magnus 67, 69
Henchoz, Stephane 55, 57
Hendrie, John *50*, 52
Heskey, Emile 26, *26*, 88, *88*
Hinchcliffe, Andy *80*, 81
Hoddle, Glenn 11, 13, 15, 20
Hodgson, Roy 21

Hopkin, David *34*, 35
Houston, Stewart 10, 11
Huckerby, Darren 15, 17, 68, *68*
Hughes, Mark *62*, 64
Hutchison, Don 35

I

Ipswich Town 35
Italy 20, *20*, 21
Iversen, Steffen 15, 112, *112*

J

James, David 24
Johansen, Martin 67, 69
Johnsen, Erland 21
Jones, Vinnie 121, *121*
Juninho 22, *25*, 26, 27, 30, 31
Juventus 33

K

Kaamark, Pontus 27
Katchuro, Petr 35
Keane, Roy 21, 96, *96*
Keegan, Kevin 12, *17*, 18, *18*, 19
Keller, Kasey 88, *88*
Kelly, Gary 85
Kinnear, Joe *13*
Kitson, Paul 21, 116, *116*
Kvarme, Bjorn 19

L

Lampard, Frank 116
Laursen, Jacob 77
Le Tissier, Matthew 12,15, 20, *106*, 108, *108*
Leboeuf, Frank 21, 64, *64*
Lee, Robert 100
Leeds United 8, 11, 17, 19, 20, 28, 82–5
Leicester City 8, 15, 19, 20–1, 23, *25*, 26, *26*, 27, *27*, 86–9
Leonardo 32
Leonhardsen, Oyvind 92
Liverpool 8, 9, 10, 11, *11*, 12, 13, 14, 15, 16, *16*, 17, 18, 19, *19*, 20, 22, 23, *23*, 24, 25, 28, 29, 90–3, *125*
Loko, Patrice 32
Lombardo, Attilio 71, 73
Luton Town 12
Manchester City 14, 15
Manchester United 8, 9, *9*, 10, 11, 12, *12*, 13, 14, 15, 17, *17*, 18, 19, *19*, 20, 21, *21*, 22, *22*, 23, 28, *28*, 29, *29*, 94–7,
Marcelle, Clint 52, *52*
Martyn, Nigel 84, *84*
McAllister, Gary 69
McAteer, Jason 92, *92*
McDermott, Terry 18
McGinlay, John 60–1, *61*
McKenzie, Leon 73
McManaman, Steve 93, *93*
Merson, Paul 10
Middlesbrough 8, 15, *16*, 17, 18, 19, 22, 23, 24, 25, *25*,

26, *26*, 27, 28, 29, 30, 31
Molenaar, Robert 19
Moller, Andreas 33
Mustoe, Robbie 30

N

Newcastle United 8, 9, 10, 11, 12, *12*, 13, *13*, 14, 16–7, *17*, *18*, 20, 21, 22, 23, 24, 25, 28, 29, *40*, 98–101
Newton Eddie 31
Nilsson, Roland 67, 69
Nottingham Forest 16, 17, 18, 20, 21

O

O'Leary, David *85*
O'Neill, Martin *25*, 27
Ogrizovic, Steve 68, *68*
Ostenstad, Egil 10–11, 108–9, *109*
Owen, Michael 92, *92*

P

Pallister, Gary 24
Paris St Germain 32
Parker, Garry 27, 89, *89*
Pearce, Stuart 16
Pearson, Nigel *31*
Pembridge, Mark 104, *104*
Perry, Chris 120, *120*
Peruzzi, Angelo 33
Petrescu, Dan 31
Play-off Final 34–5, *34*, *35*
Pleat, David 9
Poborsky, Karel 11

R

Raducioiu, Florin 19
Ravanelli, Fabrizio 9, 11, 26, 31
Reading 18, 19
Redfearn, Neil 52, *52*
Redknapp, Jamie *125*
Reebok Stadium *38–9*
Ricken, Lars 33
Riedle, Karlheinz 33, *33*
Roberts, Andy 34, 72, *72*
Roberts, Ben 30
Robson, Bobby 32
Robson, Bryan 8, 17, 23, 26
Ronaldo 32, *32*
Royle, Joe 23

S

Sammer, Matthias 33
Scales, John 17
Schmeichel, Peter 12, 20
Sellars, Scott 60, *60*
Sharpe, Lee 9
Shearer, Alan 8, 9, 13, *13*, 20, 21, 22, 25, 28, *29*, 100, *123*
Sheffield United 29, 34–5
Sheffield Wednesday 9, *9*, 10, *10*, 13, 16, 102–5
Sheridan, John 60
Sheringham, Teddy 15, 28, *29*

Shipperley, Neil 35
Slater, Robbie *109*
Solskjaer, Ole Gunnar 11, 16, *17*, 96
Soltvedt, Trond Egil 67, 69
Southampton 12, 15, 18, 19, 106–9
Southgate, Gareth 48, *48*
Souness, Graeme 18
Speed, Gary 81, *81*
Stimac, Igor 76, *76*
Stockport County 12–13, 18, 20
Stone, Steve 11
Strachan, Gordon 15
Sturridge, Dean 76, *76*
Sunderland 23, 29
Sutton, Chris 56, *56*

T

Taylor, Maik *108*, 109
Thompson, Alan 60
Thomsen, Claus 19
Tomasson, Jon Dahl 101
Tottenham Hotspur 15, 17, 110–13
Tracey, Simon 35

V

Van Hooijdonk, Pierre 23
Vega, Ramon 113
Vialli, Gianluca 9, 18, 30, 31
Vickers, Paul 31
Vieira, Patrick 8, 9, 10, 14, *15*, 42, 44–5

W

Waddle, Chris 18, 23
Walker, Ian 113, *113*
Walsh, Steve 27, *27*
Wanchope, Paolo 74
Watson, Steve 101, *101*
Wenger, Arsène 8, 10, 11, 12, 14, *15*, 22
West Ham United 18, 19, 21, 114–7
Wilcox, Jason 57, *57*
Wilkinson, Howard 11, 19
Wilkinson, Paul 52–3
Wimbledon 11, 12, *13*, 14, 16, 17, 18, 22–3, 118–21
Wise, Dennis 30, 64, *64*
Woking 18
Wolverhampton Wanderers 35, *35*
Wrexham 18, 19, 20
Wright, Ian *10*, 14, 16, 20, 44, *44*, *125*

Y

Yeboah, Tony 23
York City 11
Yorke, Dwight 49, *49*

Z

Zola, Gianfranco *14*, 15, 18, 19, *20*, 30, 31, *31*, 65, *65*